Work-Related Musculoskeletal Disorders

REPORT, WORSKHOP SUMMARY, AND WORKSHOP PAPERS

Steering Committee for the Workshop on
Work-Related Musculoskeletal Injuries:
The Research Base

Committee on Human Factors

Commission on Behavioral and Social Sciences and Education

National Research Council

NATIONAL ACADEMY PRESS
Washington, DC 1999

NOTICE: The project that is the subject of this report was approved by the Governing Board of the National Research Council, whose members are drawn from the councils of the National Academy of Sciences, the National Academy of Engineering, and the Institute of Medicine. The members of the committee responsible for the report were chosen for their special competences and with regard for appropriate balance.

The National Academy of Sciences is a private, nonprofit, self-perpetuating society of distinguished scholars engaged in scientific and engineering research, dedicated to the furtherance of science and technology and to their use for the general welfare. Upon the authority of the charter granted to it by the Congress in 1863, the Academy has a mandate that requires it to advise the federal government on scientific and technical matters. Dr. Bruce M. Alberts is president of the National Academy of Sciences.

The National Academy of Engineering was established in 1964, under the charter of the National Academy of Sciences, as a parallel organization of outstanding engineers. It is autonomous in its administration and in the selection of its members, sharing with the National Academy of Sciences the responsibility for advising the federal government. The National Academy of Engineering also sponsors engineering programs aimed at meeting national needs, encourages education and research, and recognizes the superior achievements of engineers. Dr. William A. Wulf is president of the National Academy of Engineering.

The Institute of Medicine was established in 1970 by the National Academy of Sciences to secure the services of eminent members of appropriate professions in the examination of policy matters pertaining to the health of the public. The Institute acts under the responsibility given to the National Academy of Sciences by its congressional charter to be an adviser to the federal government and, upon its own initiative, to identify issues of medical care, research, and education. Dr. Kenneth I. Shine is president of the Institute of Medicine.

The National Research Council was organized by the National Academy of Sciences in 1916 to associate the broad community of science and technology with the Academy's purposes of furthering knowledge and advising the federal government. Functioning in accordance with general policies determined by the Academy, the Council has become the principal operating agency of both the National Academy of Sciences and the National Academy of Engineering in providing services to the government, the public, and the scientific and engineering communities. The Council is administered jointly by both Academies and the Institute of Medicine. Dr. Bruce M. Alberts and Dr. William A. Wulf are chairman and vice chairman, respectively, of the National Research Council.

This project was supported by an award between the National Academy of Sciences and the Department of Health and Human Services; the project, N01-IOD-4-2139, Task Order No. 47, received support from the evaluation set-aside Section 513, Public Health Service Act. Any opinions, findings, conclusions, or recommendations expressed in this publication are those of the author(s) and do not necessarily reflect the view of the organizations or agencies that provided support for this project.

International Standard Book Number 0-309-06397-3

Additional copies of this report are available from:
National Academy Press
2101 Constitution Avenue, N.W.
Washington, DC 20418
Call 800-624-6242 or 202-334-3313 (in the Washington Metropolitan Area).

This report is also available on line at http://www.nap.edu

STEERING COMMITTEE FOR THE WORKSHOP ON WORK-RELATED MUSCULOSKELETAL INJURIES: THE RESEARCH BASE

RICHARD PEW (*Cochair*), Independent Consultant, Cambridge, Massachusetts

COLIN DRURY (*Cochair*), Department of Industrial Engineering, State University of New York, Buffalo

GUNNAR ANDERSSON, Department of Orthopedic Surgery, Rush Presbyterian-St. Luke's Medical Center, Chicago, Illinois

THOMAS ARMSTRONG, Department of Industrial and Operations Engineering, University of Michigan, Ann Arbor

DAVID CORDRAY, Department of Psychology and Human Development and Vanderbilt Institute for Public Policy Studies, Vanderbilt University

MARK CULLEN, Occupational and Environmental Medicine Program, Yale University School of Medicine

BARUCH FISCHHOFF, Department of Social and Decision Sciences and Department of Engineering and Public Policy, Carnegie Mellon University

WILLIAM HOWELL, *Liaison*, Committee on Human Factors; Department of Psychology, Arizona State University, Tempe

WILLIAM MARRAS, Institute for Ergonomics, Ohio State University

DAVID VLAHOV, Department of Epidemiology, Johns Hopkins University

ANNE MAVOR, *Study Director*

JAMES McGEE, *Senior Research Associate*

RENAE BRODERICK, *Senior Consultant*

SUSAN McCUTCHEN, *Senior Project Assistant*

ALEXANDRA WIGDOR, *Director*, Division on Education, Labor, and Human Performance

SUSAN COKE, *Administrative Associate*, Division on Education, Labor, and Human Performance

COMMITTEE ON HUMAN FACTORS

Contents

Preface   ix

I STEERING COMMITTEE REPORT

1 Introduction   3
    Background, 3
    Framework of Contributors to Musculoskeletal Disorders, 5

2 State of the Evidence   8
    Criteria to Determine Causality, 9
    Soft Tissue Responses to Physical Stressors, 11
    Work Factors and Biomechanics, 12
    Epidemiological Evidence that Physical Factors Can Cause
         Musculoskeletal Disorders, 14
    Epidemiological Evidence that Non-Biomechanical Factors
         Can Cause Musculoskeletal Disorders, 16
    Interventions, 18
    Future Research, 21

3 Seven Questions Posed by Congressman Robert Livingston   23

4 Conclusions   27

References   29

II WORKSHOP SUMMARY

Introduction   35

Organizing Framework   36

Biological Responses of Tissues to Stressors   39
    Presentations, 39
    Discussion, 42

Work Factors, Individual Host Factors, and Internal Loads:
Biomechanics of Work Stressors   45
    Presentation, 45
    Discussion, 46

Epidemiology: Physical Factors   49
    Panel Discussion, 49
    Workshop Discussion, 51

Non-Biomechanical Factors that Can Affect Musculoskeletal Disorders   52
    Presentation, 52
    Discussion, 54

Intervention to Control Musculoskeletal Disorders   56
    Presentation, 56
    Discussion, 58

Conclusion: Integration and Overview   59
    Panel Comments, 59
    General Discussion, 60

References   61

Appendix A: Invitees and Participants   63
Appendix B: Workshop Agenda   67

III WORKSHOP PAPERS

Response of Muscle and Tendon to Injury and Overuse   73
    James A. Ashton-Miller

Biological Response of Peripheral Nerves to Loading: Pathophysiology of
Nerve Compression Syndromes and Vibration Induced Neuropathy   98
    David Rempel, *Lars Dahlin*, and *Göran Lundborg*

Work Factors, Personal Factors, and Internal Loads: Biomechanics of
Work Stressors   116
    Robert G. Radwin and *Steven A. Lavender*

Epidemiology Panel: Collected Papers   152
    Bradley Evanoff, 152
    Afred Franzblau, 155
    Fredric Gerr, 159
    Laura Punnett, 162
    Howard M. Sandler (with *Richard S. Blume*), 167
    David H. Wegman, 172

Non-Biomechanical Factors Potentially Affecting Musculoskeletal Disorders   175
    Julia Faucett and *Robert A. Werner*

A Review of Research on Interventions to Control Musculoskeletal Disorders   200
    Michael J. Smith, *Ben-Tzion Karsh*, and *Francisco B.P. Moro*

Preface

This volume is the work of the Steering Committee for the Workshop on Work-Related Musculoskeletal Injuries: The Research Base, which was established in May 1998 by the National Research Council (NRC) in response to a request from the National Institutes of Health. The charge was to design a workshop to examine the scientific literature on work-related musculoskeletal disorders and to prepare a report based on the workshop discussions and the committee members' own expertise. In developing the workshop, the steering committee identified leading researchers to participate as paper presenters and discussants.

Part I of this volume presents the steering committee's report, which was published as a separate document in October 1998. It contains a general framework for examining the literature, a discussion of the state-of-the-evidence regarding both work-related and non-work-related factors, a list of issues that deserve the attention of researchers, and the committee's response to a series of questions posed by Congress. Part II provides a summary of the workshop proceedings, and Part III contains the workshop papers. Because the steering committee's report and the workshop summary were initially prepared as stand-alone documents there is some overlap in their introductory sections.

Many individuals have made significant contributions to the success of the project. First, we extend our thanks to the members of the steering committee, who were willing to work on a complex and controversial topic under extreme time pressure. Each offered a unique perspective that led to a fuller understanding of the issues and the relevance of the existing science base. Also, we thank the workshop participants for their interest in the topic and their work in writing papers and preparing discussion statements on a very constrained time schedule.

Staff of the NRC were extremely helpful in organizing the workshop and in working through various drafts of these reports. We are particularly grateful to Renae Broderick, a consultant to the project, for her work in preparing the workshop summary. We are also indebted to James McGee for his efforts in coordinating workshop participants and activities; to Susan McCutchen who was indispensable in arranging travel, compiling agenda materials, and managing the preparation of this volume; to Eugenia Grohman, associate director for reports of the Commission on Behavioral and Social Sciences and Education, whose editing greatly improved the report; and to Alexandra Wigdor for her interest, guidance, and support.

This report has been reviewed in draft form by individuals chosen for their diverse perspectives and technical expertise, in accordance with procedures approved by the NRC's Report Review Committee. The purpose of this independent review is to provide candid and critical comments that will assist the institution in making the published report as sound as possible and to ensure that the report meets institutional standards for objectivity, evidence, and responsiveness to the study charge. The review comments and draft manuscript remain confidential to protect the integrity of the deliberative process.

We wish to thank the following individuals for their participation in the review of the steering committee report, the workshop summary, or both: Peter C. Amadio, Department of Orthopedic Surgery, Mayo Clinic, Rochester, MN; David R. Challoner, Institute for Science and Health Policy, University of Florida; Richard Deyo, University of Washington Health Science Center; Michael Feuerstein, Uniformed Services University of the Health Sciences and Georgetown University School of Medicine; Mark D. Grabiner, Department of Biomedical Engineering, The Cleveland Clinic Foundation; Jay S. Himmelstein, Center for Health Policy and Health Services Research, University of Massachusetts Medical School; Frederick Mosteller, Department of Statistics (emeritus), Harvard University; Dorothy P. Rice, School of Nursing (emeritus), University of California, San Francisco; Stover H. Snook, Harvard School of Public Health; and Laura W. Welch, Department of Occupational and Environmental Medicine, Washington Hospital Center, Washington, DC.

While the individuals listed above have provided constructive comments and suggestions, it must be emphasized that responsibility for the final content of this report rests entirely with its authors and the institution.

Richard Pew, *Cochair*
Colin Drury, *Cochair*
Anne Mavor, *Study Director*

Work-Related Musculoskeletal Disorders

1

Introduction

BACKGROUND

In May 1998 the National Institutes of Health asked the National Academy of Sciences/National Research Council to assemble a group of experts to examine the scientific literature relevant to work-related musculoskeletal disorders of the lower back, neck, and upper extremities. A steering committee was convened to design a workshop, to identify leading researchers on the topic to participate, and to prepare a report based on the workshop discussions and their own expertise. In addition, the steering committee was asked to address, to the extent possible, a set of seven questions posed by Congressman Robert Livingston on the topic of work-related musculoskeletal disorders. The steering committee includes experts in orthopedic surgery, occupational medicine, epidemiology, ergonomics, human factors, statistics, and risk analysis.

This document is based on the evidence presented and discussed at the 2-day Workshop on Work-Related Musculoskeletal Injuries: Examining the Research Base, which was held on August 21 and 22, 1998, and on follow-up deliberations of the steering committee, reflecting its own expertise. We note the limitations of the project, both in terms of time constraints and sources of evidence.

Although reports on the number of work-related musculoskeletal disorders vary from one data system to another, it is clear that a sizable number of individuals report disorders and lost time from work as a result of them.[1] For example, the Bureau of

---

[1] We use the World Health Organization's definition of *work-related disorders* (World Health Organization, 1985). It characterizes work-related disorders as multifactorial to indicate the inclusion of physical, organizational, psychosocial, and sociological risk factors. A disorder is work related when work procedures, equipment, or environment contribute significantly to the cause of the disorder. There is great variation in the diagnostic criteria for musculoskeletal disorders, ranging from clinical diagnoses based on symptoms and signs for some, to diagnoses based on structural and functional criteria for others. We note that "disorder" is a broader category than "injury" and better captures the range of phenomena being considered.

Labor Statistics (1995) has reported that in 1 year there were 705,800 cases of days away from work that resulted from overexertion or pain from repetitive motion. Estimated costs associated with lost days and compensation claims related to musculoskeletal disorders range from $13 to $20 billion annually (National Institute for Occupational Safety and Health, 1996; AFL-CIO, 1997). The multiplicity of factors that may affect reported cases—including work procedures, equipment, and environment; organizational factors; physical and psychological factors of the individual; and social factors—has led to much debate about their source, nature, and severity. In light of the ongoing debate, an extensive internal review of the epidemiological research was recently done by the National Institute for Occupational Safety and Health (Bernard, 1997). That study is part of the work that was considered by the steering committee.

The charge to the steering committee, reflected in the focus of the workshop, was to examine the current state of the scientific research base relevant to the problem of work-related musculoskeletal disorders, including factors that can contribute to such disorders, and strategies for intervention to ameliorate or prevent them. Approximately 110 leading scientists were invited by the steering committee to participate in the workshop, and 66 were able to attend. The attendees represented the fields of orthopedic surgery, occupational medicine, public health, epidemiology, risk analysis and decision making, ergonomics, and human factors (see Appendix A in Part II). Several attendees presented prepared papers; many others presented oral and written responses to the papers or comments on the field of inquiry. Two criteria guided the selection of invitees: that they are involved in active research in the area and that the group, overall, represent a wide range of scientific disciplines and perspectives on the topic.

In designing the workshop, the steering committee considered several approaches to framing the topics. After careful consideration, we chose not to have the presentations focus on specific parts of the body and associated musculoskeletal disorders. Rather, we organized our examination of the evidence—and the workshop discussions (see agenda, Appendix B in Part II)—to elucidate the following sets of relationships between factors that potentially contribute to musculoskeletal disorders: (1) biological responses of tissues (muscles, tendons, and nerves) to biomechanical stressors; (2) biomechanics of work stressors, considering both work and individual factors, as well as internal loads; (3) epidemiological perspectives on the contributions of physical factors; (4) non-biomechanical (e.g., psychological, organizational, social) factors; and (5) interventions to prevent or mitigate musculoskeletal disorders, considering the range of potentially influential factors. Our belief was that this approach would provide a framework for reviewing the science base for each set of relationships, as well as the wider interactions among the sets. This approach allowed us to take advantage of both basic and applied science and a variety of methodologies, ranging from tightly controlled laboratory studies to field observations. As a result, we considered sources of evidence that extend well beyond those provided by the epidemiological literature on which the public discussion has focused.

Discussions in each of the five topics (all but topic 4) revolved around a paper commissioned for the workshop and comments of invited discussants; a panel format was used to address the epidemiology of physical factors (topic 4), given the availability of recent reviews of literature on this topic.

The next section presents a conceptual framework integrating the factors thought to be related to the occurrence of musculoskeletal disorders. We used this framework to select and organize topics covered in the workshop.

FRAMEWORK OF CONTRIBUTORS TO MUSCULOSKELETAL DISORDERS

Figure 1 outlines a broad conceptual framework, indicating the roles that various work and other factors may play in the development of musculoskeletal disorders. This framework serves as a useful heuristic to examine the diverse literatures associated with musculoskeletal disorders, reflecting the role that various factors—work procedures, equipment, and environment; organizational factors; physical and psychological factors of individuals; non-work-related activities; organizational factors; and social factors— can play in their development. Its overall structure suggests the physiological pathways by which musculoskeletal disorders can occur or, conversely, can be avoided.

The central physiological pathways appear within the shaded area of the figure. It shows, first, the biomechanical relationship between load and the biological response of tissue. Imposed loads of various magnitudes can change the form of tissues throughout the day due to changes in fatigue, work pattern or style, coactivation of muscle structures, etc. Loads within a tissue can produce several forms of response. If the load exceeds a mechanical tolerance or the ability of the structure to withstand the load, tissue damage will occur. For example, damage to a vertebral end plate will occur if the load borne by the spine is large enough. Other forms of response may entail such reactions as inflammation of the tissue, edema, and biochemical responses.

Biomechanical studies can elucidate some of these relationships. Biomechanical loading can produce both symptomatic and asymptomatic reactions. Feedback mechanisms can influence the biomechanical loading and response relationship. For example, the symptom of pain might cause an individual to recruit his or her muscles in a different manner, thereby changing the associated loading pattern. Adaptation to a load might lead individuals to expose themselves to greater loads, which they might or might not be able to bear. Repetitive loading of a tissue might strengthen the tissue or weaken it, depending on circumstances. The symptom and adaptation portions of the model can interact with each other as well. For example, symptoms, such as swelling, can lead to tissue adaptations, such as increased lubricant production in a joint. These relationships can be described in mathematical models that distinguish external load (e.g., work exposure) from internal load (dose) and illustrate cascading events, whereby

6

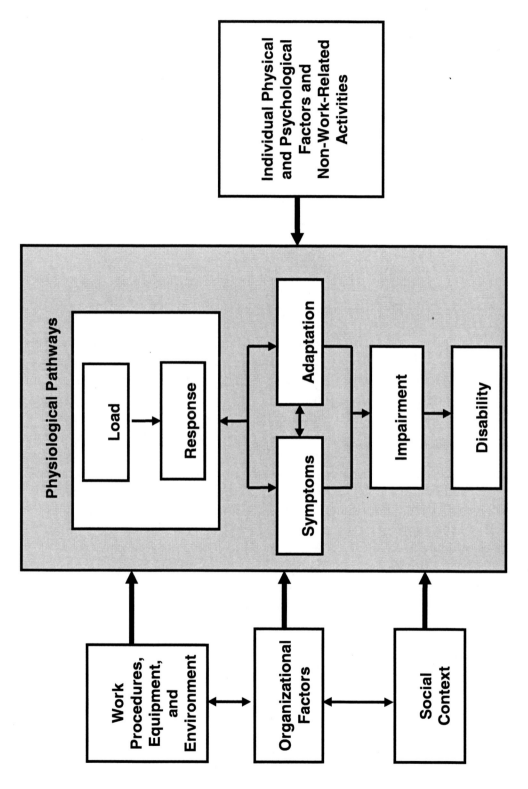

FIGURE 1 Conceptual framework of physiological pathways and factors that potentially contribute to musculoskeletal disorders.

responses to loads can themselves serve as stimuli that increase or decrease the capacity for subsequent responses.

The responses, symptoms, and adaptations can lead to a functional impairment. In the workplace, this might be reported as a work-related musculoskeletal disorder. If severe enough, the impairment would be considered a disability, and lost or restricted workdays would result.

To the left of the shaded area in Figure 1, the framework shows environmental factors that might affect the development of musculoskeletal disorders, including work procedures, equipment, and environment; organizational factors; and social context. For example, physical work factors (reaching, close vision work, lifting heavy loads) affect the loading that is experienced by a worker's tissues and structures. Organizational factors can also influence the central mechanism. Although little studied, hypothetical pathways also exist between organizational influences and the biomechanical load-response relationship, as well as the development of symptoms. For example, time pressures to complete a task might induce carelessness in handling a particular load, with consequent tissue damage. The organizational culture can also create an incentive or a disincentive to report a musculoskeletal disorder or to claim that the impairment should be considered a disability. Social context factors, such as a lack of means to deal with psychological stress (e.g., no spousal support), might also influence what a worker reports or even the worker's physiological responses.

To the right in Figure 1, the framework shows the influence of individual physical and psychological factors, as well as non-work-related activities, that might affect the development of musculoskeletal disorders. For example, psychological factors can affect a person's identification of a musculoskeletal disorder or willingness to report it or to claim that the impairment is a disability. Physical factors might involve reduced tissue tolerance due to age or gender or disease states, such as arthritis, which can affect people's biochemical response to tissue loading.

This framework can accommodate the diverse literatures regarding musculoskeletal disorders by characterizing the pathways that each study addresses. For example, an epidemiological investigation might explore the pathways between the physical work environment and the reporting of impairments or the pathway between organizational factors and the reporting of symptoms. An ergonomic study might explore the pathways between work procedures and equipment and the biomechanical loads imposed on a tissue. This framework also focuses attention on the interactions among factors. For example, the combination of a particular set of work procedures and organizational factors might produce an increase in disorders that neither would alone produce.

Looking at the evidence as a whole provides a sounder basis for understanding the overall dimensions of the problem of work-related musculoskeletal disorders than restricting an examination to any one factor or kind of evidence. It also places individual studies in context, by showing the factors and pathways that they do and do not address.

2

State of the Evidence

The goal of the steering committee was to examine the current state of the scientific research base relevant to the problem of work-related musculoskeletal disorders. As mentioned, we identified five major topics, each of which has been the subject of scientific examination. The resulting literature represents a wide variety of research designs, measures, apparatuses, and modes of analysis. Our representation of the science base therefore covers a wide range of theoretical and empirical approaches. For example, there are highly controlled studies of soft tissue responses that are based on work with cadavers, animal models, and human biomechanics; survey and cross-sectional studies that examine the relationship between musculoskeletal disorders and work, organizational, social, and individual factors; and experimental, quasi-experimental, and time-series studies that are designed to examine the effects of various interventions.

In order to make sense of such a multifaceted body of research, we have extended our analysis beyond the traditional criteria used in epidemiological studies; we rely, instead, on five commonly accepted criteria for establishing causal linkages among factors. Following the discussion of the causal criteria, this review of the evidence is divided into five sections. The first, soft tissue responses to physical stressors, covers material that corresponds to the load and response boxes in Figure 1. The second section, work factors and biomechanics, discusses the biomechanics of the load-response relationship and examines the contributions of work procedures, equipment, and environment to this relationship. The third section covers the epidemiological evidence relating biomechanical factors at work to musculoskeletal disorders. The fourth section examines the state of the evidence regarding the contributions of the non-biomechanical factors listed in Figure 1—organizational, social, and individual. The final section presents a discussion of workplace interventions; this section covers material relevant to all factors represented in the figure.

CRITERIA TO DETERMINE CAUSALITY

Five criteria are normally considered in determining whether scientific evidence supports a causal claim as internally valid—that is, that the purported cause was uniquely responsible for the effect (Campbell and Stanley, 1966; Cook and Campbell, 1979; Cordray, 1986; Einhorn and Hogarth, 1986).

- The first criterion, *temporal ordering*, requires that the cause be present before the effect is observed. It can be assessed by examining the type of control the investigator has over the timing and delivery of the causal agent in an experimental study (e.g., conducted under controlled conditions) and the course of events in an observational study (e.g., one involving systematic observation of events in the real world).
- The second criterion requires that the *cause and effect covary*. For example, when no force is applied to a tendon, it remains in a relaxed state; in the presence of the cause (a force), the tendon responds.
- The third criterion involves the *absence of other plausible explanations for the observed effect*. To the extent that confounding factors have been controlled by the design of the experiment or observation, other explanations for the observed effect are less likely. In some studies, it is possible to use random assignment of participants to conditions to control the influence of other factors, but this is not the only means for achieving control. In making a determination of whether factors other than the experimentally manipulated factor (e.g., ergonomic redesign) offer plausible explanations for the observed effect (e.g., a lower average level of sick days in the post-redesign period of observation), it is necessary to identify and test whether other plausible factors might have been operative, mimicking the effect of the target cause (e.g., change in sick leave policy, turnover in personnel). If no other such causes can be shown empirically to be responsible for the effect, it is reasonable to attribute the effect to the cause under investigation. Note that this criterion stipulates that other causal factors need to be plausible, not merely logically possible. Claims of plausibility have merit to the extent that they can be empirically supported.
- The fourth criterion, *temporal contiguity*, amplifies the first (temporal ordering). To the extent that the effect follows the cause closely in time, the plausibility that other factors are operative is reduced. For example, if a tendon reacts immediately to the presence of force, it is unlikely that other factors (e.g., gravitational pull) are responsible for the sudden elongation. On the other hand, if there is a delay between

the application of force and the response that cannot be explained by the biomechanical mechanisms associated with tendon structures, other factors may be operative, weakening the strength of the causal claim.

• The fifth criterion is that the size of the cause is related to the size or magnitude of the effect: that is, there is a *congruity between the cause and effect*. More specifically, a small force or small change in the workplace ought to correspond to a small effect and a large force or major change (e.g., multiple components of the workplace are altered) ought to be accompanied by a large effect (e.g., failure of a tissue or a substantial reduction in work-related injuries). When results from experiments or quasi-experiments violate these expectations, it is necessary to examine how the effect was modified (either enhanced, in the case of a small cause that leads to a large effect, or dampened, in the case of a large cause that produces a small effect). To the extent that a compelling explanation for these anomalies cannot be provided (e.g., delays in the implementation of a workplace redesign), it is plausible to assume that other processes (not related to the suggested cause) are responsible for some or all of the effect.

By applying these criteria to evaluate the credibility of scientific evidence, one need not place heavy emphasis on the types of research design that have been used in a given study. It is a disciplined way to take advantage of the research provided by a wide variety of methods and, thus, it has substantial implications for the manner in which a science base is considered. Rather than focusing on a study's design features, one considers the pattern of data for each study and its associated design on a case-by-case basis. For some studies, it is readily apparent that even the minimal causal criteria cannot be substantiated (e.g., it is impossible to establish that the cause came before the effect). For others, even when there is no conventional experimental control group (created through random assignment), observations before and after the introduction of an intervention can produce valid claims if coupled with other evidence about the change and with probes concerning the presence or absence of other plausible explanations.

In complex domains, single studies can seldom provide a conclusive verification of a causal proposition. It is through replication and synthesis of evidence across studies, preferably with studies that use a variety of methods (each with different strengths and weaknesses), that causal claims gain their inferential strength. In performing such syntheses, greatest weight should be given to the evidence from studies that most completely satisfy the five criteria specified above. Poorly conceptualized and executed studies may have little to offer for assessments of causal claims. In contrast, the evidence from a few well-conceived and well-executed studies can strongly outweigh the "noise" created by a large number of studies that do not satisfy the five criteria for causality. (A similar argument was made in deliberations about the evidence related to the effectiveness of a set of complex public health programs; see Normand et al., 1995).

Finally, inferential strength is gained by examining the evidence from a variety of theoretical perspectives (as well as a variety of research methods), as specified in the framework provided in Figure 1. Establishing that biological and biomechanical processes influence tissues, that these forces are present in some work environments or work-related tasks, that their presence is associated with musculoskeletal disorders, and that their influence can be reduced by workplace redesign (or other interventions) should provide a greater understanding of the evidence than can be gained by considering each factor separately. The findings presented in the rest of this section reflect the steering committee's application of the criteria to the research literature.

SOFT TISSUE RESPONSES TO PHYSICAL STRESSORS

Several well-established findings are supported by the papers of Rempel et al. (1998) and Ashton-Miller (1998), presented at the workshop. While certain loads can be tolerated and adapted to, all soft tissues, including muscle, tendon, ligament, fascia, synovia, cartilage, intervertebral disc, and nerve, fail when subjected to sufficient force. Data from cadaver studies provide ranges within which such failures occur, and animal models of some tissue provide support for the laboratory data. Even at levels of force clearly below the failure level, however, there is scientific evidence, from these types of studies, that tissue response to deformation can produce inflammation, failure at microscopic levels, and muscle fatigue.

Injuries to muscle from single-event and repetitive contractions have been documented in humans and in animal models. Local muscle fatigue occurs at low contraction levels when maintained for long periods. Inflammatory muscle responses have been documented in humans subjected to repetitive or prolonged loading. Muscles also are affected by individual factors, such as age and level of conditioning. These effects involve not only the tissue, but also the neuromuscular control system.

Ligaments and tendons also fail from single or repetitive loading. For tendons, disorders can occur at the insertion into the bone, in the tendon proper, or at the junction between tendon and muscle. Animal models have demonstrated the development of inflammatory responses in the tendon sheath and insertion areas (tendinitis and tendinosis).

Cartilage is a tissue known to deteriorate when subjected to abnormal loads. Intervertebral discs, which are a special type of cartilage, fail when loaded, as fissures develop within the substance. Age, gender, and other individual factors influence these processes.

Nerves subjected to tension or compression will respond with pain, dysfunction, and ultimately permanent tissue changes. There is good scientific evidence about both acute and chronic effects of nerve compression and about the effects of vibration on nerves. Critical pressure and duration values have been established for acute nerve compression, but they have not yet been established for chronic compression.

It is important to note that many of the well-designed experimental studies in animals and cadavers have been successfully replicated. The applicability of their findings to humans in the workplace has been addressed by observations of comparable effects in exposed humans. On all of these highly controlled studies, the causal criteria are met: the load or stress occurs before the response, confounding factors are controlled to eliminate other plausible responses, and the size and temporal proximity of the load and effect can be consistently measured and predicted.

WORK FACTORS AND BIOMECHANICS

The relationships among external work factors, loads, and responses (see Figure 1) have been studied extensively, using both theoretical models and human laboratory studies. Theoretical models make use of mathematical models that are widely applied to design mechanical structures in aircraft, automobiles, bridges, and buildings. Some human studies involve postmortem techniques to examine geometry and mechanical properties of tissues and their response and adaptation to various loads. Other human studies use force gauges and electromyography to directly measure forces produced in given activities. It has been shown that activities of work, daily living, and recreation often produce loads that approach the mechanical limits of soft tissue (discussed in the preceding section) and in some cases for some individuals exceed those limits. Up to certain limits, some tissues, such as muscle tissue, are able to adapt to repetitive loading; while the ability of other tissues, such as nerve tissue, to adapt is much less (see discussion of these in Radwin and Lavender, 1998). In general, the results of human studies meet the criteria of temporal order, temporal contiguity, covariance, and the absence of other plausible explanations.

Work entails positioning and exertion of the body to accomplish required tasks. In addition, exertion of the body against an external object may impose significant contact stresses on the surface of the body, which are transmitted to underlying tissues. If the work object vibrates, some of that vibration will be transmitted to the body. Exertion, posture, contact stress, vibration, and varying temperatures are external stressors. The intensities of the exertions are related to the weight, resistance, drag, inertia, and reaction forces of the work objects. Postures are related to the geometry of the workplace and the size of the worker; they range from neutral positions to the limits of the range of motion. Contact stresses are related to force and area of contact. Vibration is related to how a tool is powered, balanced, and mounted. Low temperatures are related to ambient air temperature and to the thermal conductivity of handles and gloves. If ambient air is cold or if a work object is cold, a worker's hand will be cooled. The frequency and duration of exertions and postures are related to production rates and quotas. These exposures may occur not only at work, but also in various recreational and living activities.

These relationships are supported by basic Newtonian mechanics, and they can be observed directly (Chaffin and Andersson, 1990). For example, posture is related to the location of parts, assemblies and controls, size and shape of handles, orientation of work objects, and visual requirements. Posture is also affected by obstructions that workers must see or reach over, under, or around. Posture variations can be observed within a given work situation, but this variation is small in relation to that attributed to the workstation. If work is located overhead, as often occurs in manufacturing settings, workers will have to stand with their hands above their heads. If the work is located on the floor, workers may have to bend or stoop. It has been observed that work capacity is greatly reduced at very high and very low locations (Snook and Ciriello, 1991; Marras et al., 1997).

It can be shown that the force required to support a work object is related to weight and friction (Armstrong, 1985). Similarly, forces required to depress the keys on a keyboard are related to the stiffness of the keys (Armstrong et al., 1994). However, there may be significant variations from person to person; one worker may strike the keys of a keyboard very forcefully, while another uses a light touch.

It can also be shown that the frequency and duration of exertions are related to work standards and quotas. Production rates are based on estimates of the time required to perform a given task. Allowances may be added to provide time for process variations and to provide sufficient recovery time. Pay incentives, which encourage faster work, may result in insufficient recovery time. The effect may be compounded by production quotas that necessitate overtime. Although external stresses can be produced by activities of recreation and daily living, the duration of exposures rarely equals the 40 to 60 hours per week that commonly occur in work settings.

External loads impose internal loads on underlying tissues (e.g., muscles, tendons, tendons sheaths, bones, ligaments, and nerves). The relationship between external and internal loads has been demonstrated with biomechanical models and observed using instrumentation. For example, intervertebral disk pressures of the lumbar spine up to 1.6 MPa have been calculated and measured. Internal finger flexor tendon tensions have been shown to be three to five times greater than external finger forces (Chaffin and Andersson, 1990).

The relationship between external and internal loads is also based on Newtonian mechanics. Internal loads have been shown to produce mechanical, physiological, and psychological responses, such as tissue deformation, altered metabolism, altered circulatory patterns, and perceived exertion (see discussion of soft tissue responses above). Depending on the duration and intensity of the loads and recovery time, the responses may cause discomfort and impair performance. Fatigue is one such example. While fatigue can significantly affect worker comfort and impair work performance, it is a transient response that dissipates rapidly when work stops. In some cases, however, loads are large enough or last long enough to stimulate acute tissue disorders. Although damaged tissue stimulates a healing response, healing may not occur if the loads continue to be applied.

These processes have been studied in all parts of the body. For example, exertions of the hand entail a complex mechanical equilibrium of the muscles in the forearm and hand that open the fist and those that close the fist. Exertions of the trunk entail a complex equilibrium among all of the muscles in the back and extremities.

The relationships among external loads and internal loads and mechanical, physiological, and psychological responses have been studied extensively, using simulation, direct instrumentation, indirect instrumentation, and epidemiological studies. The studies support several important conclusions that are in accord with the proposed multifactorial framework presented above (see Figure 1) and that provide a basis for evaluating and controlling biomechanical stresses in the workplace:

• There are numerous ways of measuring and characterizing external loads. For example, force can be measured in terms of the weight of parts, tool reaction force, perceived exertion, muscle electrical activity, or observer ratings. Posture can be measured in terms of joint angles, perceived exertion, observer ratings, or work locations (e.g., keyboard height).

• Internal loads can be estimated by using external loads. For example, a worker must bend or stoop to lift an object from the floor; a worker will exert more force on a stiff keyboard than a light touch keyboard. Understanding these relationships allows prediction of internal loads.

• Predicted internal loads generally agree with measured internal and external loads. For example, measurements of pressure at the L5S1 intervertebral disk agree with predicted values (Marras and Granata, 1997). Predictions of finger flexor tendon loads generally agree with measurements of tendon loads. Measurements of muscle loads using electromyography generally agree with predicted values.

• The importance of a particular response varies from one part of the body to another. For example, tensile, contact, and shear loads and fluid pressures are particularly important in the wrist. It has been shown that internal loads produced on tendons by repetitive handwork are sufficient to cause significant elastic and viscous strain. These loads can be associated with pathological changes in adjacent synovial and nerve tissues. Muscle force and interjoint pressures are particularly important in the low back.

• Although external loads can be measured on continuous scales, most epidemiological studies consider only two levels of exposure—high and low. This approach reflects the operational realities of field studies, which are often limited by availability of workers, exposure groups, and stability of work settings. However, continuous scales would be useful for primary prevention and work design.

EPIDEMIOLOGICAL EVIDENCE THAT PHYSICAL FACTORS CAN CAUSE MUSCULOSKELETAL DISORDERS

One of the factors prompting our review of the scientific relationship between biomechanical stressors at work and the occurrence of musculoskeletal disorders has been controversy regarding human studies in working populations. These studies, although numerous, have used diverse methods for measuring both exposure to mechanical factors and the health outcomes of interest. As results have not converged in every regard, some individuals have discounted some or all of the collective evidence.

In an effort to clarify this situation, the National Institute of Occupational Safety and Health (NIOSH) undertook a review of the epidemiological literature (Bernard, 1997), with the intent of examining critically the strengths and weaknesses of available studies. The study attempted to identify both those areas for which there is strong evidence for convergence of results linking an exposure to musculoskeletal disorders and those areas for which the evidence is weaker or divergent.

A highly representative sample of respected epidemiologists was invited to the workshop to discuss the NIOSH review and the epidemiological studies considered. Seven of these experts from within and outside the field participated in a panel discussion. Both written and presented comments of the panel have been further considered and extensively discussed by the steering committee (using the approach to evidence outlined above). See Evanoff, 1998; Franzblau, 1998; Gerr, 1998; Punnett, 1998; Sandler and Blume, 1998; and Wegman, 1998.

These presentations and discussions led us to the following summaries of the scientific evidence:

• Strong associations between measured biomechanical stressors at work and musculoskeletal disorders were observed in most studies; however, temporal contiguity between the stressors and onset of effects, as well as evidence of amelioration after reduction of stressors, could not always be established, nor could the clinical course of the observed effects. This shortcoming, though inherent to practical requirements of such research, makes it difficult to make strong causal inferences on the basis of the evidence from any individual study.

• Methods used for the assessment of exposures and health outcomes vary, rendering the task of merging and combining evidence more challenging than in some other areas of occupational risk assessment. But this variability does provide the benefit of multiple perspectives on a common set of problems.

• It is not feasible to assess the relative contribution of task and other factors to musculoskeletal disorders in the general population. In addition, high rates of workplace participation complicate characterization of the nonworking population (e.g., the prevalence of health-related reasons for not working). Therefore, evidence about the prevalence and incidence of even the most common musculoskeletal disorders in nonworking populations, which could be readily compared to results of epidemiological studies of workers, is largely lacking.

• Some published studies that show associations between biomechanical stressors and musculoskeletal disorders are difficult to interpret because of the possibility that plausible but unmeasured factors could explain some or all of the observed differences in rates of musculoskeletal disorders. In other words, whether biomechanical stressors or something else have caused higher rates of musculoskeletal disorders could not be definitively answered. This problem is common to epidemiological research in general.

Despite these limitations, however, the steering committee reached the following conclusions:

• Restricting our focus to those studies involving the highest levels of exposure to biomechanical stressors of the upper extremity, neck, and back and those with the sharpest contrast in exposure among the study groups, the positive relationship between the occurrence of musculoskeletal disorders and the conduct of work is clear. The relevant studies have not precisely determined either the causal mechanical factors involved nor the full clinical spectrum of the reported musculoskeletal disorders (which have often been lumped together nonspecifically as musculoskeletal disorders of a body region); nonetheless, those associations identified by the NIOSH review (Bernard, 1997) as having strong evidence are well supported by competent research on heavily exposed populations. Examples include the excesses of musculoskeletal disorders of the upper extremities among sawyers and auto assembly workers and the excesses of musculoskeletal disorders of the back among materials handlers and health care workers who lift patients.

• There is compelling evidence from numerous studies that as the amount of biomechanical stress is reduced, the prevalence of musculoskeletal disorders at the affected body region is likewise reduced. This evidence provides further support for the relationship between these work activities and the occurrence of musculoskeletal disorders.

• Evidence of a role for biomechanical stress in the occurrence of musculoskeletal disorders among populations exposed to low levels of biomechanical stressors remains less definitive, though there are some high-quality studies suggesting causal associations that should serve as the basis for further investigation. In cases of low levels of biomechanical stress, the possible contribution of other factors to musculoskeletal disorders is important to consider. Many of these factors are discussed below.

EPIDEMIOLOGICAL EVIDENCE THAT NON-BIOMECHANICAL FACTORS CAN CAUSE MUSCULOSKELETAL DISORDERS

The framework in Figure 1 shows individual, organizational, and social factors as sources of variation that might directly affect the physiological pathways leading from tissue load, through impairment, to disability. This section examines the evidence for and against these relationships.

We note two points about most musculoskeletal disorders: (1) it is highly unlikely that all individuals have equal susceptibility to any disorder, and (2) it would be unusual if organizational aspects of the workplace and social support factors had no role in either the incidence or the time pattern of a disorder. The issues of interest are the magnitude of such effects, relative to biomechanical effects, and the nature of interactions between biomechanical, individual, organizational, and social factors.

The literature on non-biomechanical factors is highly variable in a number of ways that complicate comparisons across studies. First, the number of non-biomechanical factors is potentially unlimited, and different studies typically have examined different, although often overlapping, sets of factors. Second, many of the variables of interest, such as job content, job control, or social support, lack consensus on standard measurement and procedures. Measurement scales are often borrowed from studies of conditions other than musculoskeletal disorders. As a result, different studies of the same topic use different measures and even different disorders, or different precursors and endpoints for the same disorder. Third, both cross-sectional and longitudinal research techniques have been used, with a variety of sample sizes and with different criteria for causality. This variability is a barrier to mechanical aggregation of studies, a task that requires careful attention to sample size and measurement error. Diversity, however, can be an asset if the findings of a variety of studies reinforce one another. Testing for such convergent validity requires an interpretative framework that acknowledges the potentially complementary strengths and weaknesses of different research methodologies.

Below we review the evidence on individual, organizational, and social factors (see Faucett and Werner, 1998, for supporting material). No evidence was presented that malingering is a large contributor to the overall incidence of musculoskeletal disorders, although it is likely there are individuals who abuse the medical and social systems in this way.

Individual Factors

Faucett and Werner (1998) and the workshop discussants agreed that individuals differ in their susceptibility to the incidence, severity, and etiology of musculoskeletal disorders. Most of the reviewed papers studied upper-extremity musculoskeletal disorders, although some focused on the low back. For some individual factors (age, prior medical conditions) there is high plausibility for the influence of biological mechanisms that could account for the strong relationships observed in epidemiological studies. For a number of other factors, there is equally strong epidemiological evidence, but the mechanism is less clear (body mass index, gender). Still other factors are less well established (genetics, general conditioning) or are limited to a single disorder (wrist physical dimensions for carpal tunnel syndrome).

Overall, the studies complement and reinforce one anothers' conclusions for particular variables that have been studied repeatedly (e.g., aging). However, it is important to note that these relationships, although often statistically significant, rarely show high predictive value. Most studies explain a relatively small percentage of the overall variance in the outcome measures. This is not a paradoxical result, but simply a reflection of the fact that even weak predictors will be statistically significant if they are measured well in large samples.

Organizational and Social Factors

A number of studies have grouped non-biomechanical factors at the workplace and within social support groups as "psychosocial factors." These are often the factors directly associated with levels of workplace stress, such as job content and demands, job control, and social support. However, variables such as job satisfaction or job enjoyment have also been included. The effects associated with these factors have been examined in the NIOSH review (Bernard, 1997), the commissioned paper prepared for the workshop (Faucett and Werner, 1998), and in a number of other recent comprehensive reviews (particularly from Europe), with quite similar conclusions (see, e.g., Bongers et al., 1993).

Organizational variables of job content and job demands include such factors as job variety, job identity, workload, and time pressure. In the study and evaluation of these variables, both objective measures and subjective perceptions of workers have been used; the latter have been collected in the form of workers' responses on scales. Generally speaking, poor job content (e.g., poor task integration, lack of task identity) and high job demands have been found to be related to higher rates of musculoskeletal disorders. In some cases, these factors covary with physical factors. For example, high levels of time pressure can increase speed of movement and hence the dynamic forces acting on tissues. The effect of job control, also called decision latitude, on reports of musculoskeletal disorders has received moderate support from the literature.

Social support is seen as a mediating variable in studies of psychological stress; it finds strong support in the NIOSH review and the commissioned review, but somewhat less in other reviews presented by workshop discussants. Across organizational and social variables, psychological stress has some causal plausibility, but in general its biological plausibility is weaker than for some other individual and biomechanical factors. Again, the conclusion is that even when statistically significant, these factors are not large.

INTERVENTIONS

There are a variety of actions that can be taken in the workplace to eliminate or reduce the risk of musculoskeletal disorders. According to the commissioned paper by Smith et al. (1998:2): "These include engineering redesigns, changes in work methods, administrative controls, employee training, organized exercise, work hardening, personal protective equipment, and medical management to reduced exposures." Numerous assessments have been undertaken to determine whether such actions, singly or taken as a program of risk reduction, actually do result in observed benefits to employees and employers.

Intervention studies differ from their epidemiological counterparts in at least one fundamental way: in intervention studies, the effects of occupational risk factors are examined by manipulating attributes of the work condition. One approach is to use the standard *experimental* paradigm. This involves creating an intervention group that receives one or more of the actions listed above and a control group that receives alternative forms of the intervention or "business as usual." Another research design is the *before-and-after* paradigm. When multiple observations are obtained before and after introduction of the intervention, the before period serves as the control condition from which the effects of changes in musculoskeletal disorders in the post-intervention period can be assessed. This design is referred to as an *interrupted time-series quasi-experiment* (Campbell and Stanley, 1966). Although it does not involve random assignment to conditions, it represents a relatively strong research design that is often able to provide internally valid evidence about the causal effects of an intervention. That is, because of the control that is exercised over the presentation of the cause (e.g., a work-related design), intervention studies generally fulfill the temporal ordering criteria (i.e., the cause precedes the effect).

Exposure to the cause can be controlled either through random assignment of conditions or through timing of the introduction of the intervention. As with most intervention research, an investigator's ability to control the influence of all plausible threats to validity is reduced as the site of the study moves from the laboratory to the workplace. However, generalization (i.e., external validity) is enhanced for studies conducted in "real-world" settings. Thus, there is a constant tradeoff between internal and external validity.

Overall, there is a great deal of diversity regarding the nature and quality of research methods used in intervention studies (Smith et al., 1998). There are a number of laboratory studies involving the use of random assignment of participants to interventions. However, these studies often involve participants who differ from the target workers of interest on key attributes (e.g., study participants have included well-conditioned athletes). Furthermore, the experimental arrangements are not always representative of the types of work-related tasks that are of most interest. The duration of exposure to a stressor is often short and therefore unrepresentative of the duration and intensity of exposure in workplaces. In assessing the effects of exposure to an intervention, laboratory-based studies often have to rely on short follow-up assessments and measures that reflect symptoms rather than the end-states of most interest (e.g., sick days). As such, the relevance of these studies, despite some of their desirable features (e.g., random assignment), is often questioned.

Field studies conducted in work environments overcome some of the shortcomings of the laboratory studies because of greater realism of the interventions that are tested, longer exposure to the redesign efforts, longer follow-up intervals, and the measurement of important end-states. A few of these studies are classified as true experiments (i.e., experimental versus control conditions); the remainder are designated as less well-controlled studies. But within this latter group, several high-quality quasi-experiments have been undertaken that provide relatively convincing evidence about the effects of multicomponent intervention actions (Aaras, 1994; McKenzie et al., 1985; Jones, 1997). Not only do these studies provide data for extended periods before and after the introduction of the intervention package, they often provide additional evidence about the operation of the causal factor (e.g., workplace redesign) in reducing the amount of load or stress on muscles. Moreover, the patterns of outcome data fulfill the conditions for causal inference: that is, they show sharp reductions in end-state measures following introduction of the intervention (indicating covariation, temporal ordering, temporal contiguity), the size of the reduction (effect) corresponds to the size of the cause (indicating cause-effect congruity), and few (if any) rival explanations can be invoked to explain the effects.

Another class of field studies involves comparisons of alternative forms of intervention (e.g., back school versus exercise) rather than pure control group conditions, where the participants receive little or no specialized attention. Given that two or more interventions are contrasted, each of which might have beneficial effects, there is an increased chance that the results will show no comparative advantage of either intervention or mixed results, where one intervention is superior on some but not all outcome measures.

In field settings, it is not uncommon for an intervention to involve multiple actions to participants in the intervention group. Under this circumstance, it is difficult to determine which of the actions was responsible for any observed effect. It may be tempting to criticize a study because the individual influence of each action could not be uniquely identified. However, from the perspective of the internal validity of the study, this criticism is not strictly applicable. Rather, it is possible to conclude that the design of the study produced valid findings about the "package" of actions. Labeling the specific cause of the findings is an issue of construct validity, a standard that is unlikely to be achieved in actual workplace environments.

The available reviews of the literature (Smith et al., 1998; Lahad et al., 1994) have not examined all of the studies (experiments and quasi-experiments) that have appeared in the literature to date. As such, it is not possible to characterize the quality of the evidence for the full collection of studies. However, there are a number of high-quality studies that can be used to determine whether interventions can reduce the risk of musculoskeletal disorders.

The literature provides evidence that interventions, of various types and complexity, *can* prevent the development of musculoskeletal disorders in specific industries and occupational groups. For example, there is a set of well-controlled studies that show that hospital workers, nurses aides, and industrial workers benefited from extended exercise programs (Lahad et al., 1994). Among these benefits were greater strength, less absenteeism, and fewer days of reported lower back pain. These effects have been seen for workers with and without prior histories of back pain. Other, less well-controlled studies revealed similar benefits. There is also some minimal evidence pointing to a positive benefit of educational strategies. Other examples are found in the poultry processing and telecommunication industries, where interventions resulted in reductions in the total number of recordable repetitive trauma disorders (according to the criteria of the Occupational Safety and Health Administration [OSHA]), lost workdays, number of days of restricted activity, and employee turnover. In these latter examples, there is also some evidence that the interventions were cost beneficial for employers.

Further evidence for effective intervention is found in several well-designed studies that show that alternative hand tool designs result in improved hand and wrist posture, thereby minimizing the risk of musculoskeletal disorder. And there is some evidence that weight handling devices reduce the risk of musculoskeletal disorders (Smith et al., 1998).

Most of the industry-specific studies used multicomponent interventions (e.g., engineering controls, training, medical management, employee empowerment). Although these studies attempted to provide insights into the relative importance of each component, it is often not possible to identify those features of the overall intervention that are most critical in achieving the observed benefits.

FUTURE RESEARCH

Although the research base contains valuable information and shows consistent patterns regarding the relationships between stressors and musculoskeletal disorders, additional research would provide a better understanding of the processes involved. Looking across the areas defined in the framework, there are five interrelated and fundamental issues that deserve additional attention by researchers:

1. In all areas, additional research would shed light on the *models and mechanisms* that underlie the established relationships between causal factors and outcomes. For example, it is obvious that a tissue will fail when loaded above its ultimate strength. How tissue responds to repetitive loading, what triggers inflammatory responses, and how these are influenced by individual factors have not been explained in detail. A similar argument can be made for intervention studies, especially those that involve multiple components. Here, the literature shows that a "bundle" of actions *can* reduce the risk of musculoskeletal disorders and associated outcomes (e.g., sick days). What is less clear are the mechanisms by which changes to work procedures, equipment, environment, and organization, as well as to social and individual factors, produce the benefits.

2. Along with a better understanding of the mechanisms that produce tissue failure and mechanisms that produce reductions in risks, the relationships between symptoms, injury reporting, impairment, and disability should be clarified, as well as how these relationships are influenced by individual, social, legal, and environmental factors. That is, there is a need to conduct more studies that consider multiple factors—workers generally are exposed to multiple factors—and there is likely to be significant interaction between factors.

3. The literature identifies a range of procedures and equipment-related intervention strategies that can be effective. It would be helpful to know more about the relationships between incremental changes of the environmental load and incremental responses. Knowledge of these relationships could help to define more efficient and better targeted interventions.

4. In order to improve the ability to assess mechanisms, change processes, and interactions among factors, it would help to have more standardization and greater detail in injury reports, better measurement of the attributes of contributors and risks, and better measurement of outcomes and other relevant variables.

5. Although a good deal is known about musculoskeletal disorders, a better understanding of the clinical courses of these disorders would be possible with improved models and measures. Better understanding of the course of these disorders would provide information that would assist in formulating strategies for tertiary intervention, by altering the clinical and economic impact of musculoskeletal disorders once they have become manifest. One potential area for research is the contribution of physical conditioning and exercise to developing human resistance and resilience.

3

Seven Questions Posed by Congressman Robert Livingston

The material in Section 2 puts in perspective the state of the evidence with respect to the range of factors that could be contributing to musculoskeletal disorders and describes the extent to which there is a scientific basis for concluding that such disorders originate in the workplace and can be reduced through programmatic interventions. This section presents the steering committee's response to the seven questions posed by Representative Livingston. As our analysis has been at the level of the family of musculoskeletal disorders, our response will be provided across disorders.

Question 1: What are the conditions affecting humans that are considered to be work-related musculoskeletal disorders?

The musculoskeletal conditions that may be caused by (non-accidental) physical work activities include disorders of inflammation, degeneration, and physiological disruption of muscles, tendons, ligaments, nerves, synovia, and cartilage involving limbs and trunk. These entities are included in categories 353-355, 722-724, and 726-729 of the *International Classification of Diseases* (commonly referred to as ICD-9) (World Health Organization, 1977). Not every disorder in these categories may be caused by mechanical stressors, but all the major musculoskeletal disorders of interest are included in these groupings. Common examples are low back strain, tenosynovitis, and carpal tunnel syndrome.

Question 2: What is the status of medical science with respect to the diagnosis and classification of such disorders?

There is great variation in the diagnostic criteria for the many musculoskeletal disorders, ranging from clinical diagnoses based on symptoms and signs for some, to diagnoses based on structural and functional criteria for others. The diagnostic criteria used in epidemiological studies are often different from those used to make treatment decisions. This difference can lead to classification of cases for research that would be unacceptable when invasive treatment alternatives are considered, but it has little influence on the conclusion of appropriately designed epidemiological surveys. In the classification of back pain, a symptom classification is often used because the precise etiology of the painful process often cannot be identified. For specific disease entities, such as herniated disks, there are accepted diagnostic criteria that are based on clinical symptoms and signs, as well as imaging information. Similarly, there are disease entities for upper extremities for which there are accepted diagnostic criteria; for other disease entities, they are classified broadly on the basis of clinical symptoms and signs.

Question 3: What is the state of scientific knowledge, characterized by the degree of certainty or lack thereof, with regard to occupational and nonoccupational activities causing such conditions?

The relationships among work factors, biomechanical loads, and responses are supported by mathematical models and direct measurements. The mathematical models are widely accepted and applied to design mechanical structures in aircraft and automotive design. Direct measurements have been used to a lesser extent than modeling because they are potentially injurious to human subjects; however, when they have been used they generally support the biomechanical models.

It has been shown that the load forces encountered over time in normal work activities often approach the physiological and mechanical tissue limits. Limits may be exceeded as a result of a single high force or as a result of repeated loads over time. Some tissues have a greater ability to adapt to repeated loads if there is sufficient recovery time between successive loads, while other tissues, e.g., nerves, are less able to adapt.

Biomechanical loads are encountered in activities of work, daily living, and recreation. The contribution of these activities to tissue response is related to their relative duration and intensity. For most people, their main exposure is at work. There is a substantial body of epidemiological literature that shows a disproportionately high incidence of musculoskeletal disorders of all types among persons exposed to high biomechanical loads. Although there can be debate about acceptable exposure limits, there can be little disagreement about the fundamental relationship between extreme work exposures and musculoskeletal morbidity.

Question 4: What is the relative contribution of any causal factors identified in the literature to the development of such conditions in (a) the general population; (b) specific industries; and (c) specific occupational groups?

Data at the population and industry level have been collected for a variety of purposes by different groups using different methods. Some data are based on survey results, some on clinical or medical diagnoses, and some on compensation claims. In the judgment of the steering committee, it is not possible to make useful comparisons on the basis of these data.

The incidence of musculoskeletal disorders in any specific occupational group can be expected to reflect the tissue loads imposed by the work, the tissue tolerances of the mix of individuals doing it, and the other activities in their lives imposing related loads. The relative contribution of the different factors in any occupational group depends on (1) the strength of these relationships across the ranges of individuals and activities in that group and (2) the variability of the individuals and activities. For example, gender will not be an important predictive factor if men and women do not, on average, have different tissue tolerances for the loads imposed in that occupational group or if workers in the group are overwhelmingly men or women. The relative contribution in a specific industry will, similarly, depend on the mix of individuals and tasks in it. Unfortunately, measurements of the relevant features of individuals and tasks are typically unavailable, limiting our ability to assess the relative contribution of different factors across groups. The evidence shows that the incidence of musculoskeletal disorders is higher among individuals who perform activities that exceed tissue tolerances. Generally speaking, the more that they perform those activities, the greater are their risks for such disorders.

Question 5: What is the incidence of such conditions in (a) the general population; (b) specific industries; and (c) specific occupational groups?

Current knowledge about the incidence of each of the conditions described in Question 1 in the general adult population is limited because (1) the conditions are clinically diagnosed, typically in doctors' offices; (2) diagnostic criteria for these conditions are not uniformly applied; (3) there are no data collection systems to capture such diagnoses in the health care system; and (4) two-thirds of the adults in the general population *are* employed, with variable occupational risks. Those who are not employed, including those with various chronic conditions and disabilities, are not a suitable reference population. Data on industry and occupational groups are based on a wide variety of methods that have been collected for different purposes. It is the steering committee's judgment that it is not possible to make useful comparisons on the basis of these data.

Question 6: Does the literature reveal any specific guidance to prevent the development of such conditions in (a) the general population; (b) specific industries; and (c) specific occupational groups?

Specific interventions can affect the reported rate of musculoskeletal disorders in specific industries and for specific occupations. Interventions can also reduce reports of musculoskeletal disorders, the presence of risk factors, and the reporting of comfort and pain associated with work. It is also clear that the effectiveness of interventions can be improved if they are tailored to specific occupations and work settings. There is a dearth of data on interventions in the general population.

Question 7: What scientific questions remain unanswered, and may require further research, to determine which occupational activities in which specific industries cause or contribute to work-related musculoskeletal disorders?

Looking at this web of evidence, we have reached three major conclusions:

- Musculoskeletal disorders are a serious national problem: estimates of costs range from $13 to $20 billion annually.
- These problems are caused by work and non-work activities.
- There are interventions that can reduce the problems.

We have also identified some focused research projects, the results of which could increase the efficacy of interventions. Some of these projects would produce useful results within specific research areas; others would increase the connections among the areas. It is a strength of the science that it points to these specific opportunities (see the discussion of future research above).

4

Conclusions

The steering committee has explored the complex problem of musculoskeletal disorders in the workplace. We have supplemented our professional expertise with workshop presentations, commissioned papers and other submissions, and discussions with invited workshop participants. We find very clear signals on some topics and weaker signals on others—but little in the way of contradiction. Thus, while there are many points about which we would like to know more, there is little to shake our confidence in the thrust of our conclusions, which draw on converging results from many disciplines, using many methods:

• There is a higher incidence of reported pain, injury, loss of work, and disability among individuals who are employed in occupations where there is a high level of exposure to physical loading than for those employed in occupations with lower levels of exposure.

• There is a strong biological plausibility to the relationship between the incidence of musculoskeletal disorders and the causative exposure factors in high-exposure occupational settings.

• Research clearly demonstrates that specific interventions can reduce the reported rate of musculoskeletal disorders for workers who perform high-risk tasks. No known single intervention is universally effective. Successful interventions require attention to individual, organizational, and job characteristics, tailoring the corrective actions to those characteristics.

• Research can (1) provide a better understanding of the mechanisms that underlie the established relationships between causal factors and outcomes so that workers who are at risk can be identified and interventions undertaken before problems develop; (2) consider the influence of multiple factors (mechanical, work, social, etc.) on symptoms, injury, reporting, and disability; (3) provide more information about the relationship between incremental change in load and incremental biological response as a basis for defining the most efficient interventions; (4) improve the caliber of measurements for risk factors, outcome variables, and injury data collection and reporting systems; and (5) provide better understanding of the clinical course of these disorders.

By and large, the controversies that we observed reflect the usual disputatiousness of science, which advances when speculative challenges lead to new and clarifying results. One feature of the discourse around musculoskeletal disorders is that it sometimes involves individuals from one discipline (or subdiscipline) who reject entirely the legitimacy of research from another. The steering committee understands the claims made by these often forceful advocates of particular research ideologies. However, we respect the contributions of properly designed research conducted by the variety of disciplines needed for the topic.

The steering committee's task has been to examine the state of the evidence. As such, we have tried to assess the plausible ranges of effects for the various factors that have been studied systematically. We have, however, deliberately avoided providing recommendations for action for three reasons:

1. The risk of musculoskeletal disorders depends on the interaction of person and task, as does the effectiveness of options for reducing those risks. A full specification would require much more detailed treatment of person-task combinations than is possible here. We have, instead, focused on the scientific principles that should guide the prediction and prevention of problems.

2. We have not reviewed the full range of consequences of musculoskeletal disorders and interventions related to them. For example, we have not evaluated the effects of ergonomics programs on employee productivity, turnover, and morale. Nor have we examined the effects of musculoskeletal disorders on the economic and psychological well-being of injured individuals and their families. Rational decision making must consider the full set of relevant consequences.

3. Rational decision making also depends on the relative importance attached to the different consequences. Different people and institutions will have different values and different opportunities for action, at the governmental, employer, and individual levels.

References

Aaras, A.
  1994 The impact of ergonomic interventions on individual health and corporate prosperity in a telecommuni-
        cations environment. *Ergonomics* 37(10):1679-1696.
AFL-CIO
  1997 *Stop the Pain.* Washington, DC: AFL-CIO.
Armstrong, T.
  1985 Mechanical considerations of skin in work. *American Journal of Industrial Medicine* 8:463-472.
Armstrong, T., J. Foulke, B. Martin, J. Gerson, and D. Rempel
  1994 Investigation of applied forces in alphanumeric keyboard work. *American Industrial Hygiene Association
        Journal* 55(1):30-35.
Ashton-Miller, J.A.
  1998 Response of Muscle and Tendon to Injury and Overuse. Paper prepared for the Steering Committee for
        the Workshop on Work-Related Musculoskeletal Injuries.
Bernard, B.P., ed.
  1997 *Musculoskeletal Disorders and Workplace Factors: A Critical Review of Epidemiologic Evidence for Work-
        Related Musculoskeletal Disorders of the Neck, Upper Extremity, and Low Back.* Cincinnati, OH: U.S.
        Department of Health and Human Services.
Bongers, P.M., C.R. de Winter, M.A.J. Kompier, and V.H. Hildebrandt
  1993 Psychosocial factors at work and musculoskeletal disease. *Scandinavian Journal of Work and Environmental
        Health* 19:297-312.
Bureau of Labor Statistics
  1995 *Workplace Injuries and Illnesses in 1994.* USDL 95-508. Washington, DC: U.S. Department of Labor.
Campbell, D.T., and J.C. Stanley
  1966 *Experimental and Quasi-Experimental Designs for Research.* Chicago, IL: Rand McNally.
Chaffin, D., and G. Andersson
  1990 *Occupational Biomechanics.* Second Edition. New York: John Wiley.

Cook, T.D., and D.T. Campbell
  1979 *Quasi-Experimentation: Design and Analysis Issues for Field Settings.* Chicago, IL: Rand McNally.
Cordray, D.S.
  1986 Quasi-experimental analysis: A mixture of methods and judgment. *New Directions in Program Evaluation* 31:9-28.
Einhorn, H.J., and R.M. Hogarth
  1986 Judging probable cause. *Psychological Bulletin* 99(1):3-19.
Evanoff, B.
  1998 Work-Related Musculoskeletal Disorders: Examining the Research Base Epidemiology: Physical Factors. Paper prepared for the Steering Committee for the Workshop on Work-Related Musculoskeletal Injuries.
Faucett, J., and R.A. Werner
  1998 Non-Biomechanical Factors Potentially Affecting Musculoskeletal Disorders. Paper prepared for the Steering Committee for the Workshop on Work-Related Musculoskeletal Injuries.
Franzblau, A.
  1998 The Epidemiology of Workplace Factors and Musculoskeletal Disorders: An Assessment of the NIOSH Review. Paper prepared for the Steering Committee for the Workshop on Work-Related Musculoskeletal Injuries.
Gerr, F.
  1998 Workshop on Work-Related Musculoskeletal Injuries: Examining the Research Base Panel on Epidemiology: Risk Factors. Paper prepared for the Steering Committee for the Workshop on Work-Related Musculoskeletal Injuries.
Jones, R.J.
  1997 Corporate ergonomics programs of a large poultry processor. *American Industrial Hygiene Association Journal* 58(2):132-137.
Lahad, A., A.D. Malter, A.O. Berg, and R.A. Deyo
  1994 The effectiveness of four interventions for prevention of low back pain. *Journal of the American Medical Association* 272(16):1286-1291.
Marras, W., and K.P. Granata
  1997 The development of an EMG-assisted model to assess spine loading during whole-body free-dynamic lifting. *Journal of Electromyography and Kinesiology* 17(4):259-268.
Marras, W.S., K.P. Granata, K.G. Davis, W.G. Allread, and M.J. Jorgensen
  1997 Spine loading and probability of low back disorder risk as a function of box location on a pallet. *International Journal of Human Factors in Manufacturing* 7(4):323-336.
McKenzie, F., J. Storment, P. Van Hook, and T.J. Armstrong
  1985 A program for control of repetitive trauma disorder associated with hand tool operations in a telecommunications manufacturing facility. *American Industrial Hygiene Association Journal* 46(1):674-678.
National Institute for Occupational Safety and Health
  1996 *National Occupational Research Agenda.* Publication No. 96-115. U.S. Department of Health and Human Services, Public Health Service, Centers for Disease Control and Prevention, National Institute for Occupational Safety and Health. Washington, DC: U.S. Department of Health and Human Services.
Normand, J., D. Vlahov, and L. Moses, eds.
  1995 *Preventing HIV Transmission: The Role of Sterile Needles and Bleach.* Panel on Needle Exchange and Bleach Distribution Programs, National Research Council. Washington, DC: National Academy Press.
Punnett, L.
  1998 Epidemiologic Studies of Physical Ergonomic Stressors and Musculoskeletal Disorders. Paper prepared for the Steering Committee for the Workshop on Work-Related Musculoskeletal Injuries.
Radwin, R.G., and S.A. Lavender
  1998 Work Factors, Personal Factors, and Internal Loads: Biomechanics of Work Stressors. Paper prepared for the Steering Committee for the Workshop on Work-Related Musculoskeletal Injuries.
Rempel, D., L. Dahlin, and G. Lundborg
  1998 Biological Response of Peripheral Nerves to Loading: Pathophysiology of Nerve Compression Syndromes and Vibration Induced Neuropathy. Paper prepared for the Steering Committee for the Workshop on Work-Related Musculoskeletal Injuries.

Sandler, H.M., and R.S. Blume
  1998 Analysis of the Scientific Approach in Assessing Epidemiological Evidence for the Relationship Between Work and Musculoskeletal Disorders. Paper prepared for the Steering Committee for the Workshop on Work-Related Musculoskeletal Injuries.

Smith, M.J., B.-T. Karsh, and F.B.P. Moro
  1998 A Review of Research on Interventions to Control Musculoskeletal Disorders. Paper prepared for the Steering Committee for the Workshop on Work-Related Musculoskeletal Injuries.

Snook, S.H., and V.M. Ciriello
  1991 The design of manual handling tasks: Revised tables of maximum acceptable weights and forces. *Ergonomics* 34(9):1197-1213.

Wegman, D.H.
  1998 Workshop on Work-Related Musculoskeletal Injuries: Examining the Research Base Panel on Epidemiology: Physical Factors: Summary Comments. Paper prepared for the Steering Committee for the Workshop on Work-Related Musculoskeletal Injuries.

World Health Organization
  1977 *World Health Classification: Manual of the International Statistical Classification of Diseases, Injuries, and Causes of Death.* 9th Revision. Geneva, Switzerland: World Health Organization.

  1985 *Identification and Control of Work-Related Diseases.* Report Series 714. Geneva, Switzerland: World Health Organization.

II

Workshop Summary

Introduction

In May 1998, the National Institutes of Health asked the National Academy of Sciences/National Research Council to assemble a group of experts for two tasks: to examine the scientific literature relevant to the issue of work-related musculoskeletal disorders of the lower back, neck, and upper extremities and to address seven questions posed by U.S. Representative Robert Livingston on this topic. The steering committee established to carry out these tasks was composed of experts in orthopedic surgery, occupational medicine, epidemiology, ergonomics, human factors, and risk analysis. It was responsible for designing and moderating a workshop, identifying and inviting participation by the leading researchers in relevant areas, and preparing two reports: one presenting the steering committee's conclusions and the other summarizing the workshop and providing the papers prepared for the workshop. The first report (National Research Council, 1998) was issued in September 1998. This is the second report.

The workshop was designed to focus on the current state of the scientific research base pertaining to work-related musculoskeletal disorders, including risk factors that can contribute to such disorders, and interventions that may alleviate or prevent such disorders. The steering committee invited approximately 90 leading scientists from the fields of orthopedic surgery, occupational medicine, public health, ergonomics, and human factors to participate in the workshop; 66 of the invitees attended. In selecting participants, the steering committee relied primarily on two criteria: experts who are

44

actively engaged in pertinent research and diversity of participants, representing a wide range of scientific disciplines, perspectives, beliefs, and approaches.

The workshop took place at the National Academy of Sciences on August 20-21, 1998. Several participants were commissioned to prepare and present papers; others provided written and oral responses to the papers. This report summarizes the papers and workshop discussions. (See Appendices A and B for the list of participants and the agenda.)

In designing the workshop and commissioning papers, the steering committee chose not to focus on specific parts of the body and associated musculoskeletal disorders. Instead, the steering committee sought to examine the many biological, biomechanical, non-biomechanical, and physical and psychological differences among individuals that might play a role in the development of musculoskeletal disorders. The steering committee believed this approach would provide a framework for reviewing the science base in each area, as well as the overlaps among them.

The steering committee organized the workshop around five major topics: (1) biological responses of tissues, specifically muscles, tendons, and nerves, to biomechanical stressors;[1] (2) work factors, individual factors, and internal loads—that is, the biomechanics of work stressors; (3) the epidemiology of physical factors; (4) nonbiomechanical factors that may affect musculoskeletal disorders; and (5) interventions to prevent or mitigate musculoskeletal disorders. For four of these topics, discussions at the workshop centered on a paper (or papers) commissioned for the workshop, followed by the comments of invited discussants. For the epidemiology of physical factors, the steering committee used a panel format to take advantage of a recent review of this literature (Bernard et al., 1997).

ORGANIZING FRAMEWORK

The steering committee developed a conceptual framework integrating the factors thought to be related to the occurrence of musculoskeletal disorders. This framework was used to organize the workshop topics and was presented to all participants at the outset of the workshop.

Figure 1 presents that framework. It diagrams the work-related and other factors most frequently involved in the development of musculoskeletal disorders. It is a useful framework for examining the diverse literatures associated with musculoskeletal disorders, each reflecting the roles that work-related biomechanical, psychosocial, organizational, and individual factors can play in the development of musculoskeletal disorders. The framework also suggests the pathways by which musculoskeletal disorders can occur and be avoided.

The central musculoskeletal disorder mechanism appears within the load-response box of Figure 1. It shows the load-response relationship that expresses the biomechanical

---

[1]Two papers were commissioned for this topic—one focusing on muscles and tendons and the other on nerves.

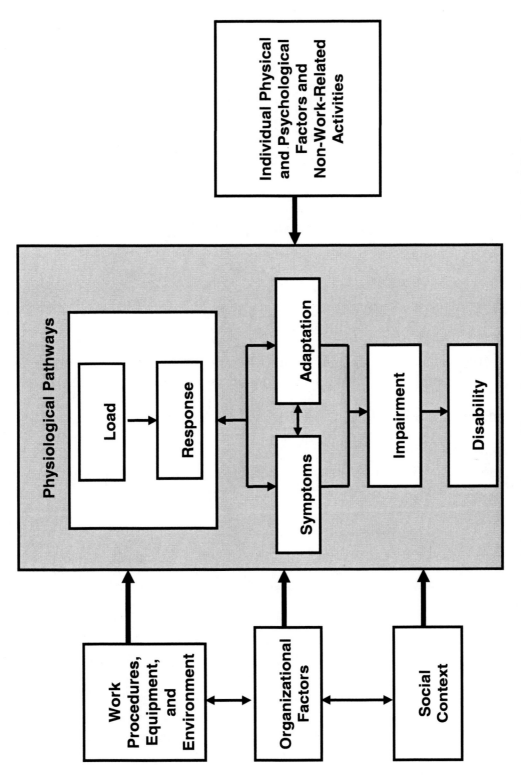

FIGURE 1 Conceptual framework of physiological pathways and factors that potentially contribute to musculoskeletal disorders.

component of musculoskeletal disorders. Loads of various magnitudes are imposed on bone or tissue in various ways. The impact of loads on tissues may change in the course of a day because of changes in fatigue, work pattern or style, coactivation of muscle structures, or other factors. The impact of loads on tissues can provoke several responses. If the load exceeds a mechanical tolerance or the ability of the tissue to withstand the load, tissue damage will occur. For example, damage to a vertebral end plate will occur if the load borne by the spine is heavy enough. Other tissue responses may include such reactions as inflammation, edema, and biochemical responses.

Systematic responses of the body to biomechanical loading may produce both symptomatic and asymptomatic reactions. Some of these reactions contain feedback mechanisms that can influence the tissue loading and response relationship, as illustrated in the gray box (physiological pathways) of Figure 1. For example, pain might cause an individual to use muscles in a different way, thus changing the associated loading pattern. Repetitive loading of a tissue might lead an individual to ignore discomfort signals and expose himself to greater loads, which he might or might not be able to bear. The symptom and adaptation portions in Figure 1 can interact with each other as well. For example, swelling might lead to a tissue adaptation, such as increased production of lubricant in a joint.

These symptoms, responses, and adaptive behaviors can lead to functional impairment. In the workplace, this might be reported as a work-related musculoskeletal disorder. If severe enough, the impairment could be considered a disability, and lost or restricted workdays could result.

In the box to the right, the framework recognizes the influence of individual factors, including physical and psychological factors, that might affect the musculoskeletal disorder sequence. For example, psychological factors can affect one's willingness to report a musculoskeletal disorder or claim that the impairment is a disability. Physical factors might involve reduced tissue tolerance due to age, gender, and overall physical condition. Disease states, such as arthritis, also can affect a person's biochemical response to tissue loading.

In the boxes to the left of the central physiological pathways, Figure 1 identifies environmental factors that might affect the development of musculoskeletal disorders, including physical work, organizational factors, and social context. For example, physical work factors (such as lifting heavy boxes or equipment) can affect the loading that is experienced by a worker's tissues and structures, and can also influence the symptoms and reported incidence of a musculoskeletal disorder. Organizational factors can also influence each component of the musculoskeletal disorder sequence. For example, time pressures to complete a task might frustrate a worker and provide an incentive or disincentive to report a musculoskeletal disorder or to claim that an impairment should be considered a disability. Although little studied, pathways exist between organizational influences and the biomechanical and body reaction (symptoms and response) components of the musculoskeletal disorder sequence.

Finally, social context is also a potential modifier of the musculoskeletal disorder sequence. For example, social factors, such as lack of support in dealing with psychological stress (e.g., no spousal support), might influence a worker's reporting behavior or even the worker's biomechanical responses.

The steering committee believes that this framework summarizes the diverse literatures regarding musculoskeletal disorders by characterizing the pathways that each literature addresses. For example, epidemiological investigations often explore the pathways between the physical work environment and the reporting of impairments or the pathway between organizational factors and the reporting of symptoms. Ergonomic studies often explore the pathways between physical work factors and biomechanical loads imposed on a tissue. The framework also provides a means to explain the interactions among factors. For example, the combination of a particular set of physical work and organizational factors might yield an increase in the reporting of symptoms that neither, considered alone, would yield.

Often the whole is greater than the sum of its parts. The steering committee deliberately sought to examine the evidence as a whole and not to restrict inquiry to one particular sector or field of inquiry. It also sought to place individual studies in context, by showing the factors that they do and do not address. The workshop was designed with these considerations in mind.

The next five sections provide summaries of each paper and the workshop discussions of them.

BIOLOGICAL RESPONSES OF TISSUES TO STRESSORS

Presentations

Soft Tissue Responses to Physical Stressors: Muscles, Tendons, and Ligaments

James Ashton-Miller

Reported soft tissue injuries can be the result of stresses (e.g., of posture, motion, or vibration) from a single, mechanical event or from repetitive events. The risk of such injury increases with acute or chronic changes in intrinsic factors (age, gender, inherited tissue anatomy, pain responses) related to an individual's physical capacity and extrinsic factors (work and life-style factors) related to the physical demands of the environment. Responses to soft tissue injuries include a complex cascade of events involving inflammatory responses, which mark the first phase of the healing process, followed by a remodeling phase in which tissues are restored. A smooth transition through these healing phases requires that physical loading of tissues be temporarily reduced, in part because of pain and discomfort. This should be followed by a careful increase of physical loading during remodeling to avoid exacerbating symptoms.

Muscles

Muscles can suffer from a variety of injuries, including contraction induced injuries, single-event muscle strain injuries, and fatigue. There is considerable scientific exploration of these types of muscle injury. Three models of muscle injury promise the most return in understanding work-related muscle disorders. The first is an "eccentric contraction model" in which muscles are subjected to a single, rapid stretch or a series of repetitive contractions. Research using this model has been conducted over the past 15 years in human and animal studies. The animal studies, in particular, have demonstrated that if a period of healing is allowed, the same forces can be later applied without reinjury. Age can affect the ability of the muscles to heal, and exercise, at any age, improves muscle strength and endurance, though it does not compensate for all the advantages of youth.

A second promising model has been developed to investigate muscle fatigue. This model is driven by theories that a muscle's ability to sustain power output is a function of its fiber composition and oxidative capacity. Recent *in vivo* laboratory studies of human muscle have used noninvasive spectroscopy to measure changes in tissue oxygenation in response to varying levels and duration of force. Decreased oxygen levels with increasing force were demonstrated (in nearly linear proportions) and also were associated with higher reports of discomfort by the study subjects.

The third model suggests that muscle stiffness, tenderness, and pain are associated with the release of substances, such as potassium chloride and lactic acid, during muscle contraction. Laboratory experiments testing this model involve either induced muscle fatigue or the injection of irritants into human muscle tissue. Both subjectively reported pain and myoelectric activity are monitored. The results of these studies also suggest that different muscle groups have different pain levels (jaw muscles, for example, are more sensitive than neck muscles).

Tendons and Ligaments

Tendons, ligaments, retinaculae, intervertebral discs, and the fasciae of muscles are all connective tissues between bone and muscles. The primary structural component of these tissues is collagen, which is demonstrably susceptible to external stresses. In the case of ligaments, theory suggests that strains can reduce the crimp or waviness of collagen fibrils in the ligaments and increase susceptibility to injury. Most studies of ligament injuries have focused on the knee; these studies show that ligaments are generally slow to heal and repair themselves (up to 2 years in animal studies). Aging also appears to affect the tensile strength and elasticity of the ligaments. Biomechanical, *in vitro* laboratory studies have shown that human hand tendons can be weakened under the friction generated by awkward hand or wrist postures when the hand is gripping an object. Animal studies show that repetitive strains on tendons can cause degenerative changes—increased inflammation, more capillaries, edema and fibrosis. These study findings could be augmented by *in vivo* evidence of the link between cumulative strain and tendon and ligament injury.

The ability to study cause and effect in overuse-related injuries is hampered by difficulties in accurately estimating the relationships between force and human muscles and tendons throughout different parts and activities of the day—commuting, work, and home and leisure activities. A laudable goal would be to reduce work-related stress on tissues sufficiently so that whether injured "on" or "off" the job, tissues can heal and repair in a reasonable time without risk of becoming chronic conditions.

Soft Tissue Responses to Physical Stressors: Nerves
David Rempel, Lars Dahlin, and Göran Lundborg

We focus on the effects of compression on peripheral nerve functioning as demonstrated in human and animal studies. Peripheral nerve dysfunction associated with nerve compression typically occurs where nerves pass through a tight tunnel formed by stiff tissue boundaries. The resulting "confined space" limits tissue movement and can lead to sustained tissue pressure. Well-known examples are compression of the median nerve at the wrist, of the ulnar nerve at the wrist or elbow, and the spinal root nerves at the vertebral foramen. Clinical reports suggest that lesions that take up some of this confined space (tumors, cysts, and so forth) can cause nerve injury. So too can edema and extracellular matrix in the soft tissues (such as those associated with pregnancy and congestive heart failure). Other conditions, such as diabetes mellitus or an inflammatory reaction, can also increase the susceptibility of nerves to compression injuries.

The studies we examined to illustrate the effects of nerve compression on peripheral nerves included human and animal laboratory studies of the physiologic, pathophysiologic, biochemical, and histologic effects of "loading." Four of these studies demonstrate the state of the evidence on peripheral nerves as well as its limitations.

The first of these studies is an histological study on laboratory rats. In this study, varying levels of nerve compression were applied to the sciatic nerves. Endoneurial fluid pressure was measured at several time intervals up to 24 hours after the removal of compression. Greater levels of compression were associated with greater and longer lasting levels of endoneurial fluid pressure. Histologic examination of nerve tissue showed edema and degenerating nerve fibers after 8 hours even at the lowest levels of induced compression used in the study.

A second, similar study examined nerve compression over longer time periods—up to 4 weeks, under relatively high levels of nerve compression. The histologic results were edema, inflammatory reactions, and fibrosis within hours of compression. After 2 to 3 weeks, marked fibrosis, demyelination, and axonal degeneration were evident.

Related studies of animals exposed to vibration of the hind limbs for 4 hours over a period of 5 days suggest similar edema and structural nerve changes.

These two studies deal with sciatic nerves. Two other illustrative studies deal with nerves in the fingers and wrists. One study examined carpal tunnel nerve pressure in 20 people by asking them to press a load cell with their index fingers and then pinch the same cell between thumb and index finger. Both the pressing and pinching tasks led to increasing extraneural pressure in the carpal tunnel, but the pinching task was associated with pressures twice as high as the pressing task. The other study involved 10 men (ages 17-30) exposed to hand vibration in their work who were matched with 12 male cadavers of similar ages without such work exposures. Biopsies of the nerve just proximal to the wrist in both the living subjects and the control group (cadavers) showed pathological changes to the nerve in all 10 subjects and in one of the controls. Nerve changes included the breakdown of myelin and fibrosis.

These studies demonstrate a clear biological effect: that nerves are particularly sensitive to loading at relatively low levels of compression and exhibit changes that can persist. Humans exposed to hand vibrations or performing certain maneuvers can experience elevated extraneural pressures that in laboratory animals would result in nerve injury. All of these studies are limited in some ways: limited exposures to compression, lack of statistical comparisons, investigation of only one area of nerve dysfunction when multiple nerves are involved, and measurement difficulties that limit understanding of precise dose-response relationships. Further research could overcome some of the limits and usefully add to our understanding of these biological effects.

Discussion

The papers provide evidence for several conclusions about soft tissue response to physical stress. Although certain loads can be tolerated or adapted to, all soft tissues, including muscle, tendon, ligament, fascia, synovia, cartilage, intervertebral disc, and nerve, fail if subjected to sufficient force. Data from cadaver studies provide ranges within which such failures occur, as do animal models of some soft tissues tested in laboratory studies. Even at levels clearly below these failure ranges, however, there is scientific evidence from laboratory studies that soft tissue responses include inflammation, muscle fatigue, and ultrastructural degeneration that does not heal without cessation or restriction of the provoking force. As Figure 1 illustrates, intrinsic factors, such as age and conditioning, can influence soft tissue response and recovery, as can extrinsic factors, including the work environment and life-style characteristics.

The discussants of the Ashton-Miller and Rempel et al. papers did not generally dispute the conclusions presented, though many believe that greater attention to some aspects of the scientific evidence on soft tissue responses to stress could provide additional, important insights on tissues responsible for work-related musculoskeletal disorders. Suggested research areas included:

• studies of the synovium (the tissue lining the tendons and joints);

- recent biological work on cytokines and growth factors considered important in tissue inflammation, healing, and repair;
- more scrutiny of studies using electromyography (EMG) to monitor muscle fatigue and pain (EMG measurement is noninvasive, objective, and can be used to establish biomarkers for muscle injury); and
- studies of the effects of peripheral tissue inflammation on the central nervous system, especially in cases where muscle pain lasts much longer than expected.

Several other themes emerged from the discussions of these papers. The need for more research and more integrative research was a major theme. The long-term or chronic effects of soft tissue responses to stressors was one area in which discussants believed further research was critical. Steven Lehman, University of California at Berkeley, raised this issue in discussing the need to better understand the physiology of low-force, long-duration work and its effects on motor control, muscle fatigue, pain, and the recovery process. Carlo de Luca, Boston University, suggested the use of electromyography as a method for studying muscle fatigue.

The clinicians among the discussants stressed that, although most of the laboratory evidence presented in the papers corroborated their own case observations, that laboratory evidence deals primarily with acute stressors while they find the most difficult cases to be those involving chronic stressors. Susan Mackinnon, Washington University School of Medicine, noted that her experience indicates that an understanding of patient symptoms requires an understanding of chronic nerve compression. She described a model of chronic nerve compression in rats and primates that closely mimics the pathological changes seen in humans. These pathological changes (ranging from edema to degeneration) are paralleled by the symptoms of patients in clinical testing. Patient complaints typically begin with intermittent numbness brought on by specific postures, but not apparent when the patient is resting. As compression continues or increases, numbness becomes more persistent and, eventually, permanent. There are also neural and physiological symptoms which begin with complaints of aching and progress to weakness and finally, to muscle atrophy.

Robert Szabo, University of California, Davis, reinforced Mackinnon's comments, noting that the Rempel et al. paper's discussion of laboratory studies on nerve compression over time did not highlight the clinical relevance of the findings. The findings show a progressive degeneration of nerve health under sustained compression, which suggests that nerve compression effects can be viewed on a spectrum divided into early, intermediate, and late categories. In clinical terms, early stages respond most favorably to conservative treatment (such as steroid injections and splinting for carpal tunnel syndrome). For intermediate stages of nerve compression, involving numbness and parasthesia, patients

> *We need a good model of chronic nerve compression.*
> (Robert Szabo, University of California, Davis)

respond well to nerve decompression via the surgical release of the carpal tunnel. In late stages, patients often have permanent sensory loss with long-standing edema and fibrosis: these patients may benefit from carpal tunnel release, but this will not eliminate all their symptoms.

Putting these clinical views on chronic nerve compression in an even broader context, Thomas Mayer, PRIDE, Dallas, Texas, reported that even when all forms of acute nerve compression and musculotendinous sprains and strains are considered, they account for a small portion of medical care and medical costs (see box).

Another common "need for research" theme among the paper discussants was the need to generate links between specific anatomically distinct disorders (as they are clinically observed) and specific underlying patterns of pathology. J. Steven Moore, Texas A&M, summarized this view by noting that models that relate (1) specific patterns of musculoskeletal loading to (2) distinct internal stress in specific anatomical structures that (3) elicit tissue

> *It has been known for 2 to 3 decades that 90 percent of the musculoskeletal claims comprise only 20 percent of the medical and indemnity expenditures. The 10 percent of cases extending beyond the acute phase of soft tissue healing account for 80 percent of the system costs for low back pain.*
>
> (Thomas Mayer, PRIDE, Dallas, Texas)

responses that (4) lead to observed tissue changes—are critical to diagnosis, treatment, and epidemiological tracking of musculoskeletal disorders and the circumstances under which people are exposed to such disorders. Echoing these remarks, Kai-Nan An, Mayo Clinic, noted that inconsistencies in the definitions and diagnosis of work-related repetitive stress injuries makes the true incidence of such injuries and the factors that provoke them difficult to identify.

Overall, the paper authors and discussants agreed that sound research shows that muscles, tendons, ligaments, and nerves can fail when subjected to sufficient force and that they can heal and repair themselves over time under the appropriate conditions (restriction or cessation of force and gradual reconditioning). However, there was also agreement that work remains to be done in establishing the links between impetus to injury to soft tissue response, on one side, and optimal conditions (either physical or environmental) for healing and repair of injury, on the other.

> *We now have the biomechanical and mechanobiological concepts and techniques to begin rigorous study that could lead to progress in prevention and treatment of these [musculoskeletal] disorders. The challenge is to bring first-rate mechanics, biology, and clinical perspectives together in order to approach the [research] problems in a unified, consistent manner.*
>
> (Dennis Carter, Stanford)

WORK FACTORS, INDIVIDUAL HOST FACTORS, AND INTERNAL LOADS: BIOMECHANICS OF WORK STRESSORS

Presentation

Work Factors and Biomechanics

Robert Radwin and *Steven Lavender*

The key tissues involved in the development of work-related musculoskeletal disorders (bone, ligament, tendon, muscle, disc, and nerve tissues) are stressed or loaded during the performance of work tasks in ways that can be predicted by theory and observed using diverse measurement methods. Tissue stress may be influenced by exertion, posture, contact stress, vibration, and variations in temperature. There is a considerable body of empirical evidence and findings, using models, that support relationships between external loads and the associated internal loads that can damage key tissues. This evidence not only supports a relationship between external and internal loads, but also demonstrates that, because of the biomechanics of the musculoskeletal system, internal loads are generally several times higher than the external loads that generate them.

Typically, theoretical models used to predict relationships between external and internal loads are mathematical representations of musculoskeletal mechanics that predict tissue reactions under external force. For example, Armstrong and Chaffin (1979) used a mathematical model of the mechanical relationships between belts and pulleys to describe the external forces, postures, and internal tendon positions that induce loads in the carpal tunnel of the wrist. If a tendon sliding over the surface of the wrist is considered analogous to a belt wrapped around a pulley, then the mathematical expression of this relationship predicts that the external force generated by the exertion of the hand is proportional to the compressive force of the internal tension developed in the tendons over the wrist and in the finger flexor muscles. This tension can affect adjacent anatomical structures such as ligaments and bones. The model also predicts that if the tissue lining the tendon (the synovia) becomes inflamed, internal tension increases. Repeated tension can further aggravate inflammation and induce swelling (Chaffin and Andersson, 1991).

Empirical observation of the relationship between external and internal loads requires a variety of measurement methods. External loads that impact internal tissues are rarely measured directly due to the obvious risks associated with subjecting people to potentially damaging levels of physical force and the invasiveness of direct measures of internal tissue responses. Direct measures are found in cadaver studies: they show the geometric and mechanical properties of tissues and their responses to external loads, including the order in which tissues respond. For example, Adams et al. (1980) found that severing ligaments in cadaver lumbar motion segments demonstrates that the supraspinous/interspinous ligament segments are the first ligament tissues to become stressed when there is forward bending of the lumbar spine. Other measures of external and internal stress relationships come from the use of force gauges and electromyography in studies of people engaged in physical activities that involve a range of exertion, posture, vibration, and temperature. These studies have been conducted both in laboratories and workplaces.

Physical stress factors in the workplace can be measured by observational surveys of the physical demands of jobs or tasks, by time and motion studies in which specific data are collected to assess physical stress, and by analytical examination of workplace layout and work processes (especially material flow and work scheduling). If hand tools are required, study of the exertion and the type of grip needed to use them can be made. These measures are considered less accurate and precise than more direct measures, partly because their ability to link external and internal stresses is limited and partly because they rely more on human observation. An example of an observational study measure is the comparison between a workplace designed so that workers must lift heavy objects from a low position and one in which the lift starts at a higher position. Biomechanical theory and laboratory studies show that the low-level lift results in greater spine and disc compression than the high-level lift. Observation and worker self-reports parallel findings from laboratory studies and from models.

Time and motion analyses indicate that the pace of work can also influence the duration and repetitiveness of exertion. These findings, coupled with laboratory results, suggest that faster pacing exacerbates the contraction of soft tissues, although it is known that their ability to perform static contraction decays rapidly over time. Planned job rotation can provide relief from potentially damaging lift, stretch, and repetition exposures. Workers can move from a task that requires shoulder abduction, for example, to one that requires low-level lifting, thus allowing both the shoulder muscles and the spine to recover.

Individuals vary in their internal tissue response to external loads or stresses. Anatomical and physiological differences—including muscle mass, tendon size, ligament range, and bone lengths, for example—can influence the impact of work tasks on individual tissues. Anatomical and physiological factors can also differ with age and gender. Moreover, exposure to physical stresses outside the workplace can influence tissue response.

There is a significant range of measurement, accuracy, precision, and reliability in studies of the relationships between external forces and their impact on internal tissue responses. Taken as a whole, these studies support the link between the physical stresses of work and their impact on the human musculoskeletal system.

Discussion

The relationships among external work factors, external and internal loads, and soft tissue responses (as shown in Figure 1) have been studied extensively, using models, human laboratory studies, and workplace analyses. Exertion, posture, contact stress, vibration, and varying temperatures are all types of external forces or loads that are associated with physical activities. The studies described by the paper and discussants demonstrate that the physical activities of work, daily living, and recreation produce external loads that can be used to estimate internal loads on soft tissues. These estimates of internal loads often approach the mechanical limits of soft tissues, and, in some cases, for some individuals, exceed those limits. The studies also show that soft tissues vary in their responses to loading. Muscle tissue, for example, is better able than nerve tissue to adapt to the types of repetitive loading that can be observed in some workplace environments. In general, the findings of these biomechanical studies, especially when combined with the earlier findings from studies of soft tissue responses, strongly support a relationship between musculoskeletal disorders and external physical stress.

There was a general consensus among the workshop participants invited to discuss the Radwin and Lavender paper. Most clearly agreed that there is enough scientific evidence to confirm that strain on musculoskeletal tissue increases when humans perform physical activities that involve forceful manual exertions, awkward postures, repetitive or prolonged exertions, exposure to vibrations, and exposure to cold temperatures. Discussants differed in their views on the soundness of methodologies used to produce the evidence, in particular, several were skeptical about the reliability of at least some of the observational and analytical methods used in workplace studies.

Several themes emerged in the workshop discussions. Some discussants reinforced and expanded on ideas addressed in the Radwin and Lavender paper; others noted omissions from the paper that, if filled in, could strengthen its conclusions. On the omissions side, several discussants noted the lack of treatment of epidemiological studies that discuss musculoskeletal injury rates in relation to biomechanics. They believe that these links help to establish dose response relationships between external factors and tissue damage, although the relationships are often only at "high/low" level of detail.

In some areas, problematic loading conditions have been clearly delineated. For example, epidemiological studies have repeatedly linked adverse health outcomes with repeated lifting and working of the trunk bent forward, to the side, or twisted.

(Carolyn Sommerich, North Carolina State University)

Richard Wells, University of Waterloo, noted that the paper does not clearly delineate the fact that different histories of external loading may produce different injuries or disorders. As an example, he noted that a single high load on a spinal motion unit may produce an end plate fracture, while low continuous loading, especially in a flexed spinal position, may lead to disc herniation. Thus, sitting in a "low demand" situation may produce injury. Similarly, in muscles, a single, high-force contraction and low-force, long-duration contractions produce different outcomes. These aspects of soft tissue responses help explain apparently paradoxical findings that both high loads and low loads (as in sitting) may be associated with low back pain and that high demand manual tasks and low demand manual tasks (such as keyboard work) may lead to upper limb disorders.

Another omission noted by several discussants was the lack of representation of the range of views on the relationships between biomechanical measures and specific injuries. Mark Redfern, University of Pittsburgh, observed that there is controversy over the biomechanical causation of carpal tunnel syndrome.

> *The carpal tunnel syndrome (CTS) may deserve more detailed [scrutiny] since there is much controversy over CTS and its biomechanical causation.*
>
> (Mark Redfern, University of Pittsburgh)

He also noted that there are differing opinions about how biomechanical measures are related to musculoskeletal disorders and about how such measures are used.

Discussant themes that reinforced and expanded on the points made by Radwin and Lavender include Robert Norman's and W. Monroe Keyserling's comments about the strengths and weaknesses of contemporary methods of workplace analysis. Robert Norman, University of Waterloo, observed that many of the workplace methods that have been used to estimate physical loads are not believed to be highly reliable. These include worker self-reports, checklists, and the use of job titles. W. Monroe Keyserling, University of Michigan, observed that many of the methods discussed in the paper (trained observations, video analysis, electromyography, and goniometry) can produce reliable risk exposure information for jobs that have relatively short cycle times (such as assembly line jobs) or for non-cyclical jobs performed primarily at a single workstation (such as those of telephone operators for an airline). However, numerous jobs remain very difficult to analyze because they involve variability in work activities, locations, and exposures to musculoskeletal stressors. Improvements in workplace analysis methods could better capture the complexities of many jobs.

Finally, all discussants agreed with the paper authors that the difficulties of directly measuring the relationships between external force and internal injury makes refinement of knowledge a challenge in this area of research. The need to more clearly isolate external work forces from those of workers' characteristics (anatomy, strength) and life-styles in their impact on musculoskeletal disorders adds to the research challenges. Carolyn Sommerich, North Carolina State University, Raleigh, called for in-

> *Many researchers . . . in this area [biomechanics of work and musculoskeletal disorders] still focus on physical or nonphysical factors. . . . [This] may influence their conclusions . . . about the relative importance of these factors. The science base . . . [is] enhanced when researchers form interdisciplinary teams . . . [make] assessments across the range of . . . influential factors.*
>
> (Carolyn Sommerich, North Carolina State University)

terdisciplinary research teams to conduct joint investigations on the range of potential factors—workplaces, life-styles, workers' physical characteristics, and a variety of methodological measures.

EPIDEMIOLOGY: PHYSICAL FACTORS

The steering committee decided to use a recent review of the epidemiological studies of work-related musculoskeletal disorders by the National Institute for Occupational Safety and Health (NIOSH) (Bernard et al., 1997) as a starting point for its review of the research literature. The review examines the strengths and weaknesses of 600 selected studies investigating exposure to musculoskeletal disorders in the workplace. The steering committee invited a group of respected epidemiologists to discuss the NIOSH review and the epidemiological studies it covered. These six experts—from within and outside the field—submitted written comments and participated in a panel discussion at the workshop.

The panelists were asked by the steering committee to use four questions to organize their reviews and comments:

1. Has NIOSH missed or overlooked any important body of epidemiological evidence it its review?

2. Describe the methodologies of the studies that have been heavily weighted in the NIOSH assessment. What is the general quality of these studies?

3. Would either the inclusion of any omitted studies or the reassessment of the quality of those reviewed substantially alter the interpretation of the epidemiological evidence that certain physical stressors in the workplace increase the risk of acquiring certain musculoskeletal disorders [MSDs]?

4. What does the evidence [in the NIOSH review] tell us about the incidence [of MSDs] in the general population versus among specific groups of workers?

In most cases, the panelists restricted their reviews to NIOSH coverage of studies involving exposure to work-related biomechanical stressors of the upper extremities, neck, and back. The panel discussion was moderated by Ronald Gray.

Panel Discussion

Bradley Evanoff, Alfred Franzblau, Fredric Gerr, Laura Punnett, Howard Sandler (with Richard Blume), and David Wegman

The general consensus of the panelists was that there is strong evidence from many studies for a positive relationship between the conduct of work and the occurrence of musculoskeletal disorders of the upper extremities, neck, and back. This relationship is especially clear in studies involving high levels of exposure to workplace biomechanical stressors. Examples include the excesses of musculoskeletal disorders of upper extremities among auto assembly workers and sawyers and the excesses of musculoskeletal disorders of the back among materials handlers and health care workers. It is also clear that in such high exposure cases the reduction of biomechanical stress also reduces the prevalence of musculoskeletal disorders. The evidence for the role of biomechanical stress in the occurrence of musculoskeletal disorders among work populations exposed to low levels of biomechanical stress is weaker, although several high quality studies suggest that further investigation is warranted.

In response to the first question—on the comprehensiveness of the NIOSH study—the panelists generally agreed in answering: No. However, some qualifications were noted. For example, NIOSH could have usefully included a listing of the studies not considered in its review but identified in its search; some specific additional studies were discussed by several panelists, but they agreed that no important body of evidence was omitted. Disagreements with the comprehensiveness of the NIOSH review also focused on the lack of assessment regarding the full range of musculoskeletal disorders, the neglect of specific dose relationships and threshold "triggers" of exposure in specific disorders, and the focus on work related factors over non-work-related factors.

In answer to the steering committee's second question—on the weighting and quality of the studies—the panelists generally agreed that the study methods most heavily weighted in the NIOSH review resulted in examination of high-quality studies. Several panelists noted that study methodology was not the sole criterion that NIOSH used to select studies and that NIOSH's comprehensive approach used multiple criteria, including: high participation rates; appropriate "blinding" of investigators; health outcomes defined by symptoms, physical examinations, and independent exposure measures; and explicit criteria for causality that met standard epidemiological practices. Many panelists noted the lack of longitudinal studies in the review, but they emphasized the strengths of well-planned cross-sectional studies, as well as the difficulties and potentially confounding factors in conducting longitudinal studies in the workplace. They noted that the review included many study designs, including ones that were population based, case control, cross-sectional, and case series.

Several panelists suggested that the diagnostic definitions of carpal tunnel syndrome used in many of the studies were problematic since evidence for this diagnosis requires electrodiagnostic measures. Others suggested that some studies of questionable quality were included in the review and that the methods NIOSH used in selecting and weighting studies were not repeatable.

Although inconsistencies and problems in the NIOSH review were noted by many panelists, their answer to the third question posed by the steering committee—on the effects of omitted studies or reassessment of the quality of included studies—were *nearly* unanimous: No. Fredric Gerr noted that more rigorous elimination of studies failing to meet all NIOSH's outlined criteria would substantially reduce the number of studies available for review, but that this smaller body of literature would not substantively change the conclusions drawn by NIOSH regarding work and musculoskeletal disorders. In dissent, however, Howard Sandler said that the NIOSH approach to their review of the evidence was sufficiently flawed to make the conclusions questionable. He stated that NIOSH failed to specify the methodology used to perform weighting, that many of the cited studies had serious deficiencies, and that the cross-sectional studies were particularly weak.

The steering committee's fourth question—on the disorders in the general population versus among specific groups of workers—was acknowledged by all the panelists to be difficult to answer. Although several panelists noted that studies show a higher than expected rate of the disorders among workers with high exposures to physical risk factors, they also agreed that there were very few studies of the incidence or prevalence of specific musculoskeletal disorders in the general population. Even the existing studies are old enough to be suspect, and virtually none are longitudinal. For example, the most recent study of carpal tunnel syndrome incidence in the general population is based on data collected from 1961 to 1980, and incidence may have greatly increased in recent years; in addition, the accuracy and completeness of the data in the study are open to question.

Workshop Discussion

Workshop participants offered both criticisms and support of the NIOSH review. For example, Robert Szabo, University of California, Davis, suggested that even though not one of the studies cited by NIOSH had implicated keyboarding as a cause of carpal tunnel syndrome, the report suggests that keyboarding is a cause. David Florence, American Academy of Orthopedic Surgeons, added that a problem that exists in practice is that workers fabricate musculoskeletal injuries, perhaps as a result of the widespread publicity such injuries have received. Thomas Mayer, PRIDE, Dallas, Texas, observed that there are also macroeconomic implications of concluding that exposure to risk factors at work is associated with higher rates of musculoskeletal disorders, making the review of any evidence in this area a political as well as a scientific discussion. Peter Nathan, Portland Hand Surgery Rehabilitation Center, Oregon, maintained that NIOSH had ignored studies examining the role of nonoccupational factors in the etiology of carpal tunnel syndrome.

I believe the NIOSH document is one of social and political interest. It is not a scientific document; it is a political statement, it is a social statement, and we should acknowledge that. For the most part, only articles suggesting a positive association between work exposure and neuromusculoskeletal symptoms are cited. If an article questioning the work-related hypothesis is presented, the discussion is highly critical. In general, the document does not discuss studies which examine nonoccupational causes of carpal tunnel syndrome.

(Peter Nathan, Portland Hand Surgery Rehabilitation Center)

In contrast, several workshop participants offered views supporting the general consensus of the panelists and the NIOSH review. For example, Paulien Bongers, TNO Prevention and Health, Netherlands, noted that the systematic reviews of the evidence that she had conducted, including both longitudinal and cross-sectional studies, supported the NIOSH conclusions. Margaret Seminario, AFL-CIO, emphasized that the question the NIOSH review, the panel, and the workshop must address is not whether the scientific evidence is perfect, but whether it is sufficient to justify interventions. She added that she finds the evidence is sufficient.

> *The world I come from is one more concerned with policy issues involving how to use the scientific research base in protecting workers. In the context of policy decisions, we do not need perfect information. We need to know that there is a scientific base showing there is risk in the workplace for exposure to factors associated with musculoskeletal risks and that interventions can reduce this risk.*
>
> (Margaret Seminario, AFL-CIO)

NON-BIOMECHANICAL FACTORS THAT CAN AFFECT MUSCULOSKELETAL DISORDERS

Presentation

Epidemiological Evidence that Non-Biomechanical Factors Can Cause Musculoskeletal Disorders

Julia Faucett and Robert A. Werner

Multiple occupational risk factors have been proposed for common musculoskeletal disorders, but a growing number of investigators around the world are reporting relationships between individual factors and non-biomechanical aspects of work and these disorders. Individual factors include age; ongoing medical conditions, such as diabetes or rheumatoid arthritis; weight and height; gender; levels of individual physical conditioning; and inherited anatomical variations, especially in the wrist. Non-biomechanical factors arise from the way work is organized, integrated, and controlled. These things can affect the psychological stress level of work, the degree of social support available, and the satisfaction workers obtain on the job.

Individual Factors

The ultimate mechanism of injury in carpal tunnel syndrome and cumulative trauma disorders is probably ischemia (or localized anemia due to contracted blood vessels) so that any individual factors influencing the health of the vascular system may compromise soft tissues. There is evidence from a number of well-designed studies to support a relationship between systemic disorders—especially diabetes and rheumatoid arthritis—and carpal tunnel syndrome and other disorders related to nerve compression and ischemia. These disorders, however, affect only a small percentage of active workers. Severe vitamin B_6 deficiencies and gynecological conditions (pregnancy, use of oral contraceptives, surgery that affects hormones) have also been posed as risk factors, but the associations with carpal tunnel syndrome and related disorders, though statistically significant, are weak, and their clinical significance is low.

Increasing age has consistently been associated with the slowing of the median nerve across the wrist that is thought to be critical in carpal tunnel syndrome. The association between increased age and other cumulative trauma disorders and low back pain is weak. Studies have generally supported a relationship between obesity (as measured by body mass index ratios) and a diagnosis of carpal tunnel syndrome, but obesity explains less than 8 percent of the variance in such diagnoses. A relationship between obesity and other cumulative trauma disorders is not consistently found in studies of the industrial worker population. General fitness has been negatively associated with obesity and older age, but as an independent factor, it does not help to explain much of the variance in diagnoses of carpal tunnel syndrome, low back pain, or other cumulative trauma disorders.

Gender has also been suggested as an independent risk factor in carpal tunnel syndrome (that is, the prevalence of carpal tunnel syndrome is higher among women). Although there is some evidence supporting this higher prevalence, there are also inconsistencies among the gender study findings that require further investigation. Inherited characteristics of wrist shape and size, carpal tunnel size, and hand size have been investigated in carpal tunnel syndrome: there is strong evidence that a narrow carpal tunnel canal is associated with a diagnosis of carpal tunnel syndrome.

Organizational and Social Factors

Organizational, technological, environmental, and directly task-related features of work systems can influence workers' perceptions of work. These perceptions can, in turn, influence their performance of work in ways that may increase or decrease the likelihood of musculoskeletal disorders. For example, a managerial decision to increase production demands among data processors may evoke fear in an individual worker that he or she cannot complete the task on time. The result may be a change in that individual's work style that includes faster, harder key strokes, higher associated levels of catecholamines and cortisol, which may harm soft tissues, and detrimental delays in awareness of musculoskeletal discomfort.

Studies of non-biomechanical factors in the workplace can be categorized according to the factor emphasized in the investigation: job demands (work load, pace, fluctuations); job content (task variability, meaningfulness, and integration); job control (decision latitude, control over work pace and breaks); work role ambiguity; social relationships and support; and job satisfaction. Workplace investigations provide moderate support for relationships between job demands, job content, and job control and musculoskeletal outcomes. Generally speaking, poorly designed job content, unpredictable and heavy job demands, and lack of decision latitude or control are associated with higher incidence of musculoskeletal disorders. Studies of social relationships have shown that worker support, especially supervisory support, can moderate psychological stress on the job.

The scientific evidence on non-biomechanical factors varies considerably in method, making direct comparisons across studies difficult. Longitudinal studies are sparse. Data on worker perceptions were most frequently measured through worker self-reports, although observational methods have also been used. Outcome measures were sometimes clinical and sometimes reported symptoms, and surveys of non-biomechanical factors used a diversity of measures. Few studies investigated interactions among non-biomechanical factors. Despite these methodological weaknesses, there were moderate, but significant relationships between non-biomechanical factors and the incidence of musculoskeletal disorders across studies. Such consistency suggests that non-biomechanical factors must be considered in investigation of work-related musculoskeletal disorders.

Discussion

Individual, organizational, and social factors (see Figure 1) are possible influences on the physiological pathways that lead from soft tissue loading to the impairment and disability of musculoskeletal disorders. In reviewing the scientific literature on non-biomechanical factors, both the paper authors and the workshop discussants universally acknowledged that the number of such factors is potentially unlimited and thus any review has to narrow the factor set to a manageable number. The broad range of non-biomechanical factors also leads to a range of study methods and measures that complicates comparisons across studies. Diversity, however, can be a strength in evaluating evidence if findings from such different kinds of studies reinforce one another. The workshop authors and discussants generally agreed that there was sufficient mutually reinforcing evidence from these studies to support several findings:

• Individuals vary in their susceptibilities to musculoskeletal disorders, especially along the dimensions of systemic vascular disorders (diabetes, rheumatoid arthritis), age, and to a more limited extent, body mass, genetics, and general conditioning.
• Organizational and psychosocial factors associated with work design, work social supports, and individual responses to workplace stress can be reasonably assumed as risk factors for higher rates of work-related musculoskeletal disorders. Studies have demonstrated that poorly designed jobs, highly demanding workloads and pace, and low levels of worker control on the job can be associated with higher rates of musculoskeletal disorders. Social support at work can lower these rates.
• Non-biomechanical factors can be thought of as moderators, but no one suggests

that they are the primary causes of injury. However, they may change the likelihood of the severity of injury.

• Non-biomechanical factors must be considered if understanding of the relationship between biomechanical work factors and musculoskeletal disorders is to expand and inform the design of workplace interventions to reduce or prevent such disorders.

There was less consensus among workshop discussants about the relative importance of non-biomechanical and biomechanical factors as risk factors in workplace musculoskeletal disorders. The paper authors and several discussants agreed that non-biomechanical factors had modest effects in explaining differences in the rates of musculoskeletal disorders reported in the workplace. Others disagreed. Peter Nathan, Portland Hand Surgery Rehabilitation Center, Oregon, observed that it is essential to observe the patterns of musculoskeletal disease in the general population and ask how those individuals who are at risk perform when challenged at work. General health risk factors must take primacy in modeling the etiology of bodily discomfort. Samuel Moon, Duke University Medical Center, offered the view that the research offers little guidance as to which factors should be most heavily weighted.

Others agreed in qualified ways with the notion that non-biomechanical factors play a modest role in workplace musculoskeletal disorders. For example, Robert Gatchel, University of Texas, Dallas, noted that the importance of non-biomechanical factors in studying workplace musculoskeletal disorders cannot be well understood without looking beyond primary risk factors to secondary and tertiary risk factors. Primary prediction of musculoskeletal disorders only looks at questions about which factors constitute risk for injuries. Secondary prediction examines questions about which workers are at risk. Tertiary prediction explores which workers with chronic injuries can be effectively returned to work. The highest costs to employers, workers, and the medical system are incurred with chronically injured workers, especially those who cannot be effectively treated to return to work. Non-biomechanical factors can play an important role in secondary and tertiary prediction.

This research base does not resolve questions of directionality. It provides ample warning that workplace musculoskeletal disorder prevention programs should not ignore psychosocial factors. . . .
(Samuel Moon, Duke University Medical Center)

Several discussants noted the lack of attention in the paper to musculoskeletal disorders involving the lower extremities. Paulien Bongers, TNO Prevention and Health, Netherlands, noted that individual factors (especially smoking) and psychosocial factors have been shown in several systematic studies to be related to low back pain. Robert Gatchel, University of Texas, Dallas, noted that workers' compensation status or personal injury status (not covered in the papers) should be considered an important predictor of the rates of musculoskeletal disorders, since it is an important predictor of related chronic disorders.

Overall, the majority of discussants and the paper authors agreed that more research integrating biomechanical and non-biomechanical factors would be useful and that more attention should be paid to multitrait, multimethod approaches in designing systematic studies of predictor factors.

INTERVENTION TO CONTROL MUSCULOSKELETAL DISORDERS

Presentation

The Research on Interventions to Control Musculoskeletal Disorders

Michael J. Smith, Ben-Tzion Karsh, and *Francisco B.P. Moro*

The purpose of interventions to control musculoskeletal disorders in the workplace is to reduce or eliminate stresses that overload the individual worker's capacity to accommodate or adapt without musculoskeletal strain and eventual disorders. Such loads can come from a variety of sources that have been discussed in other papers (see Figure 1).

There are a variety of workplace interventions that have been used to reduce or eliminate work-related musculoskeletal disorders, including: engineering redesign, changes in work methods, administrative controls, training, organized exercise and work "hardening," protective equipment, and medical management to reduce exposure. Engineering redesigns include the redesign of machinery or tools and the provision of ways to assist work. An example of machinery redesign is realignment of work station controls to allow for more natural body postures. A tool redesign example is the reduction of hand tool weight or an improved grip, both of which reduce loads on the body. Ways to assist work include lifting tables or hoists, such as those used in hospitals to lift patients. Engineering redesigns primarily involve ways to reduce biomechanical risk factors.

Work methods improvements, administrative controls, and employee training can also reduce biomechanical risk factors, and they can also influence the psychosocial work environment. An example is retraining employees in improved meat cutting techniques to reduce the frequency of cutting motions and improve body postures while cutting. Administrative control changes are designed to reduce risks by rotating workers through different jobs and tasks and by prudent use of rest breaks. Personal protective equipment is designed to block employees from contact with hazards: examples are the required use of gloves to protect against hand injuries from vibrating tools and the use of back belts in jobs that involve lifting. Finally, exercise and work hardening programs are meant to increase the capacity of employees to adapt to work conditions by increasing strength, flexibility, or tolerance of pain.

Of 720 identified intervention research articles, 43 were selected for detailed examination. Conservative criteria were followed in selecting this small group of studies: the use of controls, an accounting for confounding factors, relevant measures, randomized trials, and a blind evaluation. Although not all the examined studies met all these criteria, all met basic conditions for methodological soundness. Fifteen laboratory studies, 15 field studies of injured employees, and 13 field studies of healthy employees were examined. All the studies involved deliberate manipulation of work conditions factors to reduce exposure and risk.

Laboratory studies have the advantage of randomized trials, control over the interventions and other experimental conditions, and, often, the use of control groups. However, these studies may suffer from the use of study subjects who are different from workers of interest, they may not always involve representative work tasks, and they may involve duration and intensity of exposure to risk that is often much lower than is typical in workplaces. On the other side, field study results are often difficult to interpret because they may involve multiple interventions, low levels of control over potentially confounding factors that occur naturally in the work environment, and limited availability of true control groups not treated with the intervention(s). Given the tradeoffs between laboratory and field studies, it is clear that both are needed to gain a more complete picture of the effectiveness of interventions to control work-related musculoskeletal disorders.

Several findings can be drawn from the 43 studies examined:

1. Alternative tools designed to improve hand and wrist postures and reduce forces on the palm and fingers can reduce the risk of upper extremity musculoskeletal disorders. Weight handling devices such as hoists can also reduce these risks.

2. The evidence on both proper lifting posture and the use of backbelts is unclear.

3. Exercise, back school, and physical therapy interventions for injured workers can reduce musculoskeletal pain and symptoms, reduce the use of sick leave, and result in earlier return to work. Exercise interventions seem especially promising. However, most studies involved multiple interventions, and it is not possible to determine the effects of any one intervention.

4. Among healthy workers, ergonomic interventions appear to have positive effects on the incidence of musculoskeletal discomfort, cumulative trauma disorders, and accidents.

Despite recognized weaknesses and gaps, the intervention literature suggests that some interventions can influence the occurrence, recurrence, and severity of low back disorders and can reduce the risks associated with low back and upper extremity disorders. Physical exercise programs and hand tool and hoist designs, in particular, have shown benefits. There is value in pursuing research on interventions, especially research that deals with such questions as: Which interventions can be most beneficial for which circumstances? What are the mechanisms through which interventions produce benefits? How are multiple interventions related to each other and to the success of reducing or preventing musculoskeletal disorders?

Discussion

Workshop discussants generally agreed with the authors of invited papers that there is considerable diversity in the nature and quality of the research conducted on interventions. Martin Cherniack, University of Connecticut Health Center, noted that it is "a rapidly growing and unruly literature that highlights essential contradictions and logical inconsistencies in laboratory based and applied survey methods." Many discussants were willing to go beyond the paper authors in considering a broader range of studies as evidence that work-related musculoskeletal disorders can be reduced or prevented with interventions. Several discussants noted the many practical ergonomic programs in place at work sites around the globe that offer evidence of results. Thorough case studies of such programs, accepted for publication under peer review, meet many of the criteria set forth by well-respected methodologists.

Other discussants went even further in saying that the requirements of research for regulatory purposes are different from those of research that meets strictly methodological criteria. For example, Scott Schneider, Laborers' Health and Safety Fund of North America, noted that intervention research is hard to conduct and hard to get funded. Clinical trials, randomized controls, full-scale epidemiological investigations, and 2-year follow-up studies are not needed to say that an intervention is successful. Schneider offered several examples from an earlier NIOSH review of ergonomic interventions of engineering controls. One study showed improvements in electromyographic measurements, which had previously indicated dysfunction, and increased productivity among truck drivers using a new cab design. Schneider then posed the question: "If this type of information is sufficient for most employers to decide whether interventions are effective enough to make purchasing decisions, shouldn't they then be sufficient for us?" Several company representatives (Thomas Albin, 3M; Brad Joseph, Ford Motor Company; Wendi Latko, Xerox; and Robert Morency, L.L. Bean) offered examples of their companies' ergonomic interventions that have yielded benefits and driven company interest in further interventions.

Several discussants noted that neither technology nor industry stands still for inter-

> *The etiology of work-related musculoskeletal disorders indicates that multiple biomechanical, psychosocial, and personal factors interact, resulting in injury. Effective ergonomic interventions will need to be analyzed from a multidisciplinary approach, as well as in terms of individual effects from specific interventions.*
>
> (Linda Cocchiarella, American Medical Association)

vention studies. Stephen Burastero, Lawrence Livermore National Laboratory, observed that ergonomic product cycles outpace the publication of intervention research. Industry has often already acted on new products.

Finally, many discussants suggested that the paper authors had not examined psychosocial factors as mediators of interventions to the extent needed. They suggested that the multiple factors influencing the success of interventions should be addressed in future studies. For example, the extent of employee involvement in ergonomic interventions and the support of supervisors for using the interventions can influence their effectiveness.

CONCLUSION: INTEGRATION AND OVERVIEW

The final session of the workshop was organized around a panel invited to offer an overview of perspectives voiced throughout the workshop. Chaired by steering committee cochair Colin Drury, the panel included Jacqueline Agnew, Sidney Blair, Donald Bloswick, Fredric Gerr, W. Monroe Keyserling, Susan Mackinnon, Steven Moore, Peter Nathan, Barbara Silverstein, Richard Szabo, and Richard Wells.

Panel Comments

Substantially all of the panel's major comments and observations reinforced points previously made throughout the workshop:

• Musculoskeletal disorders are multifactorial, with work and the biomechanical aspects of work being important contributing factors. Research, especially integrative research, must continue.

• Work factors that can contribute to musculoskeletal disorders include factors beyond the boundaries of a specific job or task. They include social and organizational factors, ranging from supervisory support to redesign of work to the involvement of employees in intervention design and delivery.

• Individual factors also contribute to the incidence of musculoskeletal disorders seen in the workplace and in the general populations. This is especially true for systemic disorders (such as diabetes and rheumatoid arthritis) and age.

• Interventions to reduce or eliminate the risks of musculoskeletal disorders in the workplace have been shown to be effective in some circumstances.

• Physical conditioning programs appear to be especially promising. Ergonomic redesign of tools, workstations, and postural sequences have also been effective.

Jacqueline Agnew identified four particular issues raised during the workshop. First, with respect to interventions, there is interest in more than just primary interventions; secondary and tertiary interventions merit inquiry as well. Second, a question exists as to the outcomes that should be considered—that is, should the focus remain on medical diagnoses or also embrace reported symptoms? Third, are the musculoskeletal disorders under consideration serious enough to merit attention in a public forum and as a matter of public policy? Finally, she noted the differences that exist between the public health perspective and the clinical perspective, pointing out that during the workshop clinicians presented somewhat different viewpoints and emphasized somewhat different concerns than those of public health researchers.

Several other panelists echoed Agnew's questions about the seriousness of the musculoskeletal disorders that were the focus in the workshop (the emphasis on carpal tunnel syndrome and repetitive stress injuries had been denoted by several participants). Donald Bloswick, for example, urged that musculoskeletal disorders not be defined just in terms of carpal tunnel syndrome or upper extremity cumulative trauma disorder. He noted that the NIOSH report indicated that 700,000 workdays per year are lost due to musculoskeletal disorders, only 100,000 of which are upper extremity or repetitive trauma disorders. Susan Mackinnon suggested the need to educate the American public that keyboarding has not been shown to cause anything and that neuromusculoskeletal disorders are not dangerous and should not cause permanent disability. W. Monroe Keyserling noted that the focus of the workshop had been on injuries that result from repetitive job requirements, but that musculoskeletal disorders can result from irregular and sometimes unexpected events, which should also be seriously considered.

The importance of secondary and tertiary, as well as primary, conditions in understanding and intervening in the workplace were also reinforced and expanded on by other panelists, especially with regard to interventions. Richard Wells, for example, advocated a more applied research focus, particularly with respect to intervention research, so that ongoing changes can be better monitored and reported. Barbara Silverstein suggested that intervention research would gain from better feedback from employers and scientists to designers and manufacturers. More broadly, Peter Nathan argued that monies being spent on ergonomic assessments and many workplace interventions would be better spent on focusing and improving the overall health of workers.

General Discussion

The workshop ended with a number of comments from invited participants and the attending public. Several participants highlighted employers' perspectives. David Roy, Travelers Insurance, noted that employers must ask and get answers to questions about what to fix and how to fix it. He noted employers' uneasiness with the medical community's diagnosis of musculoskeletal disorders, especially in terms of numbers of such disorders reported, and employer concern with costs from faulty diagnosis and overreporting (coverage) above and beyond the costs of workplace preventive measures. Wendy Latko, Xerox Corporation, noted that employers cannot wait for research to be perfected before taking action in dealing with injuries and illnesses in the workplace. Xerox, for example, has taken a two-pronged approach emphasizing both wellness programs to enhance general fitness levels and the incorporation of sound ergonomic principles in job and product design. Barbara Silverstein, Washington State Department of Labor and Industries, added that her department's surveys of employers in the state indicated that approximately one-third were directly dealing with workplace injuries and illnesses through engineering, organizational, and personal fitness education programs. Waldemar Karwowski, University of Louisville, emphasized that ergonomics does indeed offer principles that enable employers to design better work places and reduce work-related injuries.

Charles Barrett, International Union of Electronic and Electrical Workers, Margaret Seminario, AFL-CIO, and Scott Schneider, Laborers Health and Safety Fund, all emphasized the employees' perspective through the lens of organized labor. They noted that work-related musculoskeletal disorders are real and that they account for many days of lost work in addition to disabling injuries and suffering at work. Seminario echoed the view of many other participants that the workshop presentation and discussions were valuable because they enabled people from different perspectives to share information and interpretations.

REFERENCES

Adams, M.A., W.C. Hutton, and J.R.R. Stott
   1980 The resistance to flexion of the lumbar intervertebral joint. *Spine* 4:245-253.
Armstrong, T.J., and D.B. Chaffin
   1979 Some biomechanical aspects of the carpal tunnel. *Journal of Biomechanics* 12:567-570.
Bernard, B.P., ed.
   1997 *Musculoskeletal Disorders and Workplace Factors: A Critical Review of Epidemiologic Evidence for Work-Related Musculoskeletal Disorders of the Neck, Upper Extremity, and Low Back.* Cincinnati, OH: U.S. Department of Health and Human Services.
Chaffin, D.B., and G.B.J. Andersson
   1991 *Occupational Biomechanics.* Second Edition. New York, NY: John Wiley and Sons.
National Research Council
   1998 *Work-Related Musculoskeletal Disorders: A Review of the Evidence.* Steering Committee for the Workshop on Work-Related Musculoskeletal Injuries: The Research Base. Washington, DC: National Academy Press. [Part I of this volume]

Appendix A

Invitees and Participants, Workshop on Work-Related Musculoskeletal Injuries: Examining The Research Base

PARTICIPANTS

Jacqueline Agnew, Johns Hopkins University

Thomas Albin, 3M Company, St. Paul, Minnesota

Kai-Nan An, Mayo Clinic and Mayo Foundation, Rochester, Minnesota

Gunnar Andersson,* Rush Presbyterian-St. Luke's Medical Center, Chicago, Illinois

Thomas Armstrong,* University of Michigan, Ann Arbor

James Ashton-Miller, University of Michigan, Ann Arbor

Bruce Bernard, National Institute for Occupational Safety and Health, U.S. Department of Health and Human Services, Cincinnati, Ohio

Sidney Blair, Loyola University Medical Center

Donald Bloswick, University of Utah, Salt Lake City

Paulien Bongers, TNO Prevention and Health, Leiden, Netherlands

Stephen Burastero, Lawrence Livermore National Laboratory, Livermore, California

Dennis Carter, Stanford University

Martin Cherniack, University of Connecticut Health Center, Farmington

Linda Cocchiarella, American Medical Association, Chicago, Illinois

David Cochran, Occupational Safety and Health Administration, U.S. Department of Labor, Washington, DC

David Cordray,* Vanderbilt University

Theodore Courtney, Liberty Mutual Insurance Company, Hopkinton, Massachusetts

Mark Cullen,* Yale University School of Medicine

Carlo De Luca, Neuro Muscular Research Center, Boston, Massachusetts

Raymond Donnelly, Occupational Safety and Health Administration, U.S. Department of Labor, Washington, DC

Colin Drury,* State University of New York, Buffalo

Bradley Evanoff, Washington University School of Medicine

Julia Faucett, University of California, San Francisco

Lawrence Fine, National Institute for Occupational Safety and Health, U.S. Department of Health and Human Services, Cincinnati, Ohio

Baruch Fischhoff,* Carnegie Mellon University

David Florence, American Academy of Orthopedic Surgeons, Rosemont, Illinois

---

*Member, Steering Committee for the Workshop on Work-Related Musculoskeletal Injuries: The Research Base

Alfred Franzblau, University of Michigan, Ann Arbor
Steven Garfin, University of California, San Diego
Arun Garg, University of Wisconsin-Milwaukee
Robert Gatchel, University of Texas, Dallas
Fredric Gerr, Emory University
Ronald Gray, Johns Hopkins University
Manny Halpern, New York University Medical Center
Steven Johnson, University of Arkansas, Fayetteville
Brad Joseph, Ford Motor Company, Dearborn, Michigan
Bentzi Karsh, University of Wisconsin-Madison
Waldemar Karwowski, University of Louisville
Michael Kerr, Institute for Work and Health, Toronto, Ontario, Canada
W. Monroe Keyserling, University of Michigan, Ann Arbor
Karl Kroemer, Virginia Tech
Mary Laedtke, U.S. Army Center for Health Promotion and Preventive Medicine,
    Aberdeen Proving Ground, Maryland
Wendi Latko, Xerox Corporation, Webster, New York
Steven Lavender, Rush Presbyterian-St. Luke's Medical Center, Chicago, Illinois
Steven Lehman, University of California, Berkeley
Thomas Mayer, PRIDE, Dallas, Texas
Susan Mackinnon, Washington University School of Medicine
William Marras,* Ohio State University, Columbus
Gary Mirka, North Carolina State University, Raleigh
Samuel Moon, Duke University Medical Center
Steven Moore, Texas A&M University, College Station
Robert Morency, L.L. Bean, Inc., Freeport, Maine
Francisco Moro, University of Wisconsin-Madison
Peter Nathan, Portland Hand Surgery Rehabilitation Center, Portland, Oregon
Robert Norman, University of Waterloo, Ontario, Canada
Lida Orta-Anés, United Automobile Aerospace and Agricultural Implement Workers
    of America, UAW, Detroit, Michigan
Richard Pew,* Independent Consultant, Cambridge, Massachusetts
Malcolm Pope, University of Iowa
Laura Punnett, University of Massachusetts, Lowell
Robert Radwin, University of Wisconsin-Madison
Mark Redfern, University of Pittsburgh
David Rempel, University of California, San Francisco
David Roy, Travelers Insurance, Hartford, Connecticut
Howard Sandler, Sandler Occupational Medicine Associates, Inc., Melville, New York
Scott Schneider, Laborers' Health and Safety Fund of North America, Washington, DC
Margaret Seminario, AFL-CIO, Washington, DC
Barbara Silverstein, Washington State Department of Labor and Industries, Olympia

Mary Lou Skovron, Genentech, Inc., South San Francisco, California, and New York University School of Medicine

Michael Smith, University of Wisconsin-Madison

Moshe Solomonow, Louisiana State University Medical Center, New Orleans

Carolyn Sommerich, North Carolina State University, Raleigh

Robert Szabo, University of California, Davis

David Wegman, University of Massachusetts, Lowell

Richard Wells, University of Waterloo, Ontario, Canada

Robert Werner, University of Michigan, Ann Arbor

INVITEES WHO WERE UNABLE TO ATTEND

Peter C. Amadio, Mayo Clinic, Rochester, Minnesota

Mohamed M. Ayoub, Texas Tech University

Susan Baker, Johns Hopkins University

Stanley J. Bigos, University of Washington

Claire Bombardier, Institute for Work and Health, Toronto, Ontario, Canada

Patricia Buffler, University of California, Berkeley

Donald B. Chaffin, University of Michigan, Ann Arbor

Harvey Checkoway, University of Washington

Jerome Congleton, Texas A&M University

Thomas Cook, University of Iowa

Marvin J. Dainoff, Miami University, Oxford, Ohio

Richard Deyo, University of Washington

Michael Feuerstein, Uniformed Services University of the Health Services, Bethesda, Maryland, and Georgetown University School of Medicine

Adam Finkel, Occupational Safety and Health Administration, U.S. Department of Labor, Washington, DC

Gary Franklin, University of Washington

Andris Freivalds, Pennsylvania State University

John Frymoyer, University of Vermont

Nortin Hadler, University of North Carolina School of Medicine, Chapel Hill

Hal Hendrick, Consultant, Englewood, Colorado

William Howell,* Arizona State University, Tempe

Morton Kasdan, Physician, Louisville, Kentucky

Jeffrey Katz, Brigham and Women's Hospital, Boston, Massachusetts

Jennifer Kelsey, Stanford University

Jess F. Kraus, University of California, Los Angeles

Steven Lamm, Consultants in Epidemiology and Occupational Health, Inc., Washington, DC

Tom Leamon, Liberty Mutual Insurance Company, Hopkinton, Massachusetts

Steven Linton, Orebro Medical Center Hospital, Orebro, Sweden

Paul Marxhausen, University of Nebraska at Lincoln
Stuart McGill, University of Waterloo, Ontario, Canada
Steven Newell, Organization Resources Counselors, Washington, DC
Robert Ochsman, Consumer Products Safety Commission, Lovettsville, Virginia
Suzanne Rodgers, Consultant, Rochester, New York
Steven L. Sauter, National Institute for Occupational Safety and Health, U.S. Department of Health and Human Services, Cincinnati, Ohio
Stover H. Snook, Harvard School of Public Health
Carol Stuart-Buttle, Stuart-Buttle Ergonomics, Philadelphia, Pennsylvania
David Vlahov,* Johns Hopkins University
Kathryn G. Vogel, University of New Mexico
Laura Welch, Washington Hospital Center, Washington, DC
Savio Woo, University of Pittsburgh
Craig Zwerling, University of Iowa

STAFF

E. William Colglazier, *Executive Officer*, National Research Council
Barbara Boyle Torrey, *Executive Director*, Commission on Behavioral and Social Sciences and Education
Alexandra Wigdor, *Director*, Division on Education, Labor, and Human Performance
Anne Mavor, *Study Director*, Steering Committee for the Workshop on Work-Related Musculoskeletal Injuries
James McGee, *Senior Research Associate*, Steering Committee for the Workshop on Work-Related Musculoskeletal Injuries
Renae Broderick, *Writer/Editor*, Cornell University, Ithaca, New York
Susan Coke, *Administrative Associate*, Steering Committee for the Workshop on Work-Related Musculoskeletal Injuries
Susan McCutchen, *Senior Project Assistant*, Steering Committee for the Workshop on Work-Related Musculoskeletal Injuries
Nat Tipton, *Senior Project Assistant*, Division on Education, Labor, and Human Performance

Appendix B

Workshop on Work-Related Musculoskeletal Injuries: Examining the Research Base

August 20-21, 1998
Auditorium, National Academy of Sciences
2101 Constitution Avenue, N.W., Washington, DC

AGENDA

Thursday, August 20

7:30 a.m.   Continental Breakfast
          Room 250: Participants A-J
          Room 280: Participants K-Z
          Public: Cafeteria is available to purchase breakfast

8:30 a.m.   Welcome and Introduction
          William Colglazier and Richard Pew

8:50 a.m.   BIOLOGICAL RESPONSE OF TISSUES TO STRESSES: MUSCLES, TENDONS, AND NERVES

          INVITED PAPER ON MUSCLES AND TENDONS: *James Ashton-Miller*

          Panel Discussion: *Kai-Nan An, Sidney Blair, Dennis Carter, Carlo De Luca, Steven Lehman, Steven Moore, Moshe Solomonow*

          Questions from Invited Participants

          INVITED PAPER ON NERVES: *David Rempel*

          Panel Discussion: *David Florence, Steven Garfin, Thomas Mayer, Susan Mackinnon, Robert Szabo*

          Questions from Invited Participants

10:50 a.m.   Break

11:15 a.m.   WORK FACTORS, INDIVIDUAL HOST FACTORS, AND
                INTERNAL LOADS: BIOMECHANICS OF WORK STRESSORS

                INVITED PAPER: *Robert Radwin and Steven Lavender*

                Panel Discussion: *Arun Garg, W. Monroe Keyserling, Robert Norman,
                Mark Redfern, Carolyn Sommerich, Richard Wells*

                Questions from Invited Participants

12:30 p.m.   Lunch
                        Room 250: Participants A-J
                        Room 280: Participants K-Z
                        Public: Cafeteria is available to purchase lunch

1:30 p.m.   EPIDEMIOLOGY: PHYSICAL FACTORS
                Panel Discussion

                Moderator: *Ronald Gray*

                Panelists: *Bradley Evanoff, Alfred Franzblau, Fredric Gerr, Laura Punnett,
                Howard Sandler, David Wegman*

                Questions from Invited Participants

3:30 p.m.   Break

4:00 p.m.   General Discussion with Paper Presenters: Invited Participants and Public

Friday, August 21

8:00 a.m.   Continental Breakfast
                        Room 250: Participants A-J
                        Room 280: Participants K-Z
                        Public: Cafeteria is available to purchase breakfast

9:00 a.m.   NON-BIOMECHANICAL FACTORS POTENTIALLY AFFECTING MUSCULOSKELETAL DISORDERS

INVITED PAPER: *Julia Faucett and Robert Werner*

Panel Discussion: *Jacqueline Agnew, Paulien Bongers, Robert Gatchel, Michael Kerr, Samuel Moon, Peter Nathan*

Questions from Invited Participants

10:15 a.m.   Break

10:45 a.m.   INTERVENTIONS TO CONTROL MUSCULOSKELETAL DISORDERS

INVITED PAPER: *Michael Smith*

Panel Discussion: *Donald Bloswick, Stephen Burastero, Martin Cherniack, Linda Cocchiarella, Brad Joseph, Lida Orta-Anés, Scott Schneider, Barbara Silverstein*

Questions from Invited Participants

12:00 p.m.   Lunch
               Room 250: Participants A-J
               Room 280: Participants K-Z
               Public: Cafeteria is available to purchase lunch

1:00 p.m.   Panel on the Integration of Workshop Presentations and Discussions

Chair: *Colin Drury*
Panelists: *Jacqueline Agnew, Sidney Blair, Donald Bloswick, Alfred Franzblau, Fredric Gerr, W. Monroe Keyserling, Susan Mackinnon, Steven Moore, Peter Nathan, Barbara Silverstein, Robert Szabo, Richard Wells*

2:00 p.m.   Questions and Comments from Invited Participants and Public

III

Workshop Papers

The papers in this part are included
as they were presented
and discussed at the workshop.

RESPONSE OF MUSCLE AND TENDON TO INJURY AND OVERUSE

James A. Ashton-Miller, Ph.D.
Senior Research Scientist, Biomechanics Research Laboratory, Department of Mechanical Engineering and Applied Mechanics, G.G. Brown 3208, University of Michigan, Ann Arbor, MI. 48109-2125, Fax: (734) 763-9332, Tel: (734) 763-2320, Email: jaam@umich.edu

Introduction

Epidemiological evidence suggests an association between certain kinds of repetitive work and musculoskeletal disorders, particularly those that can occur in upper extremity, neck or low back (Bernard, 1997). In this review we shall consider some of the biomechanical mechanisms that can lead to inflammatory, degenerative or disruptive changes in connective tissue. These changes may be linked to changes in *intrinsic* factors such as physical capacity, and to changes in *extrinsic* factors such as the physical demands placed upon the individual (Table 1). A conceptual model involving the concepts of exposure, dose, capacity and response can form a helpful framework to consider such issues (Armstrong et al., 1993). Some of the extrinsic factors include *exposure* to various forms of work-related loading as well as the *dose* or severity and duration of that loading. Intrinsic factors, on the other hand, will largely determine connective tissue stresses and strains for a given loading, while tissue *capacity* and *response* to such loading will depend upon the interaction between the intrinsic and extrinsic factors. One example of such an interaction would be tissue hypertrophy, which eventually takes place in response to a sustained loading increase, and tissue atrophy, which can occur in response to a sustained decrease in loading history.

Although work-related tissue dysfunction can occur in muscle, tendon, ligament, fascia, bursa, intervertebral disc, bone or skin, I have been asked to focus on research relating to function in the first three structures. I shall do so without consideration of the psychosocial or secondary gain issues that, while important, will be addressed in related Workshop papers.

Tissue injury and dysfunction can result from excessive stress (force per unit area) and/or strain (the relative elongation of a given length of tissue). As we shall see excessive stress or strain can result from a single forceful mechanical event, such as lifting, catching, or jerking a heavy object. Excessive tissue strain can also result from an interaction with the environment such as during a stumble, trip, or landing from a fall or jump. It can also result from accumulated strain associated with less forceful, but repetitive, loading of a structure (Wren, Beaupre, & Carter, 1998). Finally, and probably more commonly, excessive tissue strain can be caused by some combination of the two – single events superimposed upon a history of repetitive loading.

Table 1: Examples of Intrinsic and Extrinsic Factors

INTRINSIC FACTORS	EXTRINSIC FACTORS
Age	Magnitude, direction, duration, rate, and lack of variability of work-related external forces affecting tissue stress/strain history
Gender	Number, frequency and duty cycle of work-related loading cycles affecting tissue stress/strain history
Tissue anatomy – heritable factors, changes due to tissue injuries during childhood/adolescence	Work-related postural requirements affecting tissue stresses/strain history
Tissue physiology – healing/remodeling potential; response to chronic loading	Availability of rest days
Tissue state – state of hypertrophy/atrophy/remodeling as it affects relevant tissue physical capacities	Leisure/commuting activities engendering tissue stress/strain history
Muscle recruitment strategies, related functional biomechanics	
Response to psychological stress	
Response to pain state	

Soft tissue injury triggers a complex cascade of events involving an inflammatory response, which marks the first phase of the healing response, a proliferative stage, followed by a remodeling phase (Gelberman, Goldberg, An, & Banes, 1988). Uneventful transitioning through these phases usually requires a temporary reduction in physical loading because of pain or discomfort, followed by a gradual increase in physical loading to stimulate healing and subsequent tissue remodeling processes. The problem is not so much increasing physical loading again, but increasing it at a rate that does not exacerbate symptoms or, worse, cause re-injury. In some jobs workers may have considerable discretion over how and when they choose to increase the magnitude and duration of loading after injury or overuse syndromes appear so as not to aggravate symptoms. But in other jobs they may have little control over such matters, thereby increasing the risk of developing more chronic syndromes. 'Work-hardening' programs are specifically designed to minimize this risk by prescribing graduated physical training regimens to better prepare tissues for the type of work to be done.

It should not be surprising that sudden increases in activity associated with switching to a new and more physically demanding work can trigger overuse syndromes. It is always possible for an individual to increase physical loading too rapidly for tissue repair and adaptation mechanisms to be able cope with the new demands. Classic examples of this are the millions of unnecessary sports-related injuries that occur every year at all ages due to training errors. These errors are simply caused by an athlete increasing the intensity or duration of their training too rapidly for the tissue to adapt to the new regimen. Such injuries and conditions are preventable by better athlete and coach education. But a more challenging question to answer is why a worker who has performed the same job for years without symptoms now starts to report symptoms consistent with overuse. In some cases at least, an answer might be found in age-related changes in tissues and slower tissue healing and remodeling rates, so that tissues can no longer repair and remodel tissue quickly enough. Let us now examine some of the known injury mechanisms in the tissues of interest.

Muscle

Contraction-induced Injury

Contraction-induced injury is defined as morphological damage to small focal groups of sarcomeres as a result of mechanical disruption of the interdigitation of the thick and thin filament arrays or of the Z-lines of single sarcomeres (Faulkner & Brooks, 1995). The injury initiates a cascade of events that produce a more severe secondary injury after two or three days. This involves an inflammatory response, free radical damage, appearance of cytosolic enzymes in the serum, and phagacytosis of elements within the cytosol of damaged sarcomeres (Faulkner & Brooks, 1995) Human beings report pain associated with this phase as delayed onset muscle soreness. Striated muscle is rarely injured when active in isometric, or shortening contractions, but injuries are known to occur when muscle is activated and forcibly stretched (Brooks, Zerba, & Faulkner, 1995) in a so-called 'plyometric' contraction. That stretch can be caused by impact of a body segment with an external surface or object, as well as during certain self-initiated movements such as jumping up onto something. Depending upon the severity of the injury, 1 – 4 weeks is required for complete recovery of muscle structure and function (Brooks & Faulkner, 1990).

Single-event muscle strain injuries:

Stretch-related injuries in striated muscle can also be caused by a rapid movement associated with a recovery from loss of balance, a slip, trip, throw, catch, landing, or other rapid movement. Over the past fifteen years research in man, as well as in situ and in vitro animal studies, has indicated that stretch-related injuries in striated muscle are caused by a mechanical-mediated event rather than a chemical or metabolic event. Generally, this involves a single rapid stretch to actively contracting muscle (Lieber & Friden, 1993) or a series of repetitive plyometric contractions (Friden, Sjostrom, & Ekblom, 1983) (Newham, Jones, & Edwards, 1983a) (McCulley & Faulkner, 1985). At present, in animal experiments the muscle injury is best characterized by the resulting deficit in maximum force developed by the muscle, rather than by ultrastructural measures ((Newham, McPhail, Mills, & Edwards, 1983b) cited by (Brooks & Faulkner, 1996)). For single stretches the threshold for injury in mice has been estimated as a work input of 150 J/Kg muscle, corresponding to stretches in excess of 20% L_o (optimal muscle length) strain, say, at a rate of 2Lf/s (muscle fiber lengths per second). Experiments in rodents suggest that one of the factors best predicting the injury is the combination of the muscle strain and average force, or work input to the muscle, and its initial length (Macpherson, Schork, & Faulkner, 1996) (Hunter & Faulkner, 1997). Evidence from single permiabilized rat soleus muscle fibers indicates that sarcomere lengths can be heterogeneous in a contracting muscle and that regions of muscle with the longest sarcomere lengths contained the majority of damaged sarcomeres after injury (Macpherson, Dennis, & Faulkner, 1997), possibly because their length is due to reduced thick and thin filament overlap (Macpherson et al., 1996). Comparative experiments in immature, young adult and old adult mice have shown that when eccentric contractions are used to injure muscles to the same degree, then not only did muscle fibers in old muscle exhibit a greater force deficit (injury) than the younger animals, but that immature and young adult recovered within two weeks, whereas the muscles of old adult mice had not recovered after even two months (Brooks & Faulkner, 1994). To what extent postural muscle activity above a certain threshold can delay such muscle healing and/or prolong symptoms is a question of direct relevance to overuse disorders that might be explored using this type of experimental model.

Muscle Fatigue

Sustained postural muscle activity can create significant musculoskeletal problems. Epidemiological studies in assembly workers, for example, indicate that redesigning the work place in order to reduce average trapezius muscle activity below 2% MVC over an eight hour day can significantly reduce sick leave (for example, (Aaraas, 1987)).

Localized muscle fatigue has been defined as an acute impairment in performance associated with an increase in the perceived effort to produce that force and eventual inability to maintain that force(Chaffin, 1973). Muscle fatigue occurs when physical tasks demand large sustained forces, high power short-term repetitive contractions, and/or low power sustained single or repetitive contractions (Faulkner & Brooks, 1995). A detailed review of the neural and muscular mechanisms, both centrally- and peripherally-mediated, is given by Gandevia et al. (Gandevia, Enoka, McComas, Stuart, & Thomas, 1995). Enoka and Stuart have identified four factors that dictate how and whether fatigue will occur: internal and external factors affecting task dependency, muscle force-fatigue relationship, muscle synergy adaptations to counteract fatigue, and perceived sense of effort (Enoka & Stuart, 1992).

Whereas fatigue in an isometric contraction is caused by a reduction in maximum force, fatigue involving a muscle which is actively shortening or lengthening involves reductions in the force which can be developed as well as reductions in the maximum velocity of shortening (Faulkner & Brooks, 1995). One useful measure of muscle output under such conditions is muscle power (defined as force x velocity). For young human muscles at 35°C, fast muscle fibers can normally develop 225W/kg whereas slow muscle fibres can develop 65W/kg (Faulkner & Brooks, 1995). The ability to sustain power output is a function of fiber composition and the oxidative capacity of the muscle and depends upon the balance between the energy supply and energy output(Brooks & Faulkner, 1991); highly trained individuals can maintain 15% of maximal power for several hours after a warm-up period(Faulkner & Brooks, 1995).

Relatively few investigations have focused on the energy supply to the muscle during low power sustained fatiguing contractions. An important study in human quadriceps (Sjogaard, Kiens, Jorgensen, & Saltin, 1986) demonstrated considerable variability in intramuscular blood pressure during a 1 hour contraction at 5% MVC. During that contraction the blood pressure averaged approximately twice the resting pressure value, indicating an adequate blood supply pressure during the contraction. However, the pressure tracing was characterized by fluctuations perhaps indicating that different parts of the muscle were recruited sequentially to develop and maintain the given force level. After the 1 hour contraction maximum force capability was reduced by 12 % while the perceived exertion increased from 0 to 4.4 on a 0-10 scale. A more recent study (Murthy, Kahan, Hargens, & Rempel, 1997) used non-invasive spectroscopy to measure changes in tissue oxygenation *in vivo* in the human ECRB muscle. A significant decrease in oxygenation was found after a 1 min. contraction at 10 % or greater MVC effort level. The association between muscle oxygenation levels and fatigue, or between muscle oxygenation levels and subjectively perceived discomfort or pain remains unexplored.

A recent experimental investigation in humans has corroborated earlier animal and human research that muscle fatigue does affect proprioceptive acuity. In this work, the ability to discriminate different arm velocities was significantly and adversely affected at the shoulder, with proprioception in women being significantly more affected by muscle fatigue than men (Pedersen, Lonn, Hellstrom, Djupsjobacka, & Johansson, 1997). Since proprioception is known to be important for motor control, it has been hypothesized that this could be one factor underlying increased coactivation, inefficient muscle use, and an increase in the workload of the affected muscles (Pedersen, 1997), although this has yet to be shown directly.

Finally, it is important to fit the tool to the worker, rather than the worker to the tool. There are many studies showing that ergonomic interventions can reduce loading exposure. One illustrative example shows that merely selecting an appropriate power tool handle size for the size of hand of the worker can significantly reduce grip forces used (Oh & Radwin, 1993). Large-handed individuals using small handles, and small-handed individuals using large handles employed significantly larger grip forces than normal.

Muscle Pain

Increased stiffness, tenderness and muscle pain, particularly in the neck and shoulder regions, are common work-related complaints. These symptoms are often associated with work involving raised arms, repetitive motion tasks, visual control and relatively high levels of mental concentration.

One of the leading theories proposed to explain such disorders is that of Johansson and Sojka (Johansson & Sojka, 1991). Briefly, this theory starts with evidence that muscle pain, inflammation, ischemia, or sustained static muscle contractions are known to lead to the release of KCL, lactic acid, arachidonic acid, bradykinin, serotinin and histamine in the affected muscle. These substances, in turn, are known to excite chemosensitive Group III and IV afferents which, more recently, have been shown to have a potent effect on gamma - muscle spindle systems in cat limb and neck (splenius and trapezius) muscles, and the response of those spindles to stretch (Pedersen, 1997). Although not yet demonstrated directly by experiment, it is postulated that because spindles are known to play a central role in reflex-mediated stiffness, that this increased spindle output could be the genesis of the increased muscle stiffness, tension and pain symptoms reported as myalgia.

The Johannson-Sojka theory identifies specific neural pathways to explain the *circlus vitiosus* of Travell et al. who theorized that pain could lead to increased muscle tone which in turn lead to more pain (Travell, Rinzler, & Herman, 1942). Thus the Johansson –Sojka theory emphasizes fusimotor hyperactivity rather than tonic alpha motoneurone hyperactivity. The Travell tonic muscle hyperactivity theory received little support from Lund et al (Lund, Donga, Widmer, & Stohler, 1991) who have pointed out that it is rarely observed in the clinic for example in facial pain syndomes, nor was it observed in healthy volunteers in a recent placebo-controlled trial (Stohler, Zhang, & Lund, 1996). The significance of the increased fusimotor activity, on the other hand, is that it would lead to increased muscle stiffness and thence greater alpha motoneurone recruitment *whenever that muscle is used* at work, particularly whenever it is stretched actively or passively, or vibrated. Evidence of increased muscle activity during work in patients with pain and/or myalgia comes from EMG studies in Norwegian workers performing stereotyped work (Veierstad, Westgaard, & Anderen, 1990). The Johansson-Sojka model also provide a neurophysiological explanation by which the myalgia could spread to contralateral muscles as discussed and detailed by Pedersen(Pedersen, 1997).

The outcome of experimental studies conducted on patients with intermittent/chronic pain of possible muscular origin in order to ascertain underlying mechanisms are often affected by confounding factors. For this reason, a number of experimental models for studying acute muscle pain in healthy volunteers have been developed in order to better study underlying pain mechanisms. These models include electrical stimulation of the target muscle, intramuscular infusion of chemical irritants into the target muscle, and the use of fatiguing muscle contractions that include the target muscle. Because the pain derived from electrical stimulation, and delayed muscle soreness from fatiguing contractions is variable and difficult to control, one of the more successful muscle pain models has involved the infusion of hypertonic saline into the muscle. One of the advantages of such experiments in man is that it allows for the subjective rating of perceived discomfort and pain, an important dimension that is missing in animal pain experiments.

The hypertonic saline infusion model has been used in sham-controlled studies of healthy young subjects to test the Travell hypothesis that tonic muscle pain of an intensity equivalent to that reported by the majority of pain patients causes an increase in the postural myoelectric activity of the target muscle. In one case the hypothesis was tested in the jaw musculature (Stohler et al., 1996) because of its relevance to temporomandibular pain syndromes; in the other case it was tested in the neck (sternocleidomastoid) muscle (Ashton-Miller, McGlashen, Herzenberg, & Stohler, 1990) because of its involvement in neck and shoulder disorders. The resulting pain develops over a few minutes as a deep aching or burning sensation, often with referred pain, and the magnitude of the pain can be quantified subjectively using a visual analog scale. The pain intensity can be adjusted automatically over many minutes (Zhang, Ashton-Miller, & Stohler, 1993). In both sham-controlled repeated-measures experiments the development of tonic muscle pain was accompanied by reports of referred pain, and a small but significant increase in myoelectric activity in the affected muscle; however, according to rigid scientific criteria this was not greater than the sham pain used as a control in the Stohler experiment (Stohler et al., 1996).

Several points from these studies are worthy of discussion. First, the results provide little support for the tonic muscle hyperactivity (Travell) pain model which assumes a re-inforcing link between pain and muscle hyperactivity. Secondly, it is noteworthy that the jaw muscles are significantly more sensitive to pain than the sternocleidomastoid muscle because 50 times the quantity of hypertonic saline is needed to induce a similar intensity of pain. Whether the mechanism underlying this difference in pain sensitivity is due to a difference in the number of pain muscle receptors, a difference in their central projections, and/or a difference in the gain of those projections is presently unclear. The observation that different muscles have different pain thresholds deserves further research given that overuse symptoms seem to affect some muscles more than others. Thirdly, acute pain at an intensity of 5 on a VAS scale of 0-10 caused autonomic changes such as sweating and blanching in these healthy subjects. Since pain-related autonomic changes such as sweating and blanching are rarely, if ever, observed in patients with work-related overuse syndromes, yet pain scores of 5 on a 10 point VAS scale are commonly reported by them, these patients may have an average level of pain that is an order of magnitude less than that fostered in the above acute pain model. Fifth, the epidemiology of work-related disorders seems to point to an over-representation of females (see accompanying Workshop reviews). Although gender differences have been observed in tendon and ligament (Hart et al., 1998), there could also be a gender difference in the mechanisms underlying human response to pain. Data supporting such a hypothesis suggest that women did indeed perceive significantly greater pain from a standardized noxious cutaneous stimulus than men (Paulson, Minoshima, Morrow, & Casey, 1998).

Aging Effects in Muscle

The effects of age on muscle were extensively reviewed at the NIH Workshop on Sarcopenia(Holloszy, 1995). With age comes a ~20% decrease in human muscle mass, a ~20% decrease in maximum isometric specific force (Faulkner & Brooks, 1995), and a ~35% decrease in the maximal rate of developing force and power (Thelen, Schultz, Alexander, & Ashton-Miller, 1996c). This latter reduction is not due to differences in muscle recruitment strategies (Thelen, Ashton-Miller, Schultz, & Alexander, 1996b), but rather due to a change in the contractility of the muscle itself, and corroborates similar findings in animal experiments. The muscles of old animals similarly demonstrate a loss in sustained power of up to 50% which translates into an equivalent loss in endurance, a fact that is reflected in the loss of athletic performance in humans between the age of 30 and 80 years (Faulkner & Brooks, 1995). In practical terms this translates into a marked decrease in the ability to sustain power over repeated contractions in older individuals. The decline in the ability of muscles to generate force rapidly is one of the most important factors that causes elderly to have difficulty making rapid movements in time-critical situations requiring high strength (Thelen, Wojcik, Schultz, Ashton-Miller, & Alexander, 1997), particularly in elderly women (Wojcyk, Thelen, Schultz, Ashton-Miller, & Alexander, 1998) (Schultz, Ashton-Miller, & Alexander, 1997). Thus, the need to accelerate a tool of a given mass at a given acceleration will require more effort, and hence induce fatigue faster in women than in men, unless hand tools are scaled to accommodate gender differences. The same would be true of older workers vis-à-vis younger workers.

For a given provocation, the magnitude of the initial single stretch injury in rodents has been shown to be greater in muscle from older animals than in younger animals (Brooks & Faulkner, 1996). Older rodent muscle subjected to the same injuring plyometric contraction, also heals significantly more slowly than young muscle (Brooks & Faulkner, 1990), a fact that might have significance when considering age differences in overuse syndromes. These effects help explain why older athletes seem to require greater rest intervals between training sessions in order to avoid overuse problems. And the same effects could partially explain why workers in physically demanding jobs tend to change to less demanding jobs with age.

Effect of Exercise on Muscle

A large literature demonstrates that, at any age, exercise intervention programs are effective for improving muscle strength (Frontera, Meredith, O'Reilly, Knuttgen, & Evans, 1988) (Skelton, Young, Greig, & Malbut, 1995) and endurance (Overend, Cunningham, Paterson, & Smith, 1992) by from ~5 to 30% depending upon the particular muscles. But training has selective effects: while older men (70-100 years) with life long endurance training had greater power output than age-matched controls, for example, they did not have greater muscle strength than the controls (Harridge, Magnusson, & Saltin, 1997).

Estimation of Muscle and Tendon Forces

The performance of many physical activities requires humans to generate considerable muscle forces as they interact with equipment or their environment. It is these muscle forces, when combined with the external reaction forces applied to the body by its physical environment, that load the remaining soft tissues and skeleton with arrays of forces than can peak with values many times body weight. In any physical activity accurate estimation of muscle forces is the first step to characterizing the forces experienced by each tissue. In addition to posture, motion, vibration, the muscle force exerted during a task is known to be a risk factor for tendon-related disorders (Armstrong, Fine, Goldstein, Lifshitz, & Silverstein, 1987a)

There are two basic techniques for estimating muscle forces. The first, usually used in animal experiments, involves placing a tendon buckle transducer in situ to directly monitor tendon force during a given activity. Recently, this technique has been used in man to monitor finger muscle force (Dennerlein, Diao, Mote, & Rempel, 1998). Importantly, their results show a nearly three-fold variation in the finger tip-tendon tension ratio among nine subjects. This suggests that intrinsic factors can cause a tendon force to be much higher in some individuals than others performing the same task. A limitation of the method was that the forces in cocontracting muscles could not be monitored concurrently because of practical considerations at the time of surgery.

The second, non-invasive, technique involves the use of mathematical models to predict muscle contraction forces. The art of using biomechanical models has evolved over the last thirty years from using simple quasistatic two-dimensional models to three-dimensional models that direcly address the muscle indeterminancy problem using optimisation techniques in the wrist (An, Kwak, Chao, & Morrey, 1990). Those models have evolved from using optimization techniques and neural networks to predict the set of muscle forces required to establish static equilibrium while minimizing loads on the spine during lifting tasks (Schultz, Haderspek, Warwick, & Portillo, 1983) (Nussbaum, Chaffin, & Martin, 1995), to the use of myoelectrically-driven estimates of muscle activity to improve muscle force predictions during dynamic tasks (McGill & Norman, 1986) (Thelen, Ashton-Miller, & Schultz, 1996a) and muscle co-contraction patterns (Thelen, Schultz, & Ashton-Miller, 1995). Most recently, the effects of muscle stiffness are being included in order to provide for spine stability in the face of external perturbations during physical exertions (Gardner-Morse, Stokes, & Laible, 1995). In the trunk, the complexity of the muscle slip architecture and the multiplicity of muscles has precluded validation of model predictions by direct measurement of muscle forces; rather those models have had to be validated by comparing predicted spine compression forces with measured intra-discal pressures (Schultz, Andersson, Ortengren, Haderspek, & Nachemson, 1982), or by comparing predicted spine moments with measured spine moments (Thelen et al., 1996a). In simpler musculoskeletal systems such as the cat hind-limb, validation of the predictive strategies is possible by directly comparing predicted and measured muscle forces during activities such as locomotion, with errors found to be in the range 25 to 50% (Prilutsky, Herzog, & Allinger, 1997). Such direct comparisons between predicted and measured forces allow refinements to be made to the prediction method (Dennerlein et al., 1998).

However, such errors should also serve as a caveat. Even in these simpler musculoskeletal systems our ability to predict tissue loading is still far from satisfactory. Our accuracy in more complicated systems such as the spine is unlikely to be better, and may well be worse. Given those uncertain tissue loading estimates, and given additional uncertainties in tissue material properties, attempts to predict tissue strain states are currently imprecise. Inaccuracies in these estimates of tissue strain states is one of the major impediments to identifying cause and effect relationships in tissue overuse syndromes. A case in point is the difficulty of separating the effects of tool vibration on muscle and tendon from the effects of vibration on the grip force used to hold the tool(Armstrong, Fine, Radwin, & Silverstein, 1987b)

Passive Tensile Structures:

The preeminent structural component that provides tensile strength in dense regular connective tissue structures like tendons, ligaments, retinaculae, and intervertebral discs, and in the fasciae of muscles, is collagen. Parallel fibrils of Type I collagen are the main component of healthy ligaments and tendons. Like bone, collagen is an extremely active substance that is sensitive to loading history. Fluctuating loading generally promotes collagen turnover, healing, and remodeling processes, whereas static loading causes collagen to atrophy. The collagen in the peridontal ligaments, for example, turns over every few days (Alan Bailey, personal communication), whereas in an avascular structure such as the intervertebral disc, the turnover may take several years due to the transport time it takes to carry components over the large distances to the outer annulus or endplate. Each of the many types of collagen has a different turnover time.

If loading is increased beyond a certain threshold, cellular homeostasis is no longer sufficient to maintain structural integrity and the risk for accumulated damage, and hence an over use injury, increases (Frost, 1990). The mechanism by which the injury occurs is uncertain, but most likely involves a series of microscopic tears or disruptions which may not affect the gross appearance of the structure.

Ligament

Ligaments are tensile structures which interconnect bones constraining their relative motions. Excellent reviews of ligament structure and function exist (for example, (Frank et al., 1988)). Although they differ somewhat, all ligaments consist predominantly of Type I and Type III collagen, with small proportions of glycosaminoglycans, elastin, and other substances. Ligaments exhibit both elastic and creep in response to tensile loading. The mechanisms of the creep are not well understood but involve progressive fiber recruitment, as the increasing strain progressively reduces the characteristic crimp (or waviness) in the different collagen fibrils, and causes hydration shifts. While many biomechanical studies have characterized the response of certain ligaments to load, much remains to be done to elucidate the effects of age, gender, the female menstrual cycle, and repair processes on ligament function.

Much of the classic work on ligamentous response to changes in activity and injury concerns human and animal knee ligaments because they are so often involved in sports-related injuries. Measurements of human anterior cruciate ligament strains in vivo have provided valuable basic insights and data for improving rehabilitation programs so that exercises do not reinjure surgically-repaired ligaments (Renstrom, Arms, Stanwyck, Johnson, & Pope, 1986). However, the knee ligaments are rarely the site of work-related disorders, so these studies have limited relevance to the problem at hand. In addition, much of the work on ligaments has concerned responses to surgical insult which, although important, may have limited relevance to repetitive loading disorders.

The vascular response of the ligament to injury has been measured in rabbit medial collateral knee ligaments using colored microspheres. This sham-controlled study showed that by six months post-injury, the blood flow was still well over 20 times its baseline value (Bray, Butterwick, Doschak, & Tyberg, 1996). Equivalent studies for the response of ligament to repetitive loading have not yet been conducted. What is known that ligament healing and remodeling times are generally slow. After 10 months the population of collagen fibrils in a small gap made in the adult rabbit MCL were uniformly smaller than controls. At two years follow-up, even though the collagen fibrils showed evidence of slow and steady remodeling, 90% were still less than control values (Frank, McDonald, & Shrive, 1997). Again, it is unlikely that healing of this size gap in an MCL ligament has relevance to ligament overuse injuries because, according to the cumulative trauma model, trauma is more likely on a microscopic scale.

The retinaculum is a specialized type of ligament which acts as a pulley for the finger and toe tendons to prevent 'bowstringing'. Upper extremity dysfunction, for example, such as that involved in De Quervain's tenosynovitis (Moore, 1997), is associated with hypertrophy of the retinaculum covering the wrist, and is thought to be associated with repetitive and forceful thumb use. The time constants involved in the healing and remodeling of retinaculae are unknown.

Ligaments, retinaculae and joint capsules are highly sentient structures providing afferent information for reflexes involved in the control of movement (see review by Barrack and Skinner (Barrack & Skinner, 1990).

Ligament response to alterations in loading

Ligaments adapt to changes in physical loading given time and these adaptations have been studied extensively in several animal models. The most reliable animal studies utilize sham-operated controls rather than the contralateral extremity as a control, because the experimental procedure often causes abnormal loading of the uninvolved contralateral extremity. As summarized elsewhere (Woo, Wang, Netwon, & Lyon, 1990) the rabbit medial collateral ligament (MCL) showed an approximately 50 % decrease in tensile stiffness after nine weeks of immobilization (Woo et al., 1987). Upon remobilization, the rabbit MCL stiffness had returned to normal values following nine weeks of remobilization, although its ultimate tensile strength still exhibited a 20% deficit at that time point. Such experiments underline the important point that soft tissues take longer than is generally appreciated by the lay person to adapt to changes in loading regimen.

Ligamentous response to repetitive loading

Ligament viscoelasticity is evident under repetitive loading. In man, 1 hour of exercise has been observed to increase wrist laxity by approximately 30% which then returned to baseline after 24 hours (Crisco, Chelikani, Brown, & Wolfe, 1997). Frank et al report that in young rats subjected to a 1 month intensive exercise program, the collagen fibrils in the knee ligaments of the exercised rats demonstrated an increased population of medium and smaller collagen fibrils not found in unexercised controls, and this was presumed evidence of a remodeling response(Frank et al., 1988). Since the overall ligament cross-sectional area had not changed, the reduced diameters were used to help explain the acute loss in elastic modulus reported in ligaments after an intensive exercise regime.

Age-Related Changes in Ligaments

Many studies have documented age-related degradation in the mechanical properties of ligaments. In one of the most reliable studies, a significant decrease in elastic stiffness and ultimate load at failure were found when specimens with a mean age of 76 years were compared with those from donors with a mean age of 35 years (Woo, Hollis, Adams, Lyon, & Takai, 1991). The older specimens exhibited more mid-substance failures. One would anticipate that, for the same applied stress history, microstructural fatigue failures would occur at lower numbers of cycles in older ligament than young ligament, but this remains to be demonstrated.

Tendon

Work-related overuse disorders are most common in the tendons and tendon insertions of the upper extremities. The most commonly-affected tendons are in the hand, the wrist, the forearm, and the humeral epicondyles. Conversely, sport-related tendon disorders are more common in the lower extremities, particularly in those who use running as their main form of conditioning.

The structure, function and nutrition of tendons have been reviewed elsewhere (Gelberman et al., 1988) (Jozsa & Kannus, 1997). Tendons are the tensile mechanical structures that allow muscles to transfer their contractile force to bones, and vice versa, with very little elongation. In certain tasks these forces exceeds 100 N in the finger tendons (Armstrong, Foulke, Joseph, & Goldstein, 1982) and thousands of Newtons in the tendons of the large extremity muscles. Depending upon their function and location, tendon excursions can be considerable with body movements; even finger tendons can exceed 5 cm excursion between full flexion and extension.

The tendon proper consists of the epitenon, endotenon, tendon bundles, and blood vessels. The bundles consist of long, parallel, sometimes spiraling, bundles of collagen fibers separated by mature fibroblasts (tenocytes). The extracellular matrix of healthy tendon is water, collagen (primarily Type I) and glycosaminoglycans and glycoproteins. Loose areolar tissue surrounds the bundles at different hierarchical levels and contains blood vessels and nerves. The epitenon is a fine fibrous and cellular layer adherent to the tendon surface (Gelberman et al., 1988). In high friction areas, where they change direction, tendons have fibrocartilagenous regions (Vogel, 1995) to withstand the compressive stresses as well as synovial sheaths which are comprised of circumferentially arranged fibroblasts and collagen fibers – the sheaths are lined with fibroblasts. In the hand, the tendons are covered by the paratenon (Gelberman et al., 1988). To prevent 'bow-stringing' during movements of the wrists or ankles, the sheaths are held in place by a retinaculum.

The nutritional supply to tendons is complex. The perfusion of the finger tendons, for example, is accomplished by vessels running longitudinally within the tendon, entering the tendon at the proximal synovial reflection, vessels entering through long and short vinculae, and vessels entering through the ossesous insertions(Gelberman et al., 1988). One or more avascular regions can be found in healthy tendons, depending upon the specific tendon, and these are presumably nourished by diffusion much like the inner intervertebral disc or meniscus.

Tendons exhibit non-linear viscoelastic behavior (Goldstein, Armstrong, Chaffin, & Matthews, 1987) and this can affect the behavior of the muscle-tendon unit (see below), especially under conditions of repetitive, vibratory or impact loading. Because of their viscoelasticity, tendons essentially act as low-pass mechanical filters between muscle and bone, their filtering characteristic dependent on their structure, composition, size and length.

Tendon disorders can occur at the myotendinous junction (Garret, Dahners, Maynard, & Tidball, 1988), in the tendon proper and at their bony insertion, the osseotendinous junction. The structure and function of the tendon and its response to injury have been reviewed in considerable detail by Gelberman et al. (Gelberman et al., 1988) (Jozsa & Kannus, 1997).

Physicians in sports medicine have suggested tendon disorders fall into four main categories (Leadbetter, 1992), although there is, however, no consensus that this is a completely satisfactory classification system (Jozsa & Kannus, 1997).

I. *paratenonitis* (replacing the terms tenosynovitis, tenovaginitis, peritendinitis), an inflammation of the paratenon (whether synovial or non synovial); histological findings include inflammatory cells in paratenon or peritendinous areolar tissue. Clinical signs and symptoms include swelling, pain, crepitation, local tenderness, warmth, dysfunction.

II. *paratenonitis with tendinosis* (replacing the term tendinitis), paratenon inflammation together with intratendinous degeneration; histological findings include same as above, with loss of tendon collage, fiber disorientation, scattered vascular ingrowth, but no prominent intratendinous inflammation. Clinical signs include same as above with frequently palpable tendon nodule, swelling, and inflammatory signs.

III. *tendinosis* (replacing the term tendinitis), intratendinous degeneration due to atrophy (aging, microtrauma, vascular compromise, etc); histological findings include inflammatory intratendinous degeneration with fiber disorientation, hypocellularity, scattered vascular ingrowth, occassional necrosis, and/or calcification. Clinical signs include an asymptomatic tendon nodule, which might be point tender. Swelling of tendon sheath is absent.

IV. *tendinitis* (replacing the terms tendon strain or tear), symptomatic degeneration of the tendon with vascular disruption and inflammatory repair response; histological findings show three subgroups with variable signs ranging from pure inflammation with acute hemmorhage and tear, to inflammation sureimposed upon pre-existing degeneration, to calcification and tendinosis changes in chronic conditions. In chronic condition there may be: 1) Interstial microinjury, 2) central tendon necrosis, 3) frank partial rupture, and 4) acute complete rupture. Clinical signs and symptoms are inflammatory and proportional to vascular disruption, hematoma, or atrophy-related cell necrosis. The duration of symptoms defines three sub-groups: 1. Acute (<2 wks), 2. Subacute (4-6 wks), 3. Chronic (>6 weeks).

Leadbetter's histological findings in adult athletes with overuse tendon injuries requiring surgical treatment of the Achilles tendon, posterior tibial, finger flexor, lateral elbow extensors, medial elbow flexor, patellar and tricpes tendons showed (Jozsa & Kannus, 1997): (1) tenocyte hyperplasia, (2) a blastlike change in morphology from normal tenocyte appearance, (3) prominent small vessel ingrowth with accompanying mesenchymal cells, (4) paravascular collections of histiocytes or macrophage-like cells,

(5) endothelial hyperplasia and microvascular thrombosis, (6) collagen fiber disorganization with mixed reparative and degenerative changes, (7) microtears and collagen separations (Leadbetter, 1992). Inflammatory cell populations were prominent in the paratenon and tenosynovium, and reparative cells were found to be present despite the degeneration.

Tenosynovitis in upper extremity tendons most commonly occurs at the (1) extensor pollicis brevis and abductor pollicis longus at the radial styloid, (2) finger flexors at the wrist (beneath the palmar carpal ligament and flexor retinaculum), (3) flexor pollicis longus at the MCP joint, (4) extensor carpi ulnaris at the wrist beneath the extensor retinaculum, (5) flexor carpi radialis at the wrist beneath the flexor carpal ligament and the extension of the flexor retinaculum, (6) proximal long head of the biceps brachii at the intertubercular groove beneath the tranverse ligament (Jozsa & Kannus, 1997). Acute tenosynovitis can take two chronic forms that can co-exist to variable degrees: (1) stenosing tenosynovitis (marked fibrous hyperplasia which tend to hamper gliding of the tendon within its sheath) and exudative-hypertrophic tenosynovitis (synovial hypertrophy and excessive fibrin exudate in the paratendinous space, as well as adhesions between the synovial sheath and the tendon).

Although the most popular imaging modalities using ultrasonography and magnetic resonance imaging for tendon have steadily improved over the last decade to the point that they are used to aid diagnosis and treatment of tendon disorders, their resolution is still inadequate for quantitative *in vivo* studies of underlying mechanisms.

While tendons are primarily loaded by the uniaxial tensile forces generated by or transferred to muscle, they and their related paratendinous structures are also loaded in the transverse direction by reaction forces where they pass over adjacent hard and soft structures such as bursae, bony pulleys and retinaculae, especially in awkward postures or at the end of range of motion(Armstrong, Castelli, Evans, & Dias-Perez, 1984). The combination of those tensile and transverse forces result in shear forces which can affect gliding of the tendon in its sheath or over its pulley. The resulting frictional forces between the tendon and the paratendinous structures have been implicated in tendinitis. Wilson and Goodship, for example, have quantified the temperature at the tendon core as being 5.4 °C above the tendon surface temperature in the superficial digital flexor tendons of exercising thoroughbred races horses (Wilson & Goodship, 1994). Since this temperature is sufficient to cause fibroblast death in vitro, they suggest this is a possible contributor to tendon core degeneration of the horse digital tendon and possibly human Achilles tendon.

Friction between the tendon and its pulley systems is a possible cause of *surface* degeneration in tendons. Such friction is usually countered by synovial cells and related structures whose response to mechanical stimulation has been reviewed by Schumacher (Schumacher, 1995). Elegant *in vitro* biomechanical studies by Uchiyama et al have shown frictional force to be proportional to the magnitude of axial tension in the tendon (determined in the hand by the force used to grip or use a hand tool), the coefficient of friction between the tendon and its substrate (which can vary several fold between different tendons (PL vs FDL), and the change in the angle of the tendon as it passes around a tendon pulley (Uchiyama, Coert, Berglund, Amadio, & An, 1995b). Awkward hand and wrist postures can increase this pulley angle thereby increasing friction forces on the tendon. At the highest loads, extrasynovial hand tendon had approximately four times as much gliding resistance of an intrasynovial hand tendon (Uchiyama, Amadio, Coert, Berglund, & An, 1995a). Since tendon friction forces will probably be highest during plyometric contractions, it might be instructive to examine whether tasks involving plyometric contractions have higher rates of tendon dysfunction. The transverse reaction force from the pulley will tend to flatten and deform the tendon cross-sectional profile. The *in vivo* response of tendon and its bearing surfaces to fluctuations in this form of transverse loading post-injury is presently unknown. Tendons are also loaded by intermittent hydrostatic pressure in the carpal tunnel (Rempel, Keit, Smutz, & Hargens, 1997). The tissue response of tendon to these types of non-axial loads is only beginning to attract attention.

Cumulative Strain

One theory for tendon involvement in repetitive work-related disorders states that tendon strain can accumulate over the day's repeated loading. In a classic investigation of the cumulative stress-strain behavior of tendon under cyclic loading, an *in vitro* study of 25 human flexor digitorum profundus tendons from four females and three males (55-72 years) was conducted using step and cyclic loadings (Goldstein et al., 1987). Under the physiologic loads applied, elastic strains ranging from 0.2 to 1.8% were recorded using clip transducers. The stresses at the tendon-sheath and retinacular interfaces were significant for wrist positions deviated from neutral. Significantly lower (~50%) strains were found in the female tendons loaded at the same stress level. Why the female tendons were stiffer is unclear. Under repetitive loading with an 8 s loading phase and 2 sec recovery time, a significant (~40%) increase in strain occurred between the 100 and 400th loading cycle, demonstrating viscoelastic creep behavior. When the duty cycle was reversed (2 sec loading, 8 sec recovery) the strain accumulation was significantly less.

For this theory to gain acceptance, experiments are needed to provide direct *in vivo* evidence of a causal link between excessive cumulative strain and the development of histological changes consistent with tendinitis in that region of the tendon. At present, there are no figures defining what that threshold for excessive strain is in different types of tendon.

Animal models of tendon response to exercise

Many studies of tendon response to exercise (Gillis, Meagher, & Poole, 1993) (Michna & Hartmann, 1989) (Patterson-Kane, Wilson, Firth, Parry, & Goodship, 1997), though informative, involved immature animals and thus have limited relevance to work-related disorders in the adult population. In studies reviewed by Archambault(Archambault, Wiley, & Bray, 1995), young mice exposed to an intense 10 week exercise protocol initially displayed many new collagen fibrils in their flexor digitorum tendons. However, by the end of the protocol, the morphological parameters were not much different than controls, except that the exercised tendons had the largest fibrils, a broad distribution of fiber diameters and the closest packing density. In young thoroughbred horses subjected to a life-long (18 month) training program, smaller fibrils were again found in the superficial digital flexor tendon (which is particularly prone to training injury). These were taken as evidence of repeated microtrauma in a region of the tendon already weakened by the training regimen(Patterson-Kane et al., 1997). The same authors point out that approximately 30% of thoroughbreds are lost to racing because of developing tendinitis in this tendon, principally because of overuse due to excessive gallop training. In one study of pig digital extensor tendons exercised for 1 year, again in relatively young animals, Woo et al. found increases in biomechanical properties such as elastic stiffness (20%), tenson ultimate strength, ultimate strain, cross-sectional area and collagen content (Woo, Ritter, & Amiel, 1980), but a corresponding study of digital flexor studies failed to find similar increases- rather there was a slight decrease in tendon material properties, or collagen content (Woo, Gomez, & Amiel, 1981).

These and related studies indicate that tendon shows a modest, slow and variable adaptational response to increased levels of activity, suggesting that it is easy to increase loading demands more rapidly than the tendon remodeling process can keep up with. On the other hand, much larger changes are caused by immobilization which significantly and adversely affects overall mechanical properties because of alterations in collage turnover, decreased GAG content, decreased water content, and so on.

<u>Animal models for inducing tendinosis.</u>

The first experimental evidence that repetitive loading could cause changes resembling peritendinitis crepitans was provided by Rais using a rabbit hindlimb (Rais, 1961). The duration of the hyperactivity was the best predictor of the severity of the tissue abnormality. A promising model for inducing paratenonitis with tendinosis was developed in the anesthetized caged rabbit (6-9 month; 2.5-4 kg) Achilles tendon(Backman, Boquist, Friden, Lorentzon, & Toolanen, 1990). 13 rabbits were induced to kick forcefully using surface electrical stimulation of the passively lengthened triceps surae. This was achieved in a non-weight-bearing posture using a device which cyclically rotated the ankle through 20° dorsiflexion and 35° plantarflexion. The animals were exercised for 5-6 weeks at a rate of 150 flexion and extensions/min for 2 h, three times a week. The contralateral limb served as a control. Following four weeks, all animals had irregular thickening over the Achilles tendon, and most animals demonstrated palpable nodules 0.5-1 cm above the insertion to the calcaneous. The tendons of the exercised legs demonstrated degenerative changes of varying severity and distribution, most often in the central tendon region. These included alterations in the structure of the tendon, the presence of inflammatory cells, an increased number of capillaries, as well as edema and fibrosis in the paratenon. The paper provides evidence supporting the hypothesis that repetitive loading can cause histological evidence of tendonitis/osis. Limitations of the model include the use of high rates of loading, but over much shorter durations than would be the case for the human work week. In addition, Achilles tendinitis is not part of a common occupational syndrome (except for professional runners). Additional limitations include the fact that no sham-operated controls were used, only the contralateral limb was used as control. Moreover, no quantitative histological change scores were given and no gender comparison were made, even though both genders were used. Sample size was inadequate to test a gender-related hypothesis. Despite limitations, however, these papers provide evidence that repetitive loading can induce histological changes associated with repetitive stress disorders.

Measurements of Carpal Tunnel Pressure

Although large grip and pinch forces have been associated with an increased risk for developing carpal tunnel syndrome (Armstrong & Chaffin, 1979) (Silverstein, Fine, & Armstrong, 1987), the pathomechanics remain uncertain. A recent study has reported on the association between carpal tunnel hydrostatic pressures in vivo and controlled fingertip loading in man (Rempel et al., 1997). That study showed an early increase in carpal tunnel hydrostatic pressure when light finger forces were exerted, followed by smaller pressure increase with additional loading. Though carpal tunnel hydrostatic pressure was proportional to finger tip force, it was essentially independent of wrist posture. The paper thus is not in agreement with earlier studies that showed that carpal tunnel pressure increased with both pronation and wrist flexion(Smith, Sonstegard, & Anderson, 1977). One explanation could be that the Rempel study monitored hydrostatic pressures, whereas earlier studies monitored hydrostatic pressure and contact stress.

Muscle-Tendon Unit

The behavior of the muscle-tendon unit under repeated passive stretching has been examined *in situ* (Taylor, Dalton, Seaber, & Garrett, 1990). In that acute study of rabbit EDL and TA stretched to 10% past L_o, viscoelastic behavior was observed in that the unit increased in length by some 3.5% after cyclic stretching and the peak force required decreased by some 17% of ten stretches. Most of the reduction, however, occurred in the first four loading cycles. A mild rate effect was found in that peak loads increased by 30% when loading rate was increased by three orders of magnitude. There is no evidence *per se* that stretching alters the risk for developing repetitive stress disorders. However, if progressive shortening of the muscle –tendon unit were to reduce the range of joint motion to the point that tendons now received continuous loading due to reduced hand or wrist range of motion, then that could alter carpal tunnel loading. Considerable research has focussed on how tendon properties modulate muscle output to the skeleton, and vice versa.

Brief Discussion – The site of injury.

At the level of the affected muscle, tendon and ligament, the question of whether a worker is "on" or "off" the job, is irrelevant even though it is, of course, important from an insurance perspective. Tissue loading history can be severe and repetitive on the job and light off the job, light on the job and severe and repetitive off the job for some leisure activities at least, or some intermediate combination thereof. Any symptoms, pain or dysfunction that are genuinely reported as being "work-related" in reality reflect the cumulative tissue loading history on and off the job. A laudable goal would be to reduce work-related tissue loading so that, whether "on" or "off" the job, tissues can remodel in reasonable time without risk of becoming chronic conditions.

Conclusions

Tendon/ligament

1. At least two experimental studies provide evidence that repetitive loading of tendon can induce histological changes similar to those found in repetitive strain disorders. There is a need for further studies of how the various characteristics of mechanical loading (i.e., Extrinsic factors, Table 1) interact to cause tendon dysfunction and, in particular, prevent healing and adequate remodeling.
2. While cumulative microstrain is a plausible hypothesis for tendon and ligament injury in over-use syndromes, direct tests of this hypothesis are needed in vivo.
3. Results from many controlled animal model studies pertaining to exercise and injury responses of ligament and tendon, while informative as basic mechanism, have limited applicability to considering the problem of overuse disorders in industry. This is because many of the experimental studies employed immature animals. The responses of *mature* and older animals may be more relevant because of slowed healing and remodeling times associated with aging.
4. While experimental models that allow study of healing and remodeling responses following surgically-induced defects in knee ligament and Achilles tendon do provide insights into basic healing and remodeling mechanisms, they probably have little relevance for upper extremity work-related disorders because of differences in the structures involved, and the extent and type of injury involved. Better models are needed.

Muscle

5. Recent studies of muscle clearly demonstrate that plyometric contractions can lead to muscle injury and loss of function. There is a need for studies to determine whether repetitive strain disorders might be initiated by single forceful events which trigger the injury, but might be maintained by repeated loading that prevents adequate healing/remodeling.
6. The most recent decade of research has produced new insights into the mechanisms underlying myalgia. Direct experimental tests of some of the most salient hypotheses are needed.
7. There is evidence that women respond to certain types of pain differently than men do. There is a need to test this hypothesis directly with respect to muscle and tendon pain.

Future Directions

1. Biomarkers are needed that allow better localization and quantization of injury/inflammation/remodeling in muscle, tendon and ligament for in vivo studies using MRI, ultrasound or other 3-D imaging modality.

2. Several promising rodent models have been developed for studying muscle response to injury, and these could easily be used to study questions relating to how much the effects of low-level loading can delay healing and remodeling rates following single event or repetitive loading injuries.

3. In the adult animal, the effect of age is to increase the risk of injury and slow healing rates. More research is needed on how age and repetitive loading interact to affect the risk for an injury to become chronic in muscle, tendon or paratendinous structures, and ligament.

4. Recent biomechanical studies of the factors leading to friction between tendon and paratendinous structures yield opportunities for more quantitative studies of tendonitis and tenosynivitis at tendon pulley and retinaculae sites.

5. Experimental pain models should continue to be improved in the human so that perceptual and motor responses can be studied while performing tasks with pain in known structures.

6. The gender difference in some repetitive motion disorders offers a potential window of opportunity to study the differences in underlying pain mechanisms at the molecular, cellular, tissue, organ and whole-body level. A better understanding of how these systems interact with one another is desirable.

7. There are many ergonomic interventions that have been used to reduce loading exposures. Where possible, greater advantage should be taken of such interventions.

REFERENCES

Aaraas, A. (1987). Postural load and the development of musculoskeletal illness. , University of Oslo, Oslo, Norway.

An, K. N., Kwak, B. M., Chao, E. Y. S., & Morrey, B. F. (1990). Determination of muscle and joint forces: a new technique to solve the indeterminant problem. J. Biomech. Eng., 106, 364-7.

Archambault, J. M., Wiley, J. P., & Bray, R. C. (1995). Exercise loading of tendons and the development of overuse injuries. J. Sports Med., 20, 77-89.

Armstrong, T. J., Buckle, P., Fine, L. J., Hagberg, M., Jonsson, B., Kilblom, A., Kuorinka, I. A. A., Silverstein, B. A., Sjogaard, G., & Viikari-Juntura, E. R. A. (1993). A conceptual model for work-related neck and upper-limb musculoskeletal disorders. Scand. J. Work Environ. Health, 19, 73-84.

Armstrong, T. J., Castelli, W. A., Evans, G., & Dias-Perez, R. (1984). Some histological changes in carpal tunnel contents and their biomechanical implications. J. Occup. Med., 26, 197-201.

Armstrong, T. J., & Chaffin, D. B. (1979). Carpal tunnel syndrome and selected personal attributes. J. Occup. Med., 3, 202-11.

Armstrong, T. J., Fine, L. J., Goldstein, S. A., Lifshitz, Y. R., & Silverstein, B. A. (1987a). Ergonomic considerations in hand and wrist tendinitis. J. Hand Surg., 12A, 830-7

Armstrong, T. J., Fine, L. J., Radwin, R. G., & Silverstein, B. S. (1987b). Ergonomics and the effects of vibration in hand-intensive work. Scand. J. Work, Environ., Health, 13, 286-9.

Armstrong, T. J., Foulke, J. A., Joseph, B. S., & Goldstein, S. A. (1982). Investigation of cumulative trauma disorders in a poultry processing plant. Am. Ind. Hyg. Assoc. J., 21, 103-116.

Ashton-Miller, J. A., McGlashen, K., Herzenberg, J. E., & Stohler, C. S. (1990). Cervical Muscle Myoelectric Response to Acute Experimental Sternocleidomastoid Pain. Spine, 15, 1006-1012.

Backman, C., Boquist, L., Friden, J., Lorentzon, R., & Toolanen, G. (1990). Chronic achilles paratenonitis with tendinosis: An experimental model in the rabbit. J Orthop Res, 8, 541-7.

Barrack, R. L., & Skinner, H. B. (1990). The sensory function of knee ligaments (Ch. 6). In A. W. Daniel D, O'Connor J (Ed.), Knee Ligaments: Structure, Function, Injury, and Repair . New York, NY: Raven Press.

Bernard, B. P. (Ed.). (1997). Musculoskeletal Disorders and Workplace Factors. A critical review of epidemiologic evidence for work-related musculoskeletal disorders of the neck, upper extremity, and low back. (Vol. DHHS Publication No: 97-141). Cincinati, OH: U.S. Department of Health and Human Services (National Institute of Occupational Safety and Health).

Bray, R. C., Butterwick, D. J., Doschak, M. R., & Tyberg, J. V. (1996). Colored microsphere assessment of blood flow to knee ligaments in adult rabbits. J. Orthop. Res., 14, 618-25.

Brooks, S. V., & Faulkner, J. A. (1990). Contraction-induced injury: recovery of skeletal muscles in young and old mice. Am. J. Physiol, 258, C436-42.

Brooks, S. V., & Faulkner, J. A. (1991). Maximum and sustained power of extensor digitorum longus muscles from young, adult, and old mice. J. Geront.: Biol. Sci., 46, B28-33.

Brooks, S. V., & Faulkner, J. A. (1994). Skeletal muscle weakness in old age: underlying mechanisms. Med. Sci. Sports Exer., 26, 432-9.

Brooks, S. V., & Faulkner, J. A. (1996). The magnitude of the intial injury induced by strecthes of maximally activated muscle fibres of mice and rates increases in old age. J. Physiol, 497, 573-80.

Brooks, S. V., Zerba, E., & Faulkner, J. A. (1995). Injury to fibers after single stretches of passive and maximally-stimulated muscles in mice. J. Physiol. (Lond.), 488, 459-69.

Chaffin, D. B. (1973). Localized muscle fatigue - Definition and Measurements. J. Occup. Med., 15, 346-54.

Crisco, J. J., Chelikani, S., Brown, R. K., & Wolfe, S. W. (1997). The effects of exercise on ligamentous stiffness in the wrist. J. Hand Surg., 22A, 44-48.

Dennerlein, J. T., Diao, E., Mote, C. D., & Rempel, D. M. (1998). Tensions of the flexor digitorum superficialis are higher than a current model predicts. J. Biomech, 31, 295-301.

Enoka, R. M., & Stuart, D. G. (1992). Neurobiology of muscle fatigue. J. Appl. Phyiol., 72, 1631-48.

Faulkner, J. A., & Brooks, S. V. (1995). Muscle Fatigue in Old Animals: Unique Aspects of fatigue in elderly humans. In G. S. e. al. (Ed.), Fatigue (pp. 471-80). New York, NY: Plenum Press.

Frank, C., Andriacchi, T., Brand, R., Dahners, L., DeHaven, K., Oakes, B., & Woo, S. L.-Y. (1988). Ligament: Normal Ligament: Structure, Function, and Composition (Ch. 2). In W. SL-Y (Ed.), Injury and Repair of the Musculoskeletal Soft Tissues (pp. 42-101). Park Ridge, IL: Am. Acad. Orthop. Surg.

Frank, C., McDonald, D., & Shrive, N. (1997). Collagen fibril diameters in the rabbit medial collateral ligament: A longer term assessment. Conn. Tiss. Res., 36, 261-9.

Friden, J., Sjostrom, M., & Ekblom, B. (1983). Myofibrilar damage following intense eccentric exercise in man. Intl. J. Sports Med., 4, 170-6.

Frontera, W. R., Meredith, C. N., O'Reilly, K. P., Knuttgen, H. G., & Evans, W. J. (1988). Strength conditioning in old men: skeletal muscle hypertrophy and impaired function. J. Appl. Physiol., 64, 1038-44.

Frost, H. M. (1990). Skeletal structural adaptations to mechanical usage: 4. Mechanical influences on intact fibrous tissues. Anat. Rec., 226, 433-9.

Gandevia, S., Enoka, R., McComas, A., Stuart, D., & Thomas, C. (Eds.). (1995). Fatigue, neural and muscular mechanisms. (Vol. 384?). New York: Plenum Press.

Gardner-Morse, M., Stokes, I. A. F., & Laible, J. P. (1995). Role of muscles in lumbar spine stability in maximum extension efforts. J. Orthop. Res., 13, 802-8.

Garret, W., Dahners, L., Maynard, J., & Tidball, J. (1988). Myotendinous Junction. In B. J. Woo SL-Y (Ed.), Injury and Repai of the Musculoskeletal Soft Tissues. Park Ridge, IL: Am. Acad. Orthop. Surg.

Gelberman, R., Goldberg, V., An, K.-N., & Banes, A. (1988). Tendon. In B. J. Woo SL-Y (Ed.), Injury and Repair of the Musculoskeletal Soft Tissues (pp. 1-40). Park Ridge, IL: Am. Acad. Orthop Surg.

Gillis, C. L., Meagher, D. M., & Poole, R. R., et al. (1993). Ultrasonographically-detected changes in equine superficial digital flexor tendons during the first months of race training. Am. J. Vet. Res., 54, 1797-1802.

Goldstein, S. A., Armstrong, T. J., Chaffin, D. B., & Matthews, L. S. (1987). Analysis of cumulative strain in tendons and tendon sheaths. J. Biomech., 20, 1-6.

Harridge, S., Magnusson, G., & Saltin, B. (1997). Life-long endurance-trained elderly men have high aerobic power, but have similar muscle strength to non-active elderly men. Aging, 9, 80-87.

Hart, D. A., Archambault, J. M., Kydd, A., Reno, C., Frank, C. B., & Herzog, W. (1998). Gender and neurogenic variables in tendon biology and repetitive motion disorders. Clin. Orthop. Rel. Res., 351, 44-56.

Holloszy, J. O. (1995). Workshop on Sarcopenia: Muscle Atrophy in Old Age. J. Gerontol.: Med. Sci., 50A(Special Issue), 1-161.

Hunter, K., & Faulkner, J. A. (1997). Pliometric contraction-induced injury of mouse skeletal muscle: efect of initial length. J. Appl. Physiol., 81, 278-83.

Johansson, H., & Sojka, P. (1991). Pathophysiological mechanisms involved in genesis and spread of muscle tension in occupational muscle pain and in chronic musculoskeletal pain syndromes: A hypothesis. Medical Hypothesis, 35, 196-203.

Jozsa, L., & Kannus, P. (1997). Human Tendons: Anatomy, Physiology and Pathology. Champaign, IL: Human Kinetics.

Leadbetter, W. B. C. (1992). Cell-matrix response in tendon injury. Clin. Sports Med., 11, 533-78.

Lieber, R. L., & Friden, J. (1993). Muscle damage is not a function of muscle force but active muscle strain. J. Appl. Physiol., 74, 520-6.

Lund, J. P., Donga, R., Widmer, C. G., & Stohler, C. S. (1991). The pain-adaption model - a discussion of the relationship between chronic musculoskeletal pain and motor activity. Can. J. Physiol. Pharmac., 69, 683-94.

Macpherson, P. C. D., Dennis, R. G., & Faulkner, J. A. (1997). Sarcomere dynamics and contraction-induced injury to maximally activated single muscle fibres from soleus muscles of rats. J. Physiol., 500, 523-33.

Macpherson, P. C. D., Schork, M. A., & Faulkner, J. A. (1996). Contraction-induced injury to single fiber segments from fast and slow muscles of rats by single stretches. Am J. Physiol., 271, C1438-46.

McCulley, K. K., & Faulkner, J. A. (1985). Injury to skeletal muscle fibres of mice following lengtheing contractions. J Appl Physiol, 59, 119-26.

McGill, S. M., & Norman, R. W. (1986). Partitioning of the L4-L5 dynamic moment into disc, ligamentous, and muscular components during lifting. Spine, 11, 666-78.

Michna, H., & Hartmann, G. (1989). Adaptation of tendon collagen to exercise. Int . Orthop., 13, 161-5.

Moore, J. S. (1997). De Quervain's tenosynovitis. JOEM, 39, 990-1002.

Murthy, G., Kahan, N. J., Hargens, A. R., & Rempel, D. M. (1997). Forearm muscle oxygenation decreases with low levels of voluntary contraction. J Orthop Research, 15, 507-11.

Newham, D. J., Jones, D., & Edwards, R. H. T. (1983a). Large delayed creatine kinase changes after stepping exercise. Muscle and Nerve, 6, 380-5.

Newham, D. J., McPhail, G., Mills, K. R., & Edwards, R. H. T. (1983b). Ultrastructural changes after concentric and eccentric contractions of human muscle. J. Neurol. Sci., 61, 109-22.

Nussbaum, M. A., Chaffin, D. B., & Martin, B. J. (1995). A back propagation neural network model of lumbar muscle recruitment during moderate static exertions. J. Biomech., 28, 1015-24.

Oh, S., & Radwin, R. G. (1993). Pistol grip power tool handle and trigger size effects on grip exertions and operator preference. Human Factors, 35, 551-69.

Overend, T. J., Cunningham, D. A., Paterson, D. H., & Smith, W. D. (1992). Physiological responses of young and elderly men to prolonged exercise at critical power. Eur. J. Appl. Physiol., 64, 187-93.

Patterson-Kane, J. C., Wilson, A. M., Firth, F. C., Parry, D. A., & Goodship, A. E. (1997). Comparison of collagen-fibril populations in the superficial digital flexor tendons of exercized and nonexercised thoroughbreds. Equine Veterinary J, 29, 121-5.

Paulson, P. E., Minoshima, S., Morrow, T. J., & Casey, K. L. (1998). Gender differences in pain perception and patterns of cerebral activation during noxious heat stimulation in humans. Pain, 76, 223-9.

Pedersen, J. (1997). Effects exerted by chemosensitive muscle afferents and muscle fatigue on the gamma-muscle spindle system and on proprioception: Implications for the genesis and spread of muscle tension and pain. Unpublished Monograph, University of Umea, Umea, Sweden.

Pedersen, J., Lonn, J., Hellstrom, Djupsjobacka, M., & Johansson, H. (1997). Alterations in movement sense acuity in the human shoulder during muscle fatigue. Submitted for publication.

Prilutsky, B. I., Herzog, W., & Allinger, T. L. (1997). Forces of individual cat ankle extensor muscles during locomotion predicted using static optimization. J. Biomech., 30, 1025-33.

Rais, O. (1961). Heparin treatment of peritendinits crepitans. Acta chir. scand., Suppl. 268.

Rempel, D., Keit, P., Smutz, W. P., & Hargens, A. (1997). Effects of static fingertip loading on carpal tunnel pressure. J. Orthop. Res., 15, 422-6.

Renstrom, P., Arms, S. W., Stanwyck, T. S., Johnson, R. J., & Pope, M. H. (1986). Strain in the anterior cruciate ligament during hamstring and quadriceps activity. Am. J. Sports Med., 14, 837.

Schultz, A. B., Andersson, G. B. J., Ortengren, R., Haderspek, K., & Nachemson, A. (1982). Loads on the lumbar spine - validation of a biomechanical analysis by measurements of intradiscal pressures and myoelectric signals. J. Bone Jt. Surg., 64A, 713-20.

Schultz, A. B., Ashton-Miller, J. A., & Alexander, N. B. (1997). What leads to age and gender differences in balance maintenance and recovery. Muscle and Nerve, Supplement 5, S60-64.

Schultz, A. B., Haderspek, K., Warwick, D., & Portillo, D. (1983). Use of lumbar trunk muscles in isometric performance of mechanically comlex standing tasks. J. Orthop. Res., 1, 77-91.

Schumacher, H. R. (1995). Morphology and Physiology of Normal Synovium and the Effects of Mechanical Stimulation (Ch. 18). In B. S. Gordon SL, Fine LJ (Ed.), Repetitive Motion Disorders of the Upper Extremity (pp. 263-76). Rosemont, IL: American Academy of Orthopaedic Surgeons.

Silverstein, B. A., Fine, L. J., & Armstrong, T. J. (1987). Occupational factors and carpal tunnel syndrome. Am. J. Ind. Med., 11, 343-58.

Sjogaard, G., Kiens, B., Jorgensen, K., & Saltin, B. (1986). Intramuscular pressure, EMG and blood flow during prolonged low-level static contraction in man. Acta Physiol. Scand., 128, 475-84.

Skelton, D. A., Young, A., Greig, C. A., & Malbut, K. E. (1995). Effects of resistance training on strength, power, and selected functional abilities of women aged 75 and older. J. Am. Ger. Soc., 43, 1081-7.

Smith, E. M., Sonstegard, D. A., & Anderson, W. H. (1977). Carpal tunnel syndrome: contribution of flexor tendons. Arch. Phys. Med. Rehabil., 58, 379-85.

Stohler, C. S., Zhang, X., & Lund, J. P. (1996). The effect of experimental jaw muscle pain on postural muscle activity. Pain, 21, 215-2.

Taylor, D. C., Dalton, J. D., Seaber, A. V., & Garrett, W. E. (1990). Viscoelastic properties of muscle-tendon units. The biomechanical effects of stretching. Am J. Sports Med., 18, 335-42.

Thelen, D. G., Ashton-Miller, J. A., & Schultz, A. B. (1996a). Lumbar trunk loads in rapid three-dimensional pulling tasks. Spine, 21, 605-13.

Thelen, D. G., Ashton-Miller, J. A., Schultz, A. B., & Alexander, N. B. (1996b). Do Neural Factors Underlie Age Differences in Rapid Ankle Torque Development. J. Am. Geriatr Soc., 44, 804-8.

Thelen, D. G., Schultz, A. B., Alexander, N. B., & Ashton-Miller, J. A. (1996c). Effects of Age on Rapid Ankle Torque Development. J. Gerontol.: Med. Sci, 51A, M226-32.

Thelen, D. G., Schultz, A. B., & Ashton-Miller, J. A. (1995). Co-contraction of lumbar muscles during the development of time-varying triaxial moments. J. Orthop. Res., 13, 390-8.

Thelen, D. G., Wojcik, L. A., Schultz, A. B., Ashton-Miller, J. A., & Alexander, N. B. (1997). Age Differences in Using a Rapid Step to Regain Balance During a Forward Fall. J. Geront: Med. Sci, 52A, M8-13.

Travell, J., Rinzler, S., & Herman, M. (1942). Pain and disability of the shoulder and the arm: Treatment by intramuscular injection with procaine hydrochloride. JAMA, 120, 417-22.

Uchiyama, S., Amadio, P. C., Coert, J. H., Berglund, L. J., & An, K.-N. (1995a). Gliding resistance of extrasynovial and intrasynovial tendons through the A2 pulley. J. Bone Jt. Surg., 79A, 219-24.

Uchiyama, S., Coert, J. H., Berglund, L., Amadio, P. C., & An, K.-N. (1995b). Method for measurement of friction between a tendon and its pulley. J. Orthop. Res., 13, 83-9.

Veierstad, K. B., Westgaard, R. H., & Anderen, P. (1990). Pattern of muscle activity during sterotyped work and its relation to muscle pain. Arch. Occup. Environ. Health, 62, 31-41.

Vogel, K. G. (1995). Fibrocartilage in Tendon: A response to compressive load. In B. S. Gordon SL, Fine LJ (Ed.), Repetitive Motion Disorders of the Upper Extremity (Ch. 14) (pp. 205-15). Rosemont, IL: American Academy of Orthopedic Surgeons.

Wilson, A. M., & Goodship, A. E. (1994). Exercise-induced hyperthermia as a possible mechanism for tendon degeneration. J. Biomech., 27, 899-905.

Wojcyk, L. A., Thelen, D. G., Schultz, A. B., Ashton-Miller, J. A., & Alexander, N. B. (1998). Age-and Gender Differences in the Single-Step Recovery From a Forward Fall. J. Gerontol.: Med. Sci., In Press.

Woo, S. L.-Y., Gomez, M. A., & Amiel, D. e. a. (1981). The effects of exercise on the biomechanical and biochemical properties of swine digital flexor tendons. J. Biomech. Eng., 103, 51-6.

Woo, S. L.-Y., Gomez, M. A., Sites, T. J., Newton, P. O., Orlando, C. A., & Akeson, W. H. (1987). The biomechanical and morphological changes in the medial collateral ligament of the rabbit after immobilization and remobilization. J. Bone Jt. Surg., 69A, 1200-11.

Woo, S. L.-Y., Hollis, J. M., Adams, D. J., Lyon, R. M., & Takai, S. (1991). Tensile properties of the human femur-anterior cruciate ligament-tibia complex. Am. J. Sorts Med., 19, 217-225.

Woo, S. L.-Y., Ritter, M. A., & Amiel, D., et al. (1980). The biomechanical and biochemical properties of swine tendons: long-term effects of exercise on the digital extensors. Connect. Tiss. Res., 7, 177-83.

Woo, S. L.-Y., Wang, C. A., Netwon, P. O., & Lyon, R. M. (1990). The response of ligaments to stress deprivation and stress enhancements. In A. W. Daniel D, O'Connor J. (Ed.), Knee Ligaments: Structure, Function, Injury, and Repair (pp. 337-350). New York, NY: Raven Press.

Wren, T. R., Beaupre, G. S., & Carter, D. R. (1998). A model for loading-dependent growth, development, and adaptation of tendons and ligaments. J. Biomech, 31, 107-14.

Zhang, X., Ashton-Miller, J. A., & Stohler, C. S. (1993). A Closed-Loop Control System for Maintaining Constant Experimental Muscle Pain in Man. I.E.E.E. Trans. on Biomed. Eng, 40, 344-52.

BIOLOGICAL RESPONSE OF PERIPHERAL NERVES TO LOADING: PATHOPHYSIOLOGY OF NERVE COMPRESSION SYNDROMES AND VIBRATION INDUCED NEUROPATHY

David Rempel, MD, MPH
Department of Medicine, Division of Occupational and Environmental Medicine,
University of California, San Francisco

and

Lars Dahlin, MD, PhD and Göran Lundborg, MD, PhD
Department of Hand Surgery, Malmö University Hospital, Malmö, Sweden

Introduction

Nerve compression syndromes involve peripheral nerve dysfunction due to localized microvascular interference and structural changes in the nerve or adjacent tissues. Although a well known example is compression of the median nerve at the wrist (e.g., carpal tunnel syndrome) other nerves are vulnerable (e.g., ulnar nerve at the wrist or elbow, spinal nerve roots at the vertebral foramen, etc.).

When tissues are subjected to pressure, they deform and create pressure gradients, redistributing compressed tissue toward areas of lower pressure. Nerve compression syndromes usually occur at sites where the nerve passes through a tight tunnel formed by stiff tissue boundaries. The resultant 'confined space' limits tissue movement and can lead to sustained tissue pressure gradients. Based on case reports, space occupying lesions (e.g., lumbricle muscles, tumors, cysts, etc.) can cause nerve compression injury, as can conditions associated with the accumulation of fluid (edema) or extracellular matrix in soft tissues (e.g., pregnancy, congestive heart failure, acromegally, myxedema hypothyroidism, muscle compartment syndromes, etc.). Although nerve injuries related to vibration occur near the region of vibration exposure, they may be manifested at constriction sites. Other conditions, such as diabetes mellitus may increase the susceptibility of the nerve to compression. In addition, an inflammatory reaction may occur which may impair the normal gliding of the nerve. Basic knowledge of the microanatomy of the peripheral nerve and the neuron and their complex reactions to compression are essential to understanding, preventing, and treating nerve compression injuries.

Structure and Function of Peripheral Nerves

Microanatomy

The neuron consists of the nerve cell body which is located in the anterior horn of the spinal cord (motor neuron) or in the dorsal root ganglia (sensory neuron), and of a process extending into the periphery - the axon - which is surrounded by Schwann cells arranged in a longitudinal continuous chain forming myelinated nerve fibers (Figure 1 (from Lundborg G and

98

Dahlin L 1996)). Between the Schwann cells, non-myelinated nerve fibers are located in a large number. Myelinated and non-myelinated nerve fibers are organized in bundles, called fascicles, and surrounded by a mechanical strong membrane consisting of laminas of flattened cells, the perineurial membrane. The bundles are usually organized in groups, held together by a loose connective tissue called the epineurium. In between the nerve fibers and their basal membrane is located an intrafascicular connective tissue - the endoneurium. The amount of the connective tissue components may vary between various nerves and also between various levels along the same nerve. For example, nerves located superficially in the limb or parts of the peripheral nerve that cross a joint contain an increased quantity of connective tissue, possibly as a response to repeated loading (Sunderland 1978).

The normal propagation of impulses in the nerve fibers as well as the communication and nutritional transport system in the neuron - axonal transport – require a sufficient energy supply. The peripheral nerve therefore contains a well developed microvascular system with vascular plexa in all connective tissue layers of the nerve (Lundborg 1970, 1975). The vessels approach the nerve trunk segmentally and these vessels have a coiled appearance so that the vascular supply is not impaired during the normal gliding or excursion of the nerve trunk. When the vessels reach the nerve trunk they divide into branches running longitudinally in various layers of the epineurium and also form numerous collaterals to vessels in the perineurial sheath. When the vessels pass through the perineurium into the endoneurium, which primarily contains capillaries, they often go through the perineurium obliquely thereby constituting a possible "valve mechanism" (Lundborg 1970, 1975).

The perineurial layer and the endoneurial vessels play an important role in protecting the nerve fibers in the fascicles. The endoneurial milieu is preserved by a blood-nerve barrier, and the tissue pressure in the fascicle - endoneurial fluid pressure - is slightly positive (Myers et al. 1978). This is obvious when there is injury to the perineurium; following a transsection a "mushrooming" effect is observed. There are no lymphatic vessels in the epineurial space, therefore problems occur when an edema is formed in the endoneurial space. Following such an edema the pressure in the fascicle may increase and rapidly interfere with the endoneurial microcirculation (Lundborg and Dahlin 1996). The epineurial vessels are more vulnerable than the endoneurial vessels to trauma and even to surgical handling of the nerve.

The neuron itself is, as mentioned above, a unique cell with the cell body and the extending process (axon). The length of the axon may be 10 to 15,000 times the diameter of cell body. Therefore, there is a need for an intraneuronal transport system - axonal transport - where essential products are produced and constantly transported from the nerve cell body down the axon (anterograde transport), and disposal materials and trophic factors are also transported in the opposite direction (retrograde transport) (Grafstein and Forman 1980). The axonal transport consists of various components where fast axonal transport (up to around 410 mm per day) involves various enzymes, transmitter substance vesicles and glycoproteins and the various slow components (up to 30 mm per day) involve mainly cytoskeletal elements such as subunits of microtubules and neurofilaments. It should be noted that axonal transport is energy depend and disturbances in axonal transport may be involved not only in the development of diabetic neuropathy but also in nerve compression injuries (Dahlin et al. 1986).

Normal Gliding of Nerve Trunks

Outside the peripheral nerve trunk there is a conjunctive like "adventitia" that permits an excursion of the nerve trunk which is a feature of normal nerve functioning during, for example, joint movements. Such an extraneural gliding surface together with the normally occurring sliding of fascicles against each other in deeper layers - intraneural gliding surfaces - make the normal gliding of the nerve possible. The median and ulnar nerve may glide 7.3 and 9.8 mm respectively during full elbow flexion and extension, and the extent of excursion of the nerve just proximal to the wrist is even more pronounced (14.5 and 13.8 mm respectively) (Wilgis and Murphy 1986). In relation to the flexor retinaculum the median nerve may move up to 9.6 mm during wrist flexion and to a slight degree in wrist extension but the nerve also moves during finger moments (Millesi et al. 1990).

Purpose of this Report - Database Search

The epidemiologic evidence linking repetitive loading to nerve injuries will be reviewed elsewhere. The purpose of this report is to review human and animal studies which examine the physiologic, pathophysiologic, biochemical and histologic effects of loading on the peripheral nerve.

The database PubMed was searched on August 3, 1998 for peer-reviewed articles from scientific journals from 1965 to 1998 using the following query:

(english[Language]
AND
((((("nerve compression syndromes/etiology"[MeSH Major Topic]
OR "nerve compression syndromes/pathology"[MeSH Major Topic])
OR "nerve compression syndromes/physiopathology"[MeSH Major Topic])
OR Nerve Compression Syndromes/prevention and control[MeSH Terms]))
OR ("hand arm vibration syndrome" AND nerve))

The search produced 3025 citations. On a case by case review, the following citations were eliminated: case reports, reviews, surgical techniques or complications, nerve crush studies, and nerve conduction techniques. All citations with titles suggesting study of physical exposures, loading, vibration, etiology, mechanisms of injury, biological response, and histology were retained. Total citations identified: 190.

In addition, the files of the authors were searched and a request was made to the seven discussants of this topic to provide 5 to 10 key citations. One discussant responded and provided 5 citations. These citations had been captured by the PubMed query, providing some confidence in the database search.

Experimental devices for nerve compression in animals

Various methods have been used to induce an acute or chronic compression of a peripheral nerve in animal models. There are advantages and disadvantages with all used methods. For acute compression, tourniquets can be used to apply compression around, for example, the hind limb of rabbits where it is possible to induce compression/ischemia of a limb (Lundborg et al. 1970). By this method, as well as the later presented invasive methods to induce acute graded compression of rat and rabbit nerves, the magnitude as well as the duration of the pressure can be varied (Dahlin 1986; Rydevik and Lundborg 1977; Lundborg 1970). Tourniquets have also used to induce and to evaluate structural changes in peripheral nerves in baboons (Ochoa et al. 1972; Fowler & Ochoa 1975). However, in the latter report very high pressures of 67 to 133 kPa were used. A small compression chamber, used by Rydevik and Dahlin (Rydevik and Lundborg 1977; Dahlin 1986) to induce acute, graded compression, consisted of two Plexiglas halves onto which thin rubber membranes were glued. It was applied around a mobilized nerve segment to apply low magnitude pressures for two to eight hours (for results see below). Similar methods have been used by others (Dyck et al. 1990).

Chronic nerve compression models have involved compression of mobilized nerve segments by using tightly fitting arteries (Weiss and Davis 1943), metal spring clips (Denny-Brown and Brenner 1944), compression clamps, where it is possible to grade the applied pressure (Nemoto et al. 1983; Horiutchi et al. 1983) and tubes of various materials such as polyethylene (Weisl and Osborn 1964) and silicone (Dahlin and Kanje 1992; Kanje et al. 1995; MacKinnon et al. 1985). By using tubes of varying inner diameters it is possible to obtain a graded compression but it is not possible to relate the compression to a specific pressure level as can be done in acute compression models. Furthermore, the implantation of foreign materials may generate an inflammatory response induced by the material (Kanje et al. 1995, Kajander et al. 1996). A normal developing chronic entrapment of the median nerve at the wrist in guinea pigs has also been used to study the structural changes of myelinated fibers (Ochoa and Marrot 1973), but as with the other chronic models neither the external load nor extraneural pressure has been measured.

Table 1. Pressures are frequently reported in units of mmHg. The units used in this paper are SI units (kPa). Conversions between the two units are listed.

mmHg	kPa
20	2.7
30	4.0
40	5.3
50	6.7
80	10.7
150	20.0
500	66.7
1000	133.3

Nerve Compression – Acute Effects (Hours)

Low-magnitude extraneural compression can decrease intraneural microvascular flow, impair axonal transport, and alter nerve structure and function in animal experiments. Miniature inflatable cuffs are used to apply controlled local compression around a nerve in vivo. Pressures of 2.7 can reduce epineurial venule blood flow (Rydevik et al. 1981). At pressures of 10.7 kPa all intraneural blood flow ceases. Likewise, pressures of 4.0 kPa inhibit both fast and slow anterograde as well as retrograde axonal transport (Dahlin et al. 1986). Therefore, cell nutrition and the intraneuronal communication system will be compromised at elevated extraneural pressures. Extraneural compression to 6.7 kPa applied for 2 minutes alters the shape of myelin sheaths and at higher pressures the myelin is severely split and distorted (Dyck et al. 1990). The role of pressure applied cyclically on nerve function has been evaluated in a rat tibial nerve model (Szabo et al. 1993). Static extraneural pressures of 4.0 kPa caused a decline in nerve function. The <u>mean</u> value of a pressure applied cyclically (e.g., mean 4.7 kPa; 2.7 to 6.7 kPa peak to peak) at 1Hz for 20,000 cycles had a similar effect as the continuous pressure on nerve function.

In healthy human volunteers, the extraneural pressure within the carpal tunnel was experimentally controlled by applying an external pressure over the palm (Gelberman et al. 1983a, 1983b, Szabo et al. 1983). Nerve function was followed for up to 4 hours. Some nerve function loss occurred at 5.3 kPa and complete nerve function was blocked at 6.7 kPa. In subjects with different blood pressures, the critical pressure threshold occurred at 4 kPa below the diastolic pressure, supporting an ischemic mechanism for acute nerve dysfunction. In addition, carpal tunnel syndrome may manifest with the treatment of hypertension (Emara and Saadah 1988).

Nerve Compression – Short-Term Effects (Days)

A persistent edema due to the increased vascular permeability of the epineurial and endoneurial vessels has been observed following compression at low pressures (Rydevik and Lundborg 1977). Using a pressure cuff the extraneural pressure around the rat sciatic nerve was elevated to 4 or 10.7 kPa for periods of 2, 4, 6, and 8 hours (Lundborg et al. 1983). The endoneurial fluid pressure was measured with a micropipette one hour and 24 hours after removal of the cuff, then the nerve underwent histologic analysis. A sham intervention was performed for 2 to 8 hours without inflating the cuff. A compression of 4 kPa led to elevated endoneurial pressures at 1 hour which increased with increasing duration of compression. A greater effect was observed with 10.7 kPa compression. The endoneurial pressures were similarly elevated at 24 hours. Nerve histology demonstrated endoneurial edema after 8 hours compression at 4 kPa but not with shorter durations. Greater edema and degenerating nerve fibers were observed at 10.7 kPa of compression. The endoneurial pressures measured after 8 hours of extraneural compression at 4 kPa can reduce intraneural blood flow (Myers et al. 1982). Limitations of the study were: (1) the short duration of follow-up, (2) small number of animals, (3) lack of quantitative histologic technique, and (4) no statistical testing. The study demonstrated that endoneurial fluid pressures can increase rapidly following extraneural compression and persist for at least 24 hours. A dose response effect of both compression magnitude and duration was demonstrated. Other studies have demonstrated that ischemia alters endothelial and basement membrane structure over a similar time course (Benstead et al. 1990)

Nerve Compression – Long-Term Effects (Weeks)

The same model was used to study the long-term biological effects of brief, graded nerve compression (Powell et al. 1986). Extraneural pressure of 10.7 kPa was applied for 2 hours to the sciatic nerve of the rat. At intervals of 4 hours, 1, 2, 5, 6, 7, 10, 14, and 28 days the nerves were excised for histologic analysis. In a smaller number of animals pressures of 1.3 and 4 kPa were applied for 2 hours with follow-up intervals of 5 to 7 days. Sham intervention in the contralateral limb of the low pressure animals was performed by inserting the uninflated chamber. Sham surgery without insertion of the chamber was also performed. Edema within the subperineurial space was visible within 4 hours in all compression groups and persisted for the entire time of the study. Inflammation and fibrin deposits occurred within hours of compression followed by a proliferation of endoneurial fibroblasts and capillary endothelial cells. Within days, vigorous proliferation of fibrous tissue was noted with marked fibrosis at day 28 and sheets of fibrous tissue extending to adjacent structures. Endoneurial invasion of mast cells and macrophages were noted, especially at day 28. Axonal degeneration was notable at days 10 to 18 at 10.7 kPa compression and to a lesser extent at 4 kPa with rare observations at 1.3 kPa. Axonal degeneration was correlated with degree of endoneurial edema. Demyelination was increased, especially on days 7 to 10 with remyelination observed on days 14 and 28. Demyelination was associated with Schwann cell necrosis. Demyelination was prominent with 4 kPa compression and to a lesser extent at 1.3 kPa. The sham intervention also demonstrated demyelination in regions close to the cuff surface, thought by the authors due to the tense but uninflated rubber cuff pressing the nerve. The sham surgery demonstrated no lesions. Limitations: (1) primarily a descriptive study, (2) unequal numbers of animals per group, (3) lack of follow-up of low pressure groups beyond 7 days, (4) Table II missing, (5) no quantification of fibrosis or edema, (6) pressure likely applied to nerve for the first sham intervention, and (7) statistical methods no clear.

In a similar model using the peroneal nerve of rats, pressures of 6.7 and 20 kPa applied for 2 minutes led 10 days later to demyelination under the cuff and degeneration distal to the cuff (Dyck et al. 1990). The effect was greater at the higher pressure and for pressures applied for 30 minutes. Structural changes in myelin were also observed immediately at the end of compression leading the authors to conclude that the long term effects of brief compression are due to mechanical shear forces disrupting the myelin. Limitations: single nerve per exposure group, therefore, no statistical comparisons and no very low pressure compression as control.

Effects on the nerve cell bodies have also been observed in ganglion cells of rabbits 7 days following compression at 4.0 kPa for two hours. The changes consisted of decrease in nuclear volume density, an eccentric position of the nucleus in the cell and frequent dispersion of the Nissl substance (Dahlin et al. 1987). Such changes may be followed by a change in the tubulin transport in the neurons (Dahlin et al 1993) as well as functional changes in the neuron and in the nerve trunk itself (conditioning lesion effect; Dahlin and Kanje 1992; Dahlin and Thambert 1993). Such changes may be involved in conditions where one part of the nerve trunk is compressed and thereby making other parts of the same nerve more susceptible to compression at another level (double crush and reverse double crush syndrome; Dahlin and Lundborg 1990).

To model chronic nerve compression other investigators have placed short silicon tubes of varying internal diameters or loose ligatures around the rat sciatic or sural nerve (Mackinnon et al. 1984, Mosconi et al. 1996). The tube inner diameters or ligature tensions are generally selected so that blood flow is not restricted. At regular intervals, up to a year later, the animal behavior, nerve electrophysiology and histology are evaluated. Although these are primarily observational studies, they provide some insight into the biological response of the nerve to continuous low-grade compression.

The response of nerve to compression in these studies is similar to the cuff experiments. For example, Sommer et al. (93) used loose ligatures around the sciatic nerve in one limb and very loose ligatures as a sham intervention on the contralateral side. In the sham ligatures there were no changes in the endoneurium at 1 and 4 weeks but fibrous tissue was increased in the epineurium near the ligatures but did not compress the nerve fascicles. In the exposed nerve perineurial edema was observed in the first days with proliferating endothelial cells and demyelination. Within a week increased proliferation of endothelial cells, fibroblasts and macrophages, continued demyelination and distal nerve fiber degeneration and the beginning of nerve sprouts. At 2 weeks, invasion by fibrous tissue and remyelination. At 4 weeks, less edema, thickened endothelium, remyelination. At 6 weeks regenerated nerve fibers, thickened perineurium and vessel walls. At 12 weeks remyelination of distal nerve segments. This model has been used to study pain related behavior (Mosconi et al. 1996). The limitations of this model are (1) the effects of the tissue inflammatory reaction to the device (e.g., foreign body reaction) are not usually considered but do occur (Kanje et al. 1995) and (2) it is not possible to measure the applied pressure in these chronic compression models.

Similar biological responses to compression are observed after chronic, low grade compression of the cauda equina and spinal nerve roots (Toh & Mochida 1997; Yoshizawa et al. 1995; Cornefjord et al. 1997). It should also be noted that, especially at the nerve root, increasing age is associated with increasing presence of fiber degeneration and regeneration but not with changes in number of myelinated fibers per nerve or fascicle (Knox et al. 1989). Fiber degeneration is more common in compressed nerve roots from older rabbits than younger ones (Toh & Mochida 1997).

Histology of Human Nerve Compression

A biopsy of the nerve is likely to lead to permanent nerve dysfunction, therefore there are few human histologic studies of nerves at common sites of compression. In a few case reports (surgical resection of nerve, autopsy with known disease) the nerve at the site of injury was compared to a site proximal or distal to the injury (Thomas 1963; Mackinnon et al. 1986; Neary et al. 1975a). In each case, the site of injury demonstrated thickening of the walls of the microvessels in the endoneurium and perineurium along with epineurial and perineurial edema, thickening and fibrosis. Myelin thinning was also noted along with evidence of fiber degeneration and regeneration. These reports are from patients with advanced stage of compression. In earlier disease a segment of the medium nerve is usually compressed with disturbed microcirculation which is immediately restored after the transection of the flexor retinaculum. There is usually both an immediate and delayed return of nerve function indicating the importance of ischemia in the early stages of the compression syndrome (Lundborg et al. 1982).

Increased connective tissue density has also been observed along the median nerve from six elderly cadavers wrists, without knowledge of medical history (Armstrong et al. 1984). The greatest density of connective tissue was observed at the level of the wrist crease with a fall in density 40 mm proximal and distal to the crease. Similar findings are observed in the ulnar nerve at the elbow (Neary et al. 1975b). These findings suggest that extracellular matrix is deposited within the nerve at sites of bending.

The tissues which lie next to a nerve, within a confined space, are more easily harvested and can provide information on the response of adjacent tissues to compression. For example, synovial tissue has been harvested from within the carpal tunnel next to the median nerve for histologic and biochemical analyses (Yamaguchi et al. 1965, Phalen 1972, Neal et al. 1987, Faithful et al. 1986, Sclesi et al. 1989, Schuind et al. 1990, Fuchs et al. 1991, Kerr et al. 1992). In the Fuchs study, one of the few to include a control group, synovium from 147 patients was harvested at time of carpal tunnel release and compared to synovium from 19 controls. The significant findings were greater edema and vascular sclerosis (endothelial thickening) in patient samples. Inflammatory cell infiltrates (lymphocytes, histiocytes) were observed in only 10% of samples. Surprisingly, the observed incidence of 3% with fibrosis was much less than the 36% to 100% reported in other studies. The authors conclude that tenosynovitis is uncommon in patients undergoing surgery for idiopathic carpal tunnel syndrome. Limitations: case definitions did not include nerve conduction findings, only ten controls were age appropriate and four of these were cadavers without history, no definition of primary endpoints (e.g., edema, fibrosis..), and the histology was semi-quantitative. The lack of definition of histologic endpoints in this and the other studies and differences in subject selection may account for differences in observed incidence of inflammation and fibrosis. The most consistent histologic features of synovium from the carpal tunnel of patients with CTS are edema and thickening of the vascular walls. To a limited degree these findings correspond to biological responses to nerve compression observed in the later stages of the animal models.

Vibration and Nerve – Short-Term Effects (Days)

Work with handheld vibrating tools can lead to a complex of symptoms known as the hand-arm vibration syndrome in which sensori-neural disturbances are prominent (Strömberg et al. 1996). The pathophysiological process associated with a vibration induced neuropathy remains still to be clarified but there is evidence that the injury may be located along the whole length of the neuron. Animal models have been developed to evaluate the events taking place in peripheral nerves following vibration exposure. Acute vibration (82 Hz, peak-to-peak magnitude of 0.21 mm) with an exposure time of five hours per day up to five days induces an intraneural edema as well as transient structural changes in thin non-myelinated fibers in the nerve trunks close to the vibration exciter (Lundborg et al. 1990; Lundborg et al. 1987). Other studies indicate that demyelination is an early event in the process and later a loss of axons may occur (Ho and Yu, 1989; Chang et al. 1994). Functional changes of both nerve fibers and non-neural cells such as Schwann cells may also occur following vibration exposure and are noted as an increased regenerative capacity following a nerve injury (Bergman et al. 1995; Dahlin et al. 1992).

Histology of Human Vibration Induced Neuropathy

Biopsies from fingertips of patients who have been exposed to vibrating handheld tools demonstrate nerve demyelination, loss of axons and fibrosis in small nerve trunks (Takeuchi et al. 1986, 1988). Recently, biopsies were taken from the dorsal interosseus nerve just proximal to the wrist from 10 men exposed to hand vibration at work and from 12 male age matched necropsy controls (Strömberg et al. 1997). In all 10 exposed and 1 control, pathological changes such as breakdown of myelin and presence of interstitial and perineurial fibrosis were observed. The histology results suggest that demyelination may be a primary lesion in the neuropathy which is followed by fibrosis associated with incomplete regeneration or with organization of an edema. Limitations: (1) detailed exposure information not available, (2) use of necropsy controls, (3) semi-quantitative endpoints, and (4) no statistical analyses. This study demonstrates that vibration exposure at work can induce structural changes in a peripheral nerve trunk at the wrist. Such changes may occur to the median nerve in the carpal tunnel among people exposed to vibration.

Nerve Excursion in Nerve Compression Syndromes

Longitudinal gliding of the nerve trunk occurs normally during joint motions and has been measured using ultrasound in humans or with markers placed in the nerve in cadavers. In patients with CTS, nerve excursion during wrist flexion/extension or finger flexion is restricted in comparison to healthy controls (Nakamichi et al. 1995; Valls-Solé et al. 1995). The basis for this limited motion is unknown. If the limited motion is due to adhesions to adjacent tissues, local regions of limited microvascular flow may occur due to nerve strain. A strain of 6 to 8% can limit blood flow or alter nerve function in a nerve (Clark et al. 1992; Ogata et al. 1986, Lundborg et al. 1973). Based on a cadaver study it may be that elevated pressures in the carpal tunnel do not restrict median nerve excursion (Bay et al. 1997).

Extraneural Pressure in Nerve Compression Syndromes

The hydrostatic pressures in the tissue next to a nerve can be measured with a small diameter wick or saline filled catheter. A number of studies have measured extraneural pressure in patients with carpal tunnel syndrome in comparison to controls (Table 2). The extraneural pressure is almost always higher in patients with CTS than in normal subjects. However, in one study, the mean pressure in patients with very severe or 'end-stage' CTS was low (Szabo et al. 1989). Differences in selection criteria and measurement techniques (e.g., catheter type, catheter location, use of patients with paraplegia, anesthesia, forearm postures, etc.) may explain differences in pressure measured. Taken together, these studies demonstrate that the extraneural pressure is elevated in patients with carpal tunnel syndrome in comparison to controls.

Effects of Joint Posture and Hand Loading on Extraneural Pressure in Normal Subjects

In many of the same studies, the wrist was moved either passively or actively to full flexion and extension and the pressures were measured. In patients with CTS the pressures increased by a factor of two to ten with flexion or extension. Although in normal subjects the pressures were of lower magnitude a similar response to extension and flexion has been consistently observed (Table 1).

A similar pattern of increasing extraneural pressure with increasing joint deviation from neutral has been reported for other nerves. For example, in 10 cadavers the extraneural pressure adjacent to the ulnar nerve at the elbow, with the elbow extended, was 1.0 ± 0.3 kPa and rose to 6.3 ± 2.5 kPa when the elbow was flexed to 150 degrees (Macnicol et al. 1982). In normal humans the extraneural pressure response to joint posture appears to be independent of gender and age (Kumar et al. 1988).

In normal subjects the simultaneous recording of posture and extraneural pressure in the carpal tunnel has been performed to investigate the dose-response effects of finger posture (Keir et al. 1998a, Werner et al. 1997), wrist extension/flexion (Werner et al. 1997, Weiss et al. 1995, Keir et al. 1998a), and forearm rotation (Werner et al. 1997, Rempel et al. 1998) to pressure. For example, extraneural pressure was measured in 17 normal volunteers while they slowly repeated forearm rotations of supination to pronation (Rempel et al. 1998). Hand and finger postures were held constant and the pressure was recorded at specific angles of pronation/supination as measured with a manual goniometer. The sweeps were repeated with different finger metacarpophalangeal flexion angles. The lowest pressures were recorded between 0 degrees and full pronation, while pressures up to 7.3 kPa were recorded in full supination. The limitations of this and the other studies are (1) due to the invasiveness of the procedure sample sizes are small for controls, leading to difficulty evaluating the effects of gender, age and other demographic factors, (2) selection biases are not addressed, (3) source of high inter-subject variability is unknown, (4) the tasks studied are difficult to generalize to working populations. Significant findings: increasing wrist extension and to a lesser degree wrist flexion, increasing forearm supination, and increasing metacarpophalangeal deviation from 45 degrees flexion increase extraneural pressure in the carpal tunnel.

Finger loading also increases carpal tunnel pressure in normal subjects and in cadavers. In cadavers, the extraneural pressures rise in the carpal tunnel when the flexor tendons are loaded (Smith et al. 1977; Cobb et al. 1996). Similarly, in normal volunteers the pressures rise during simulated holding and gripping tasks. In the Serage et al. (95) study the pressure rose to 10.1 ± 8.7 kPa when subjects held a 10.5 cm cylinder and rose further to 31.2 ± 1.32 kPa when an active fist was made. Similar findings have been observed by others (Okutsu et al. 1989; Hamanaka et al. 1995; Werner et al. 1997). During a task of loading and unloading 1 lb cans from a box at a rate of 20 cans per minute, the carpal tunnel pressure was measured in 19 subjects (Rempel et al. 1994). The pressures fluctuated, with peak pressures occurring during can gripping. The mean pressure rose significantly from 1.1 ± 0.8 kPa at rest to 2.4 ± 1.7 during the task. In two subjects the mean pressure was greater than 4.0 kPa.

In two studies, fingertip load and extraneural pressure in the carpal tunnel were quantified simultaneously in normal volunteers to investigate the dose-response relationships (Rempel et al. 1997, Keir et al. 1998b). Fingertip loads increased extraneural pressure independent of wrist posture (Rempel et al. 1997). In the other study (Keir et al. 1998b), 20 subjects (10 male, 10 female, mean age 30 yrs) pressed with the index finger on a load cell then pinched the load cell between the index finger and the thumb. Increasing fingertip load led to increasing extraneural pressure, in a dose-response manner, with the mean highest pressure of 6.6 kPa, occurring during the pinching task at 15 N force. The pinch task led to extraneural pressures that were twice those of the pressing task. Limitations: (1) incomplete knowledge of catheter tip location may have contributed to inter-subject variability and (2) no simultaneous evaluation of effects of hand postures. Conclusions: in healthy subjects relatively low fingertip loads during pinching (e.g., 5, 10, 15 N) elevate mean extraneural pressures in the carpal tunnel to 4.0, 5.6, and 6.6 kPa, respectively.

CONCLUSIONS

Elevated extraneural pressures can, within minutes or hours, inhibit intraneural microvascular blood flow, axonal transport, nerve function, and cause endoneurial edema with increased intrafascicular pressure and displacement of myelin, in a dose-response manner. Pressures of 2.7 kPa can limit epineurial blood flow, pressures of 4.0 kPa can limit axonal transport and cause cause nerve dysfunction and endoneurial edema, and pressures of 6.7 kPa can alter the structure of myelin sheaths.

In several animal models, low magnitude, chronic nerve compression causes a biological response of: endoneurial edema, demyelination, inflammation, distal axon degeneration, extensive fibrosis, new axon growth, remyelination, and thickening of the perineurium and endothelium. Axonal degeneration was correlated with degree of endoneurial edema.

In a animal model, extraneural pressures of 4 kPa applied for 2 hours can initiate a process of nerve injury and repair and can cause structural tissue changes that persist for at least one month. While a dose-response relationship with pressure occurs, the critical pressure/duration values for nerve injury are unknown.

No animal model has been developed to evaluate the effects of repetitive hand-finger loading on nerve structure and function in order to study mechanisms of injury and dose-response relationships.

In healthy humans, non-neutral finger, wrist and forearm postures and fingertip loading can elevate extraneural pressure in the carpal tunnel in a dose-response manner. For example, fingertip pinch forces of 5, 10, 15 N can elevate pressures to 4.0, 5.6, and 6.6 kPa, respectively. Extraneural pressures in healthy humans performing repetitive tasks at the workplace are unknown.

In a rat model, exposure of the hind limb to vibration for 4 to 5 hours per day for 5 days can cause intraneural edema, structural changes in myelinated and unmyelinated fibers in the sciatic nerve, as well as functional changes of both nerve fibers and non-neuronal cells.

Exposure to vibrating hand tools at work can lead to permanent nerve injury with structural neuronal changes in finger nerves as well as the nerve trunks just proximal to the wrist. The relationships between duration of exposure, vibration magnitude and nerve structural changes are still unknown.

References

Armstrong TJ, Castelli WA, Evans FG, Diaz-Perez R. Some Histological Changes in Carpal Tunnel Contents and Their Biomechanical Implications. J Occup Med 1984; 26(3):197-201.

Bay BK, Sharkey NA, Szabo RM. Displacement and strain of the median nerve at the wrist. J Hand Surg 1997; 22A:621-627.

Benstead TJ, Sangalang VE, Dyck PJ. Acute endothelial swelling is induced in endoneurial microvessels by ischemia. J Neurol Sci 1990; 99:37-49.

Bergman S, Widerberg A, Danielsen N. Lundborg G, Dahlin LB. Nerve regeneration in nerve grats conditioned by vibration exposure. Restorative Neurol and Neurosci 1995; 7:165-169.

Chang KY, Ho ST, Yu HS. Vibration induced neurophysiological and electron microscopical changes in rat peripheral nerves. Occup Environ Med 1994; 51:130-135.

Clark WL, Trumble TE, Swiontkowski MF, Tencer AF. Nerve tension and blood flow in a rat model of immediate and delayed repairs. J Hand Surg 1992; 17A:677-687.

Cobb TK, Cooney WP, An KN. Aetiology of work-related carpal tunnel syndrome: the role of lumbricle muscles and tool size on carpal tunnel pressure. Ergonomics 1996; 39:103-107.

Cornefjord M, Sato K, Olmarker K, Rydevik B, Nordborg C. A Model for Chronic Nerve Root Compression Studies. Spine 1997; 9:946-957.

Dahlin LB, McLean WG. Effects of graded experimental compression on slow and fast axonal transport in rabbit vagus nerve. J Neurol Sci 1986; 72:19-30.

Dahlin LB, Meiri KF, McLean WG, et al. Effects of nerve compression on fast axonal transport in streptozotocin-induced diabetes mellitus. Diabetologia 1986; 29:181.

Dahlin L, Kanje M. Conditioning effect induced by chronic nerve compression. An experimental study of the sciatic and tibial nerves of rats. Scand J Plast Reconstr Surg Hand Surg 1992; 26:37-41.

Dahlin LB, Necking LE, Lundstrom R, Lundborg G. Vibration exposure and conditioning lesion effect in nerves: an experimental study in rats. J Hand Surg (Am) 1992; 17:858-861.

Denny-Brown DE, Brenner C. Lesion in pripheral nerve resulting from compression by spring clip. Arch Neurol Psychiatry 1944, 52:1-19

Dyck PJ, Lais AC, Giannini C, Engelstad JK. Structural alterations of nerve during cuff compression. Proc Natl Acad Sci USA 1990, 87:9828-9832.

Emara MK, Saadah AM. The carpal tunnel syndrome in hypertensive patients treated with beta-blockers. Postgrad Med J 1988; 64:191-192.

Faithful DK, Moir DH, Ireland J. The micropathology of the typical carpal tunnel syndrome. J Hand Surg 1986; 11B(1):131-132.

Fowler TJ, Ochoa J. Recovery of nerve conduction after pneumatic tourniquet observations on the hindlimb of the baboon. J Neurol Neurosurg Psychiatry 1975, 35:638.

Fowler TJ, Ochoa J. Unmyelinated fibres in normal and compressed peripheral nerves of the baboon: a quantitative electron microscopic study. Neuropath and Appl Neurobiol 1975; 1:247-265.

Fuchs P, Nathan P, Myers L. Synovial histology and carpal tunnel syndrome. J Hand Surg 1991; 16A:753-8.

Gelberman RH, Szabo RM, Williams RV, Hargens AR, Yaru NC, Minteer-Convery MA. Tissue pressure threshold for peripheral nerve viability. Clin Orthop 1983; 178:285..

Gelberman RH, Szabo RM, Williamson RV, Dimick MP. Sensibility testing in peripheral—nerve compression syndromes—A human experimental study in humans. J Bone Joint Surg 1983; 65A:632

Gordon SL, Blair SJ, Fine LJ (editors) Repetitive Motion Disorders of the Upper Extremity. American Acad Orthop Surgeons, Rosemont, Il. 1995.

Grafstein B and Forman DS. Intracellular transport in neurons. Physiol Rev 1980; 1167.

Hamanaka I, Okutsu I, Shimizu K, Takatori Y, Ninomiya S. Evaluation of Carpal Canal Pressure in Carpal Tunnel Syndrome. J Hand Surg 1995; 20A:848-854.

Ho St, Yu HS. Ultrastructural changes of the peripheral nerve induced by vibration: an experimental study. Br J Ind Med 1989; 46:157-164.

Horiuchi Y. An experimental study on peripheral nerve lesions – compression neuropathy. J Japanese Orpthop Assoc 1983; 57:789-803.

Kajander KC, Pollock CH, Berg H. Evaluation of hindpaw position in rats during chronic constriction injury (CCI) produced with different suture materials. Somatosens Mot Res 1996; 13:95-101.

Kanje M, Stenberg L, Ahlin A, Dahlin LB. Activation of non-neuronal cells in the rat sciatic nerve in response to inflammation caused by implanted silicone tubes. Restorative Neurol and Neuroscience 1995; 8:181-187.

Keir P, Bach J, Rempel D. Effects of finger posture on carpal tunnel pressure during wrist motion. J Hand Surg 1998a (in press)

Keir PJ, Bach JM, Rempel DM. Fingertip Loading and Carpal Tunnel Pressure: Differneces between a Pinching and a Pressing Task. J Ortho Res 1998b; 16:112-115.

Kerr CD, Sybert DR, Albarracin NS. An analysis of the flexor synovium in idiopathic carpal tunnel syndrome: a report of 625 cases. J Hand Surg 1992; 17:1028-1030.

Knox CA, Kokmen E, Dyck PJ. Morphometric alteration of rat myelinated fibers with aging. J Neuropathol Exp Neurol 1989; 48:119-139.

Kumar K, Deshpande S, Jain M, Mayak MG. Evaluation of various fibro-osseous tunnel pressures (carpal, cubital and tarsal) in normal human subjects. Indian J Physiol Pharmacol 1988; 32:139-145.

Luchetti R, Schoenhuber R, De Cicco G, et al. Carpal-tunnel pressure. Acta Orthop Scand 1989; 60:397-399.

Lundborg G. Ischemic nerve injury: Experimental studies on intraneural microvascular pathophysiology and nerve function in a limb subjected to temporary circulatory arrest. Scand J Plast Reconstr Surg 1970; 6(Suppl):1-113.

Lundborg G, Rydevik B. Effects of stretching the tibial nerve of the rabbit. A preliminary study of the intraneural circulation and the barrier function of the perineurium. J Bone Joint Surg 1973; 55B(2):390-401.

Lundboar G. Structure and function of the intraneural microvessels as related to trauma, edema formation and nerve function. J Bone Joint Surg 1975; 57A:938.

Lundborg G, Myers R, Powell H. Nerve compression injury and increased endoneurial fluid pressure: a "miniature compartment syndrome". J Neuro Neurosurg Psy 1983; 46:1119-1124.

Lundborg G, Dahlin LB, Danielsen N, Hansson HA, Necking LE, Pyykko I. Intraneural edema following exposure to vibration. Scand J Work Environ Health 1987; 13:326-329.

Lundborg G, Dahlin LB, Hansson HWA, Kanje M. Necking LE. Vibration exposure and peripheral nerve fibert damage. J Hand Surg (Am) 1990; 15:346--351.

Lundborg G, Dahlin LB: Anatomy, Function, and Pathophysiology of Peripheral Nerves and Nerve Compression. Hand Clinics 1996; 12(2):185-193.

Mackinnon SE, Dellon AL, Hudson AR, Hunter DA. A primate model for chronic nerve compression. J Reconstr Microsurg 1985; 1(3):185-194.

Mackinnon SE, Dellon AL, Hudson AR, Hunter DA: Chronic Human nerve compression - a histologic assessment. Neuropathology and Appl Neurobiology 1986; 12:547-565.

Mackinnon SE, Dellon AL, Hudson AR, Hunter DA. Chronic Nerve Compression—an Experimental Model in the Rat. Ann Plast Surg 1994, 13(2):112-120.

Macnicol MF. Extraneural pressures affecting the ulnar nerve at the elbow. The Hand 1982; 14:5-11.

Millesi H, Zöch G, Rath T. The gliding apparatus of peripheral nerves and its clinical significance. Ann Hand Surg 1990; 9:87.

Mosconi T, Kruger L. Fixed-diameter polyethylene cuffs applied to the rat sciatic nerve induce a painful neuropathy: ultrastructural morphometric analysis of axonal alterations. Pain 1996; 64:37-57.

Myers RR, Powell HC, Costello ML, et al. Endoneurial fluid pressure: Direct measurement with micropipettes. Brain Res 1978; 148:510.

Myers RR, Mizisin AP, Powell HC, Lampert PW. Reduced nerve blood flow in hexacholorophene neuropathy. Relationship to elevated endoneurial fluid pressure. J Neruopathol Exp Neurol 1982; 41:391-399.

Nakamichi K, Tachibana S. Restricted motion of the median nerve in carpal tunnel syndrome. J Hand Surg 1995; 20B:460-464.

Neal NC; McManners J; Stirling GA. Pathology of the flexor tendon sheath in the spontaneous carpal tunnel syndrome. J Hand Surg, British Volume, 1987; 12(2):229-232.

Neary D, Eames RA. The pathology of ulnar nerve compression in man. Neuropathol Appl Neurobiol 1975a; 1:69.

Neary D, Ochoa J, Gilliatt RW. Sub-clinical entrapment neuropathy in man. J Neurol Sci 1975b; 24:283.

Nemoto K. An experimental study on the vulnerability of the peripheral nerve. Journal of the Japanese Orthopaedic Association, 1983; 57(11):1773-1786.

Ochoa J, Fowler TJ, Gilliatt RW. Anatomical changes in peripheral nerves compressed by a pneumatic tourniquet. J Anat 1972; 113:433-455.

Ochoa J, Marotte L. The nature of the nerve lesion caused by chronic entrapment in guinea pig. J Neurol Sci 1973; 19:491-495.

Ochoa J. Nerve fiber pathology in acute and chronic compression. In GE Omer, M Spinner (Eds): Management of peripheral nerve problems. W.B. Saunders Co., Philadelphia, 1980, pp 487.

Ogata K, Naito M. Blood flow of peripheral nerve effects of dissection, stretching and compression. J Hand Surg 1986; 11B:10-14.

Okutsu I, Ninomiya S, Hamanaka I, Kuroshima N, Inanami H. Measurement of Pressure in the Carpal Canal before and after Endoscopic Management of Carpal Tunnel Syndrome. J Bone Joint Surg 1989; 71A(5):679-683.

Phalen GS. The Carpal-tunnel Syndrome. Clinical Orthopaedics and Related Research 1972; 83:29-40.

Powell HC, Myers RR. Pathology of Experimental Nerve Compression. Laboratory Investigation 1986, 55(1):91-100.

Rempel D, Bach JM, Gordon L, So Y. Effects of Forearm Pronationa/Supinatin on Carpal Tunnel Pressure. J Hand Surg 1998; 23A:38-42.

Rempel D, Keir PJ, Smutz WP, Hargens AR. Effects of static fingertip loading on carpal tunnel pressure. J Orthop Res 1997; 15:422-426.

Rempel D, Manojlovic R, Levinsohn DG, Bloom T, Gordon L. The effect of wearing a flexible wrist splint on carpal tunnel pressure during repetitive hand activity. J. Hand Surg (Am) 1994; 19:106-110.

Rydevik B, Lundborg G. Permeability of intraneural microvessels and perineurium following acute, graded experimental nerve compression. Scand J Plast Reconstr Surg 1977; 11:179-187.

Rydevik B, Lundborg G, Bagge U. Effects of graded compression on intraneural blood flow. An in vitro study on rabbit tibial nerve. J Hand Surg 1981; 6A:3.

Scelsi R, Zanlungo M, Tenti P. Carpal tunnel syndrome: Anatomical and clinical correlations and morphological and ultrastructural aspects of the tenosynovial sheath. J Orthop Traumatology 1989; 15:75-80.

Schuind F, Ventura M, Pasteels JL. Idiopathic carpal tunnel syndrome: Histologic study of flexor tendon synovium. J Hand Surg 1990; 15A:497-503.

Serage H, Jia YC, Owens W. In vivo measurement of carpal tunnel pressure in the functioning hand. J Hand Surg (Am) 1995; 20:855-859.

Smith EM, Sonstegard DA, Anderson WH. Carpal tunnel syndrome: contribution of flexor tendons. Arch Phys Med Rehabil 1977; 58:379-385.

Sommer C, Gailbraith JA, Heckman HM, Myers RR. Pathology of experimental compression neuropathy producing hyperesthesia. J Neuropathol Exp Neurol 1993; 52(3):223-233.

Stromberg T, Dahlin LB, Brun A, Lundborg G. Structural nerve changes at wrist level in workers exposed to vibration. Occup and Environ Med 1997; 54:307-311.

Stromberg T, Lundborg G, Holmquist B, Dahlin LB. Impaired regeneration in rat sciatic nerves exposed to short term vibration. J Hand Surg (Br) 1996; 21:746-749.

Sunderland S. Nerves and nerve injuries. Edinburgh, Churchill-Livingstone, 1978.

Szabo RM, Chidgey LK. Stress carpal tunnel pressures in patients with carpal tunnel syndrome and normal patients. J Hand Surg 1989; 14A(4):624-627.

Szabo RM, Gelberman RH, Williamson RV, Hargens AR. Effects of increased systemic blood pressure on the tissue fluid pressure threshold of peripheral nerve. J Orthop Res 1983; 1:172.

Szabo RM, Sharkey NA. Response of Peripheral Nerve to Cyclic Compression in a Laboratory Rat Model. J Ortho Res 1993; 11:828-833.

Takeuchi T, Futatsuka M. Imanishi H, Yamada S. Pathological changes observed in the finger biopsy of patients with vibration-induced white finger. Scand J Work Environ Health 1986; 12:280-283.

Takeuchi T, Takeya M, Imanishi H. Ultrastructural changes in peripheral nerves of the fingers of three vibration-exposed persons with Raynaud's phenomenon. Scand J Work Environ Health 1988; 14:31-35.

Thomas PK. The connective tissue of peripheral nerve: An electron microscope study. J Anat 1963; 97:35.

Toh E, Mochida J. Histologic analysis of the lumbosacral nerve roots after compression in young and aged rabbits. Spine 1997; 22:721-726.

Valls-Solé J, Alvarez R, Nuñez M. Limited longitudinal sliding of the median nerve in patients with carpal tunnel syndrome. Muscle Nerve 1995; 18:761-767.

Weisl H, Osborne GV. The pathological changes in rats' nerves subject to moderate compression. J Bone Joint Surg 1964; 46:297-306.

Weiss ND, Gordon L, Bloom T, So Y, Rempel DM. Position of the wrist associated with the lowest carpal-tunnel pressure: implications for splint design. J Bone Joint Surg (Am) 1995; 77:1695-1699.

Weiss P and Davis H. Pressure block in nerves provided with arterial sleeves. J Neurophysiol 1943; 6:269.

Wilgis S and Murphy R. The significance of longitudinal excursions in peripheral nerves. Hand Clin 1986; 2:761.

Werner CO, Elmqvist D. Ohlin P. Pressure and nerve lesion in the carpal tunnel. Acta Orthop Scand 1983; 54:312-316.

Werner R, Armstrong TJ, Bir C, Aylard MK. Intracarpal canal pressures: the role of finger, hand, wrist and forearm position. Clin Biomech 1997; 12:44-51.

Yamaguchi DM, Lipscomb PR, Soule EH. Carpal Tunnel Syndrome. Minnesota Medicine 1965; 22-33.

Yoshizawa H, Kobayashi S, Morita T. Chronic Nerve Root Compression. Spine 1995; 20(4):397-407.

Table 2. Mean (S.D.) extraneural pressure within the carpal tunnel in patients and control subjects with the wrist moved passively to three postures. Pressures are reported in kPa.

	Patients with Carpal Tunnel Syndrome				Control Subjects			
	No. of wrists (subjects)	Neutral	Flexion	Extension	No. of wrists (subjects)	Neutral	Flexion	Extension
Gelberman et al. 1981[24,1]	15	4.3 (0.5)	12.5 (4.5)	14.7 (2.9)	12 (12)	2.5	—	—
Werner et al. 1983[92,2]	16	4.1	10.0	14.0	—	—	—	—
Szabo et al. 1989[81,3]	22 (22)	1.3	4.3 (na)	6.8 (na)	6 (6)	0.7 (na)	2.1 (na)	3.6 (na)
Okutsu et al.1989[62,4]	62 (46)[1]	5.7 (2.3)	25.6 (8.5)	29.6 (5.9)	16[2](16)	1.9 (1.3)	19.2 (8.8)	21.1 (8.7)
Luchetti et al. 1989[36,5]	30 (26)	5.9 (2.7)	—	—	4 (4)	2.0 (2.4)	—	—
Rojviroj et al. 1990[68,6]	61 (33)	1.6 (1.6)	3.6 (2.6)	4.4 (3.3)	16 (32)	0.5 (0.3)	1.2 (0.8)	1.7 (0.9)
Seradge et al. 1995[73,7,9]	81 (72)	5.8 (4.3)	10.6 (5.3)	13.5 (6.8)	21 (21)	3.2 (2.1)	13.1 (9.2)	15.9 (10.0)
Hamanaka et al. 1995[26,8]	957 (647)	8.0 (4.2)	—	—	31 (31)	2.0 (1.4)	—	—

[1] carpal tunnel syndrome: 11 male, 4 female, mean age 56 years; control: information not available

[2] carpal tunnel syndrome: 1 male, 15 female, mean age 46 years

[3] carpal tunnel syndrome: 6 male, 16 female, mean age 51 years; control: 6 male, mean age 32 years

[4] carpal tunnel syndrome: 16 male, 30 female, mean age 51 years; control: 10 male, 6 female, mean age 36 years

[5] carpal tunnel syndrome: 1 male, 25 female, mean age 51 years; control: 1 male, 3 female, mean age 48 years

[6] carpal tunnel syndrome: 8 male, 25 female, mean age 46 years; control: 12 male, 4 female

[7] carpal tunnel syndrome: 18 male, 54 female, mean age 46 years; control: 10 male, 11 female, age range 20 to 74 years

[8] carpal tunnel syndrome: 253 male, 394 female, mean age 54 years; control: 19 male, 12 female, mean age 38 years

[9] active wrist flexion and extension during pressure measurements

WORK FACTORS, PERSONAL FACTORS, AND INTERNAL LOADS: BIOMECHANICS OF WORK STRESSORS

Robert G. Radwin, Ph.D.
University of Wisconsin-Madison
Department of Biomedical Engineering and Department of Industrial Engineering

and

Steven A. Lavender, Ph.D.
Rush Presbyterian St. Luke's Medical Center
Department of Orthopedic Surgery

1.   Introduction

Physical stress imparted to internal tissues, organs and anatomical structures in manual work is rarely measured directly. Due to the obvious complexities and risks associated with invasive internal physical stress measurements, investigations often employ indirect internal measures or external measurements that are physically related to internal loading of the body. Indirect internal physical stress measures include electrophysiological measurements such as electromyograms, or non-specific physiological measures such as heart rate, oxygen consumption, substrate consumption, or metabolite production. More commonly, external loads are assessed either from measuring (1) the kinetics and kinematics of the body, (2) the physical and temporal aspects of the work performed, or (3) correlates to physical and temporal characteristics used as surrogate measures of internal load. The strength of the association between these measures and internal loads generally decreases from the former to the later.

External kinetic and kinematic measurements include physical properties of exertions (forces actually applied or created) or the motions that individuals make. These measurements have the most direct correspondence to internal loads because they are physically and biomechanically related to specific anatomical structures of the body. When kinetic and kinematic measures cannot be obtained, quantities that describe the physical characteristics of the work are often used as indirect measures of the kinetics and kinematics including: (a) measures of loads handled, (b) the forces that must be overcome in performing a task, (c) the geometric aspects of the workplace which govern posture, (d) the characteristics of the equipment used, or (e) the environmental stressors produced by the workplace or objects handled. Alternatively less directly correlated aspects of the work, such as production and time standards, classifications of tasks performed, or incentive systems are sometimes used to quantify the relationship between work and physical stress.

The objective of this manuscript is to review the state of available scientific evidence concerning the relationships between work factors, including host factors, and the resulting internal tissue loads. The paper will focus on the biomechanical stresses placed on the tissues and the methodological issues encountered when estimating tissue loads as people perform work tasks.

116

2.   Internal Tissue Loading

The musculoskeletal system is the load bearing structure within vertebrate animals. Boney structures resist gravitational forces and maintain the body's shape. As such, bones are the primary load bearing tissue within the body. Forces applied to the body, including gravity, attempt to compress or bend the bones. Ligaments hold together the bony structure by crossing articulations where bones inter-connect. Ligaments also act as a pulley system by guiding tendons around articulations. Tendons are the connective tissues that attach muscle to bone and therefore transmit muscle forces to the skeletal system to produce voluntary movements and exertions. A consequence of force exerted by the body, or acting against the body, is that adjacent tissues are subjected to mechanical loads. These include cartilage, disc, bursa, and nerve. A detailed examination of how each of the tissues is subjected to mechanical loading follows.

2.1.   Bone

When an individual performs a movement or exertion, forces are generated within the body to initiate and control it. The bones must resist tensile, compressive, shear, and torsional forces, in addition to bending moments. Bone is an adaptable tissue that acts according to Wolf's Law, which states that bone material is added where there is increased stress and bone material is resorbed where stresses on the tissue are reduced.

Relatively little emphasis has been placed on the injuries created by the repetitive loading of bone during occupational activities. Although, recent studies have shown that stress fractures in the lower extremities are not uncommon in new military recruits (Linenger and Shwayhat, 1992; Anderson, 1990; Giladi et al, 1985, Jordaan and Schwellnus, 1994). This suggest that the bone remodeling associated with Wolf's Law is a slow process and that the vigorous training that occurs during the initial weeks of boot camp does not allow this adaptation to occur.   Others have reported that osteoarthritis (OA) in the hip and knees is more prevelant in individuals employed in occupations that experience greater loading of the lower extremity (Kohatsu and Schurman, 1990; Lindberg and Axmacher, 1988; Lindberg and Montgomery, 1987; Vingard et al., 1991).   Anderson and Felson (1988) found a relationship between the frequency of knee bending and OA.   These same authors also report that knee strength demands were also predictive of knee OA in women aged 55 to 64 years. Taken together, these studies begin to demonstrate the link between workplace activities and changes in bone tissues.

2.2.   Ligaments and Connective Tissues

By their nature, as the connective tissues linking bones within the skeletal system, ligaments are primarily exposed to tensile loads. A typical stress strain curve for ligamentous tissue reveals that the tissue initially offers little resistance to elongation as it is stretched, however, once the resistance to elongation begins to increase, it does so very rapidly. Thus, the ligaments, while loosely linking the skeletal system, begin to resist motion as a joint's full range of motion is approached. Adams et al. (1980),by severing ligaments in cadaveric lumbar motion segments, showed the supraspinous/interspinous ligaments segments are the first ligamentous tissues to become stressed with forward bending of the lumbar spine. Stability and movement of the spine or any other articulation within the low tensile region of the ligamentous stress-strain curve must be accomplished using muscular contraction. This is not to say that ligaments don't contribute to joint loading. Several authors have showed that with extreme flexion (forward bending) of the torso there is an electrical silence in the spinal musculature (Floyd and Silver, 1955; Golding, 1952; Kippers and Parker, 1984, Toussaint et al, 1995). This finding suggests that at times ligaments are used to resist the bending moments acting on the spine. The degree of ligamentous contribution to the forces placed on the inter-vertebral disc during manual material handling tasks has been debated in the scientific literature (Cholewicki and McGill, 1992; Dolan et al., 1994; Potvin et al., 1994). Nevertheless, there is consensus that ligaments are subjected to tensile stress with extreme movements, and hence, can contribute to the mechanical loads placed on the body's articulations including the inter-vertebral disc.

When ligaments act as a turning point for tendons (pulleys), they are exposed to shear forces and contact stresses. For example the transverse carpal ligament, in bridging the carpal bones in the wrist forms a pulley by which the path of the finger flexor tendons is altered when the wrist is flexed. Similarly, the palmer ligaments maintain the path of the tendons from the finger flexor muscles to the distal phalanges. Goldstein et al. (1987) showed that the tendon strain on the proximal side of the transverse carpal ligament was greater than the strain on the distal side of the ligament. This finding indicates that the friction between the tendon and the ligament results in the ligament being exposed to shear loads in addition to normal loads. Even though ligaments act as pulleys, the ligaments themselves are rarely the tissues damaged in work related musculoskeletal injuries. Instead, it is the tendons that experience the morphological changes which result in symptoms and injuries.

2.3. *Tendons*

Tendons are a collagenous tissue that forms the link between muscle and bone. The orientation of the collagen fibers in tendons is in the form of parallel bundles (Chaffin and Andersson, 1991). This arrangement of fibers minimizes the stretch or creep in these tissues when subjected to tensile loading. With repeated loading tendons can become inflamed, particularly where the tendons wrap around bony or ligamentous structures. In more severe cases the collagen fibers can become separated and eventually pulverized wherein debris containing calcium salts creates further swelling and pain (Chaffin and Andersson,1991).

Mechanical relationships between external forces, postures and internal tendon loading were demonstrated by Armstrong and Chaffin (1979) for the carpal tunnel of the wrist using the analogy of a pulley and a belt. A tendon sliding over a curved articular surface may be considered analogous to a belt wrapped around a pulley. That model reveals that the force per arc length F_l, exerted on the trochlea is a function of the tendon tension F_t, the radius of curvature r, the coefficient of friction between the trochlea and the tendon m, and the included angle of pulley-belt contact q such that:

$$F_l = \frac{F_t\, e^{\mu\theta}}{r}.$$

(1)

When the extrinsic finger flexor tendons wrap around the trochlea, the synovial membranes of the radial and ulnar bursas surrounding the tendons are compressed by forces in both flexion and extension. The resulting compressive force is directly proportional to the tension developed in the tendons and the finger flexor muscles, which are related to the external force of exertion by the hand.

Normally the coefficient of friction between the tendon and trochlear surface would be expected to be very small. The model predicts that if the supporting synovia became inflamed and the coefficient of friction m increased, F_l would increase (Chaffin and Andersson, 1991). This would also result in increased shearing forces F_s as the tendons attempt to slide through their synovial tunnels, since shear forces are generally proportional to F_l and the coefficient of friction:

$$F_s = F_l \mu \, . \tag{2}$$

This gives rise to the concept that repeated compression could aggravate further synovial inflammation and swelling.

Armstrong and Chaffin (1979) also showed that the total force transmitted from the belt to a pulley F_R, depends on the wrist angle q, and the tendon load F_t as described by the equation:

$$F_R = 2F_t \sin(\theta/2) \tag{3}$$

Consequently the force acting on adjacent anatomical structures such as ligaments, bones, and the median nerve, depends on the wrist angle. The greater the angle is from a straight wrist, the greater the resultant reaction force on the tendons. The same equation also shows that the resultant force transmitted by a tendon to adjacent wrist structures is a function of tendon load.

2.4. Muscles

2.4.1. Force Generation and Biomechanics

Skeletal muscles provide locomotion and maintenance of posture through the transfer of tension by their attachment to the skeletal system via tendons. Tension is developed through active contraction and passive stretch of contractile units, or muscle fibers.

The musculoskeletal system employs simple mechanics, such as levers, to produce large angular changes in adjoining body segments. Consequently the amount of muscular force required to produce a desired exertion or movement depends on the external force characteristics (resistance or load dynamics handled), and the relative distance from the fulcrum to the point of external force application and from the fulcrum to the point of muscular insertion. While the effective distance between the fulcrum and the point of insertion for a specific muscle varies depending on the angle of the joint, the leverage of the muscles is almost always very small relative to the load application point, hence the internal muscle forces are usually several times larger than the external forces. As a result, most of the loads experienced by the joints within the body during exertions result from the internal muscle forces as they work in opposition to the external forces.

2.4.2. Co-contraction

The synergistic activation of the muscles controlling an articulation is often referred to as co-contraction. In many cases the co-contraction is between muscles working fully or partially in opposition to one another. From a biomechanical perspective, co-contraction is a way in which joints can be stiffened, stabilized, and moved in a well-controlled manner. Co-contraction, however, also has the potential to substantially increase the mechanical loads (compression, shear, or torsion) or change the nature of the loads placed on the body's articulations during an exertion or motion. This is because any co-contraction of fully or partially antagonistic muscles requires increased activation of the agonistic muscles responsible for generating or resisting the desired external load. Thus, the co-contraction increases the joint loading first by the antagonistic force, and second by the additional agonist force required to overcome this antagonistic force. Therefore, work activities where co-contraction are more common impose greater loads on the tissues of the musculoskeletal system.

2.4.3. Localized Muscle Fatigue

As muscles fatigue the loadings experienced by the musculoskeletal system change. In some cases the changes result in alternative muscle recruitment strategies or substitution patterns where-in other secondary muscles, albeit less suited for performing the required exertion, are recruited as replacements for the fatigued tissues. This substitution hypothesis has received experimental support from Parnianpour and colleagues (1988) who showed considerable out of plane motion in a fatiguing trunk flexion/extension exercise. It is believed that the secondary muscles are at greater risk of over-exertion injury in part due to their smaller size or less biomechanically advantageous orientation, and in part due their poorly coordinated actions. Alternatively, larger adaptations may occur which result in visible changes in behavior. For example, changes in lifting behavior have been shown to occur when either quadriceps or erector spinae muscles have be selectively fatigued (Novak et al., 1993; Trafimow et al., 1993; Marras and Granata, 1997). Fatigue may also result in balistic motions or exertions in which loads are poorly controlled and rapidly accelerated, which in turn, indicates there are large impulse forces within the muscles and connective tissues.

Localized muscle fatigue can also occur in very low level contractions, for example those used when supporting the arms in an elevated posture. In this case the fatigue is further localized to the small, low force endurance fibers (slow twitch) within the muscle. Because the recruitment sequence of muscle fibers during exertions works from smaller to larger fibers, the same small slow twitch fibers are repeatedly used and fatigued even during low level contractions (Sjogaard, 1996). Murthy et al. (1997), using near infrared spectroscopy to quantify tissue oxgenation as an index of blow flow, found reduced oxygenation within 10 to 40 seconds of initiating sustained contractions at values as low as 10 percent of the muscles maximum capacity, thereby indicating an interference with the metabolic processes.

2.5. Inter-vertebral Disc

The intervertebral disc serves as a joint since it permits rotation and translation of one vertebra relative to another. It also maintains the space between vertebrae so that spinal nerves remain unimpinged, and protects the upper body and head from the large peak forces experienced in the lower extremities. Anatomically, the disc is comprised of two parts: the nucleus pulposus, and the annulus fibrosis. The nucleus pulposus is in the central region of the disc and is comprised of a gelataneous mixture of water, collagen, and proteoglycans. The annulus fibrosis is comprised of alternating bands of angled fibers oriented approximately 30 degrees relative to the horizontal (White and Panjabi, 1990). In essence, the disc behaves as a pressure vessel and transmits force radially and uniformly. Thus, the disc is capable of withstanding the large compressive forces that result from muscular recruitment. Hutton and Adams (1982) found that cadaver discs from males between the ages of 22 and 46 could, on average, withstand single loads of over 10,000 N before failure occurred. In most cases, the failure was in the thin bony membrane which forms the boundary between the disc and the vertebral body (vertebral endplate) rather than through nuclear prolapse. Since the disc is an avascular structure, the health of the endplate is critical for nutrient exchange, and even small failures may hasten the degenerative process.

Researchers have found that prolapsed discs occurred more frequently when the vertebral segments were wedged to simulate extreme forward bending of the spine (Adams and Hutton, 1982). In this position the anterior portion of the annulus fibrosis undergoes compression while the posterior portion is under tensile stress. Over 40 percent of the cadaver discs tested by Adams and Hutton (1982) prolapsed when tested in this flexed posture, and with an average of only 5,400 N of compression force applied. This finding shows that the disc is particularly susceptible to bending stresses. In a later study where Adams and Hutton (1985) simulated repetitive loading of the disc, previously healthy discs failed at 3,800 N, again mostly through endplate fracture. Taken together, these studies show that the disc, especially the vertebral endplate, is susceptible to injury when loading is repetitive or when exposed to large compressive forces while in a severely flexed posture.

It should be clear from earlier discussions of muscle that the internal forces created by the muscles can be quite large in response to even modest external loads. When the muscles which support, move, and stabilize the spine are recruited, forces of significant magnitude are placed on the spine. Several investigators have quantified spine loads during lifting and other material handling activities. The earliest attempts to quantify the spinal loads used static sagittal plane analyses (Morris et al., 1961; Chaffin, 1969). Validation for these modeling efforts came from disc pressure and electromyographic studies (Nachaemson et al., 1964). More advanced models have been developed to quantify the three dimensional internal loads placed on the spine. Schultz et al. (1982a) developed and validated an optimization model to determine the three dimensional internal spine loads that results from asymmetric lifting activities. Compression estimates ranged from 520 N for upright unloaded standing, to 1560 N for unloaded subjects flexed 30 degrees, and up to 2660 N for the same group of subjects, flexed 30 degrees while holding an 80 N weight with their arms extended (Schultz et al., 1982b). In asymmetric tasks, for example lateral bending or resisted twisting, the lateral shear forces ranged exceeded 150 N, depending in part upon the optimization criteria used (Schultz et al., 1982c). Others have sought to predict the internal muscle forces directly from electromyographic signals, and then used these muscle forces in conjunction with a geometric models of the torso to compute the resulting forces acting on the spine. Typically these models have been validated using computed moments from a link segment model (McGill and Norman, 1986), or by measured external torque (Marras and Sommerich, 1991). McGill and Norman reported compression values on the L4/L5 disc ranging between 6 and 8 thousand Newtons as their subjects lifted 450 N loads. Anterior shear forces ranged between 200 and 1200 Newtons for the same lifts. During lateral bending exertions McGill (1992) reported compressive loads of 2500 N, lateral shear forces over 80 N, and anterior shear forces as high as 239 N. Marras and Granata (1997) have shown that the compression and shear values during lateral bending (extension) are dependent upon the movement speed. Similar velocity effects were reported for twisting exertions (Marras and Granata, 1995).

Others have quantified spine loads indirectly by examining the reaction forces and moments obtained with linked segment models. McGill et al. (1996) have shown that there is a very strong predictive relationship (r^2=.94) between the external spine moments and the spine reaction forces generated by their electromyographic assisted model. This indicates that the changes observed in the more readily quantifiable spine reaction moments, due to changes in the modeled task parameters, are representative of the changes in actual spine loading. Increased lifting speed, lower initial lifting heights, and longer reach distances all significantly increase the spine reaction moments, and hence, have a significant impact on the compressive and shear forces acting on the disc (De Looze et al., 1993; Frievalds et al., 1984; Leskinen et al., 1983; McGill and Norman, 1985; Schipplein et al., 1995; Buseck, et al. 1988; De Looze et al., 1994; Dolan et al., 1994; Tsuang et al., 1992). More recently, three-dimensional dynamic linked segment models have been developed to evaluate the spine loading during asymmetric tasks (Gagnon et al., 1993; Gagnon and Gagnon, 1992; Kromodihardjo and Mital, 1987; Lavender et al., 1998). These later models have been useful for documenting the spine loads (indirectly) that stem from lifting activities that involve twisting and lateral bending.

2.6.   Nerves

Nerves, while not contributing either actively or passively to the internal forces generated by the body, are exposed to forces, vibration, and temperature variations that affect their function. Carpal tunnel syndrome is believed to result from a combination of ischemia and compression of the median nerve within the carpal canal of the wrist. Evidence of compression of the median nerve by adjacent tendons has been reported by direct pressure measurements (Tanzer, 1959; Smith, et al., 1977). Electrophysiological and tactile deficits consistent with carpal tunnel syndrome has been observed under experimentally induced compression of the median nerve (Gelberman, et al., 1981; Gelberman, Szabo, and Williamson, 1983). The biomechanical model of the wrist developed by Armstrong and Chaffin (1979) in Equation 3 predicts that median nerve compression will increase with increased wrist flexion and extension, or finger flexor exertions. Increased intra-carpal canal pressure was observed by Armstrong, et al. (1991) wrist and finger extension and flexion, and for increased grip exertions. Rempel (1995) reports similar findings and for repetitive hand activity and during typing.

Environmental stimuli, for example cold temperatures and vibration, have been shown to affect the response of peripheral nerves. Low temperatures, for example, can affect cutaneous sensory sensitivity and manual dexterity. Vibratory stimuli, with repeated exposure, is believed to cause via a reflex response (nerve) contraction of the smooth muscles of the blood vessels associated with Reynaud's Syndrome (Chaffin and Andersson, 1991). Less severe nerve damage resulting from, vibratory stimuli has been associated with paresthesias and tingling sensations.

3.   External Loading Factors

The literature contains numerous methodologies for measuring physical stress in manual work. Studies from different disciplines and research groups have concentrated on diverse external factors, workplaces, and jobs. Factors most often cited include forceful exertions, repetitive motions, sustained postures, long vibration exposure and cold temperatures. An example of the variety of factors cited is contained in Table 1. Although the literature reports such a great diversity of factors, it is possible to group these methodologies into a coherent body of scientific inquiry. A conceptual framework is now presented for organizing the physical parameters in manual work.

3.1. Physical Stress

Physical stress can be described in terms of fundamental physical quantities of **motion, force, vibration**, and **temperature**. These basic quantities comprise the kinematic, kinetic, oscillatory and thermal aspects of work and energy produced by, or acting on the human in the workplace.

3.1.1. Motion

Motion describes the displacement of a specific articulation or the relationship between adjacent body parts. Motion of a body segment relative to another segment is most commonly quantified by angular displacement, velocity or acceleration of the included joint. Motion is specific to each joint and therefore motions of the body are fully described when each individual body segment is considered in total. Motions create internal stress by imposing loads on the involved muscles and tendons in order to maintain the position, transmitting loads to underlying nerves and blood vessels, or creating pressure between adjacent structures within or around a joint.

3.1.2. Force

Force is the mechanical effort for accomplishing an action. Voluntary motions and exertions are produced when internal forces are generated from active muscle contraction in combination with passive action of the connective tissues. Muscles transmit loads through tendons, ligaments and bone to the external environment when the body generates forces through voluntary exertions and motions. Internal forces produce torques or rotation about the joints, and tension, compression, torsion, or shear within the anatomical structures of the body.

External forces act against the human body, and may be produced by an external object or in reaction to the voluntary exertion of force against an external object. Force is transmitted back to the body and its internal structures when opposing external forces applied against the surface of the body. Localized pressure against the body can transmit forces through the skin to underlying structures such as tendons and nerves. Pressure increases directly with contact force over a given area and decreases when the contact area is proportionally increased.

Contact stress is produced when the soft tissues are compressed between bone and external objects. This may occur when grasping tools, parts or making contact with the work station. Contact stress may be quantified by considering contact pressure (force/area). An increase in contact force or a decrease in contact area will result in greater contact stress. Pounding with the hands or striking an object will give rise to stress over the portion of body contact. Reaction forces from these stress concentrations are transmitted through the skin to underlying anatomical structures.

3.1.3. Vibration

Vibration occurs when an object undergoes oscillatory motion. Human vibration, the term commonly used, is produced by the acceleration of an external object. Vibration is transmitted to the human body through physical contact either with seat or the feet (whole body vibration), or by grasping a vibrating object (hand-arm vibration). Whole-body vibration is associated with vibration from riding in a vehicle or from standing on a moving platform. Hand-arm, or segmental vibration may be introduced when using power hand tools or operating controls such as steering wheels on off-road vehicles. Physiological responses to human-transmitted vibration include endocrine and metabolic, vasodilatation/constriction, motor, sensory, central nervous system and skeletal responses.

External vibration transmits from the distal location of contact to proximal locations of the body and sets into motion the musculoskeletal system, receptor organs, tissues and other anatomical structures. Vibration transmissibility is dependent on vibration magnitude, frequency, and direction. Dynamic mechanical models of the human body describe the transmission characteristics of vibration to various body parts and organs. Such models consider the passive elemental properties of body segments, such as mass, compliance, and viscous damping. Vibration transmission is affected by these passive elements and is modified by the degree of coupling between the vibration source and the body. The force used for gripping a vibrating handle and the posture of the body will directly affect vibration transmission. Vibration can introduce disturbances in muscular control by way of a reflex mediated through the response of muscle spindles to the vibration stimulus. This reflex is called the tonic vibration reflex which results in a corresponding change in muscle tension when vibration is transmitted from a vibrating handle to flexor muscles in the forearm (Radwin, Armstrong and Chaffin, 1987).

3.1.4. Temperature

Heat loss occurs at the extremities during work in cold environments, such as in food processing, handling cold materials, working outdoors, or exposure to cold air exhaust from pneumatic hand power tools. Local peripheral cooling inhibits biomechanical, physiological, and neurological functions of the hand. Exposure to localized cooling has been associated with decrements in manual performance and dexterity, tactility and sensibility, and strength. These effects are attributable to various physiological mechanisms.

3.2. Physical Stress Properties

The physical stresses described in Section 3.1 may be present at varying levels. These variations can be characterized by three properties: **magnitude**, **repetition**, and **duration**. The relationship between physical stresses and their characteristic properties are illustrated in Figure 1.

Magnitude is the extent to which a physical stress factor is involved. Magnitude quantifies the amplitude of the force, motion, vibration, or temperature time-varying record, and has the physical units of the corresponding physical measure.

Repetition is the frequency or rate that a physical stress factor repeats. The frequency that the physical stress in Figure 1 repeats is the inverse of the period between repeated exertions, motions, vibration, or cold temperature, and the physical units of $time^{-1}$.

Duration refers to the time that one is exposed to a physical stress and is quantified in physical units of time.

3.3. Interactions

The characteristic properties of physical stresses together quantify exposure to external stress. Combinations of different physical stresses and properties can be used to represent factors that are commonly reported for quantifying exposure. These relationships are summarized in Table 2. Physical stresses are quantified in a similar manner as shown in Table 3. Force measurements quantify force amplitude, in addition to the rate and time of force application. Motion of individual joints include the magnitude of angular displacement, velocity or acceleration, the frequency of motions and the time the motion is sustained. Vibration magnitude is quantified as acceleration of the vibrating objects, and repetition and duration is a measure of the frequency and time the vibration occurs. Similarly, cold temperature and associated frequencies and amplitudes quantify cold exposure.

This organization is useful because it provides a construct for comparing and combining studies using different measurements and methodologies, as represented in Table 1, into a common framework. For example, physical stress measurements using a survey methodology that simply assesses the presence and absence of highly repetitive wrist motions can therefore be compared with a study that measures the frequency of motions using an electrogoniometer. This is possible because both studies have quantified the repetition property of wrist motion. Similarly a study that considers the weight of objects lifted may be compared with a study that assesses muscle force using electromyography because both studies quantify the magnitude of force. Therefore, a body of scientific knowledge from diverse investigations emerges.

External physical stress factors described in Sections 3.1 and 3.2 relates to distinct internal physical stress factors. This relationship is summarized in Table 4. For example, force magnitude is directly related to the loading of tissues, joints and adjacent anatomical structures, as is the metabolic and fatigue processes of contracting muscles. The strength of these relationships depends on the particular measurement and the type of stress. Biomechanical and physiological mathematical models have been developed to quantitatively describe some of these relationships. Similar relationships between external and internal factors have been recognized by Moore, Wells and Ranney (1991) and Armstrong, et al. (1993).

4.   Assessment of Workplace Factors

Physical stress factors in the workplace have been evaluated at different levels of detail, depending on the specific research instrument and measurement methodology used. Survey methods involve observational study at the job or task level. Production and time data may be obtained from existing records such as time standards and process planning data, or from measured data using work sampling or time and motion studies. More detailed job analysis methods analyze the job at the element or micro level using by direct physical measurements. These analyses involve breaking down the job into component actions, measuring and quantifying physical stress factors.

4.1.   Survey Methods

Survey methods include interviews, self-reported questionnaires, or observation and checklists. Questionnaires, diaries and interview techniques are easily administered and are commonly used for quantifying physical work load. The method relies on the firsthand observations and experiences of the employee /supervisor. An employee interview consists of asking questions regarding job/task attributes and associated physical stress exposures (Bernard, et al., 1994). One advantage of these methods are their ability to assess exposure over long time intervals, infrequently performed tasks, or multiple methods at performing tasks. which is a feature not usually available for other methodologies. However the method depends on subjective data.

Observational methods are the most common method employed. The most developed methodologies are for postures and motions of different articulations and use of the hands. These include posture classification systems like OWAS (Karhu, et al., 1977; Karhu, et al., 1981). Some observational methods integrate posture classification and a checklist of exertions, tool use and assessment of repetition with a breakdown of task elements (Keyseling, et al., 1993; McAtamney, and Corlett, 1993).

4.2.   Production and Time Data

Many of these methods are rooted in traditional work measurement, which is historically based on time and motion study that is used for quantifying the temporal aspects of work. Time data is important for understanding the duration of work and rest, for quantifying repetition, and for determining the duration that work is performed. Suitable time data may be available to investigators at various levels of detail. The average daily time allotted for performing a job can be estimated from the shift time. The average time for specific tasks may be obtained from a task rotation or production schedule. Cycle time describes the time for completing a single cycle of production, and may be determined from production rate data. The time to perform a specific element may be available from a time and motion study.

Although use of production or cycle time data may be convenient and easily obtained, it is limited in that the motions and exertions performed in completing the task may be related to these data, but may not correspond directly. For example, a manual assembly operation may involve fastening four screws using a power screwdriver for every unit assembled. Consequently the production rate would indicate one quarter of the actual number of repetitive motions performed each cycle. Alternatively, use of production data for a similar assembly operation where the work is distributed among two operators in a cell who alternate the fastening operation would indicate a greater amount of repetitions over the course of a work day. The necessity to directly observe the work performed when using production data becomes apparent. Job rotations and other work organization aspects of the job further complicate the use of these data.

Some investigators collect original time and motion data specifically for assessing the temporal aspects of physical stress exposure. Work sampling can be used for estimating the proportion of time that an employee is engaged in specific activities or tasks. Keyserling (1986) combined time study with posture classification for estimating the time that specific postures are assumed.

4.3. Detailed Analysis

Several techniques are available for describing and quantifying postures. They range from simple gross descriptions, for example pinching or pressing (Armstrong et. al., 1979), to categorical descriptions joint angles (Armstrong et al., 1982; McAtamney and Corlett, 1993), to full quantitative measurement of three dimensional angles. Joint angles are most often described in terms of the orthopedic angles as defined by the American Academy of Orthopedic Surgeons (1965). Other systems quantify postures by determining each body segment's orientation relative to a global coordinate system. This type of postural description is required to use the 2D and 3D Static Strength Prediction Models developed by the University of Michigan (Chaffin, 1970; Chaffin et al., 1977). In general, however, the better you can describe the problem that exists the better chance that your will solve the problem. Thus, the more quantitative the description the better the reading of the true problem.

When measuring orthopedic angles a goniometer can be used to quantify postures. However, it is imperative that the measurements be obtained without interfering with the work process. Therefore, most of the time postural measurements are made from videotapes rather than from the observed individuals directly. This introduces a number of errors into the process however. Ideally the video camera is oriented in a plane orthogonal to the plane of measurement and adjusted such that the center of the image corresponds to the articulation of interest. With two dimensional motions, for example lifting tasks within the mid-sagittal plane, locating the camera in an orthogonal plane is a possibility. High contrast adhesive markers attached to the limbs and the torso facilitate the extraction of measurements from videotape by providing consistent reference marks on the limbs and joint center locations. In reality most studies need to quantify the posture of multiple body parts at the same time thereby leading to wider camera angles and increased error in measuring postures further from the center of the video camera lens.

With tasks that create postural deviations in three dimensions it becomes very difficult to accurately measure postures from the screen directly. The necessary information can be extracted from a two dimensional image on the video monitor to simulate the observed posture.

The simulated posture is then measured. The use of multiple video cameras increases the accuracy of three dimensional postural descriptions. A synchronization signal is used to insure that video data are describing the same motion or posture.

When the evaluation is focused on specific body parts, for example the spine or the wrist, electrical goniometers may be used. The simplest version of an electrogoniometer consist of two rigid tangs that can be affixed to the adjacent body segments hinged by a potentiometer. These devices are usually strapped or taped to the skin such that the axis of rotation aligns with the joint's axis of rotation. For the elbow an electrical goniometer designed to measure flexion should be should be positioned such that it is on the lateral side of the upper and lower arm with the potentiometer centered over the joint between the humerus and the radius. A single axis potentiometer works well if the joint can be conceptualized as a hinge joint. With the knee, for example, this assumption may not be valid as there can be three dimensional motion in addition to a shifting center of rotation as the femur tibial contact point changes with knee flexion. Thus, for extremely accurate measurements a more complex arrangement of goniometers may be needed (Chao, 1976).

Trunk postures and motions have been measured using various types of instrumentation. Nordin et al. (1984) reported a flexion analyzer that was essentially an inclinometer strapped on the back. This device provides data indicating the duration of the working time that was spent in 5 flexed postures consisting of 18 degree intervals between 0 and 90 degrees. This device is useful for obtaining an overall picture of the trunk postures required in a job across many tasks and work cycles. The device clearly distinguished the difference between dentists, who flexed forward only moderately, and warehouse workers who worked in deeply flexed postures. The same device was later used by Magnusson et al. (1990) to study the trunk postures in assembly line workers performing highly repetitive work. Snijders et al. (1987) reported on the development of a device that can be worn beneath the clothing and can collect three-dimensional trunk postural data throughout a work shift of eight hours or more. The data are stored on a multi-channel tape recorder and can be analyzed at a later time. Marras et al. (1992) have developed the Lumbar Motion Monitor, which in addition to measuring the instantaneous posture of the lumbar and lower thoracic spine in three dimensions, provides the angular velocities and accelerations associated with the movements. The LMM gives very precise information regarding the postures and motions from each individual activity sampled. If one is looking at primarily static task then the postural data is the primary focus of the analysis. If one is looking at a dynamic material handling task then the motion parameters such as range of motion, velocities, and accelerations become the focus of the analysis.

4.3.1.1 Force

The force associated with industrial tasks are sometimes estimated from indirect measurements of the task requirements rather than measuring the exertions of individuals performing the task. These include measuring the weight of objects carried or lifted, or measuring the force necessary to do work, such as pushing or pulling a control. Direct force measurements should consider variability among individuals.

At the most detailed level, force is measured for specific operations, such as grasps or moves. Less detailed analyses may measure forces exerted for individual elements. An estimate of specific exertions in a task may suffice for many practical analysis purposes.

Instruments applicable to force measurements range from simple mechanical instruments to electromechanical devices. Simple mechanical devices such as a spring scale or dynamometer can be used to estimate lift/pull/push forces in many instances. Direct force measurements are often difficult to obtain. Forces can often be roughly calculated using the weight of the objects, estimates of the frictional forces, the power settings on tools, and simple physics equations.

Mechanical force transducers are most suitable for static force measurements such as determining the weight of a stationary object or for measuring quasi-static, or very slowly changing forces such as the force needed to overcome friction and push or pull a rolling cart along the floor. Electronic force transducers overcome many of the limitations of mechanical force transducers. Strain gage load cells are capable of measuring static force, and they are much better suited for measuring forces that change with time than mechanical spring scales.

Internal muscle forces are difficult to measure directly, but can be estimated with electromyography (EMG). Under controlled conditions, internal muscle forces can be estimated by simulating the motions and exertions in a laboratory setting. If internal forces are measured, sufficient replicate measurements should be made to account for variability within and between individuals performing the task.

Pressure and force can be measured using ink force sensors and strain gages, but this is rarely done due to difficulties in using the equipment. The conditions that cause high contact stresses are well recognized and are usually eliminated without measuring the level of stress.

Exertions in industrial tasks may be directly measured by installing strain gage force sensors directly inside handles and objects grasped. For example, Armstrong, et al. (1994) installed strain gage load cells directly underneath computer keyboards for measuring finger exertions during typing., and Radwin, et al. (1991) investigated the grip forces involved in operating a pistol grip power hand tools. Although direct measurements are possible, it is very limited in practicality for most situations because of the great amount of preparation required.

4.3.1.2 Vibration

Vibration acceleration may be measured using accelerometers mounted on objects contacting the body. Accelerometers contain a small mass and a piezoelectric or piezoresistive element that measures the resulting force when the mass accelerates. Therefore accelerometer sensitivities are generally proportional to their mass. It is important that the total mass of an accelerometer is sufficiently small not to interfere with the measurement by loading the vibrating body. The smaller the accelerometer, the less sensitive it is. Smaller accelerometers have greater resonant frequencies and are usable over a greater frequency range. Accelerometers are also influenced by temperature changes, humidity, and other harsh environmental conditions.

Human occupational vibration exposure is usually assessed by measuring vibration acceleration and determining acceleration magnitude, frequency characteristics, and exposure time (duration).

The relative effects of hand-transmitted vibration and other physical stress factors are often difficult to separate because many jobs using vibrating hand tools also involve considerable use of the upper limb. For instance, vibrating hand tool operators may also have to assume extreme postures dictated by a specific tool-handle location and work piece orientation.

Vibrating power tool handles and triggers may introduce contact stress from sharp edges against the fingers or palm. The hands may also be exposed to cold air produced from pneumatic tool exhaust outlets.

Furthermore, physical stress factors can adversely affect vibration transmission exposure. For example, forceful exertions will result in increased vibration transfer to the tool operator's hand and arm because of improved coupling between the vibrating handle and the hand. Highly repetitive work can affect vibration exposure through accumulated doses of repeated vibration exposures.

4.3.1.3   Cold

Ambient temperature is measured by a thermometer. A thermistor or thermocouple sensor is used to measure surface temperature readings (e.g. measuring cold exhaust of an air tool venting across the wrist).

5.   Workplace Design Factors and Physical Stress Exposure

5.1.   Workplace Layout

The previous discussion has shown that the postures assumed and forces exerted affect internal tissue loading. Given that the design of the workplace affects the forces exerted and postures and motions exhibited by an individual, it is reasonable to expect that the tissue loads are, in part, a function of the way in which the work and the workplace is designed. The strength of these relationships will depend upon how much variation is possible in work methods and other anthropometric considerations. For example, lifts from low levels typically result in greater torso flexion than do lifts from higher levels. Thus, low level lifts result in greater spine moments and disc compressive forces than higher level lifts (Drury et al., 1989b; Schipplien et al, 1991), which in turn, leads to greater spine compression due to muscle recruitment (McGill et al., 1996). Although, the actual amount of forward bending that occurs in a particular lift, and hence, the magnitude of the forward bending moment, will be affected by the lifting technique used (De Looze et al., 1993; Buscek, 1988; Bush-Joseph et al., 1988), the lengths of various body segments, and the relative strengths and endurance of the muscles recruited for task performance (Novak et al., 1993; Trafimow et al., 1993).

How material flows through a work place can have a profound impact on the tissue loads people experience. Clearly the weight of the objects (material) handled in performing one's job has a direct impact on internal tissue loads. Thus, decisions as to the size and weight of shipping containers have a direct influence on tissue loads. In addition to increased weight that typically accompanies increases in object size, larger objects result in greater horizontal distances between the object's center of mass and the body's articulations, and consequently greater external moments (Schipplein et al., 1995). Likewise, the orientation of objects, and the accessibility of objects impacts the reach distance and the magnitude of the external moments.

How well an object can be grasped, often referred to as the "coupling" between the object and a worker, affects the internal loads on the spine and lowers the strength demands (Frievalds et al., 1984; Garg and Saxena, 1980; Drury et al., 1989a,b). Lower strength demands implies a reduction in the internal forces generated by the body. In addition, several other material flow issues affect tissue loading including:

1. <u>Adhesion between items</u>- modifies the actual external force required to handle an object.
2. <u>Pacing</u> – affects movement speed, and hence, internal forces. May be controlled by conveyor speeds or time allowances in a work standard.
3. <u>Coefficient of friction between an item and a person</u> – affects the amount of internal force used to grasp and hold an object.

5.2. Interactions with Objects

The use of hand tools and handling of containers and other objects should be considered in evaluating physical stress since there are numerous aspects of these objects that affect force, posture, vibration and cold exposure. The combined effects of hand tool geometry, work location, orientation and operator position can have a dramatic effect on upper limb posture. How tool operators hold a particular hand tool might affect their posture and the manner in which the hand grips the tool. Posture can affect muscle length relative to its resting length, introduce passive forces from tendon strain, and alter biomechanical aspects of exertions involved in operating the tool.

It is not simply the use of a particular tool, but the way the tool is used that imposes physical stress on the tool operator. The relative effects of various physical stress factors involving work with hand tools are difficult to separate because many jobs using hand tools also involve extensive use of the upper limbs. For instance, hand tool operators may have to assume extreme postures dictated by a specific tool handle shape and workpiece orientation. The same tool may be used for repetitive, short-cycle tasks, resulting in exposure to repetitive exertions and motions. Some power hand tools can also introduce vibration, and triggers may cause contact stress from sharp edges against the fingers and palm. The hands may also be exposed to cold air produced from pneumatic tool exhaust outlets.

5.3. Work Scheduling

The duration of and the time between exertions are critical parameters when evaluating the impact of work scheduling on tissue loads. The ability to perform static contractions decays rapidly over time. Static contractions result in reduced blood flow, ischemia, and metabolite retention in the contractile tissues. The scheduling of work can have a significant impact on the duration of muscular exertions. Job rotation, when well planned, provides for relief of affected body parts so that tissue recovery processes can occur throughout the day. Job rotation schemes should be evaluated carefully to insure that these goals are met. For example, an employee may move from a set of tasks that requires shoulder abduction to a set of tasks that require low level lifting and thereby allow the shoulders to be in a non-flexed and non abducted posture. Job enlargement, or the adding of tasks to relatively simple jobs allows for tissue recovery within the on-going work process. Clearly, tasks must be carefully selected to allow insure exposure to risk factors is reduced.

5.4. Force Requirements

The force applied to the work material to accomplish a task is only one aspect of force that affects the operator. Power hand tools also generate forces, which in turn act against the operator. The torque at a power screwdriver blade, for example, transfers a force back to the tool handle. The human operator must react against this force by exerting an equal and opposite force to hold onto the tool handle as the tool is operated.

The amount of force exerted by the muscles on the tendons and fingers is related to the hand posture. Armstrong (1986) argues that since muscle force is less when objects can be grasped using a power grip posture, than exertion of force with a power grip will be less stressful than exerting an equivalent amount of force with a pinch grip posture.

5.5. Individual Factors

There are several individual factors the modulate the tissue loads experienced by an individual. For example, Giladi et al (1991) reported the influence of individual factors on the incidence of fatigue fractures, specifically, they found individuals with narrow tibiae, and / or a grater external rotation of the hip were more likely to experience fatigue fractures. Cowan and colleagues (1996) reported the relative risk of "overuse" injuries was significantly higher in military recruits with most valgus knees. Moreover, these authors showed the "Q" angle, which defines the degree of deviation in the patellar tendon from the line of pull on the patella by the quadriceps muscles, was predictive of stress fractures. Thus, anthropometric differences, differences in the strength capacities between individuals, and variations in the work methods used will all affect the tissue loads experienced by an individual as work tasks are performed.[1]

Variation in the anthropometric characteristics between individuals will have an impact on the biomechanical properties of the musculoskeletal system, which in turn will impact the internal loads that anatomical structures experience. Sources of anthropometric variation that impact tissue loading include:

1. Bone lengths-Affects the leverage of the external loads and the postures attained while performing a work task.
2. Tendon Attachment points relative to joint centers of rotation- Affects the leverage of the muscles.

---

[1]   The reader will note that gender has not been specifically listed as an individual factor affecting tissue loading. However, we believe that much of variation due to gender is due to underlying differences in strength capacities and anthropometric characteristics.

3. Muscle mass-One of the determinants as to how much force can be generated by an individual.

4. Muscle Fiber type distributions- Determines an individuals relative capacity for high power versus endurance work.

5. Ligament laxity – Determines range of motion and force production within the normal working range of a joint.

6. Disc cross sectional area- Affects the stress on the disc (force per unit area) .

7. Fluidity of the disc nucleus: Affects forces transmission through disc tissues.

8. Variations Tendon size – Affects stress within the tendon, may directly or indirectly affect the frictional forces between the tendon and other anatomical structures.

9. Size of the carpal tunnel-Affects frictional forces within the tunnel.

Numerous factors between individuals can affect vibration transmission to the body. Physical differences between individuals affect the dynamic responses of their bodies, and consequently the variability in vibration transmission. While body size and mass can influence the physical response to vibration, changes in body posture often have the greatest affect on vibration transmission. Age and gender may have an effect because of varying biodynamic responses (Griffin, 1990).

The internal loads on the tissue should be independent of strength capacity, assuming all individuals have at least enough strength capacity to use similar work methods. This is because the tissue loads are largely governed by the biomechanical characteristics of the exertion being performed. The physiological consequences of the loading could be quite different since one individual may be capable of exerting much more force than another. Hence, one individual may be working closer to his or her maximal capacity relative to that individuals co-workers. Thus, fatigue rates would be expected to vary. Likewise, strength capacity differences are also affected by the relative distributions or fast and the slow twitch muscle fibers within the contractile tissues used. Individuals with a preponderance of slow twitch fibers may be able to perform sustained tasks requiring low muscular force over an extended period without fatigue, however, they may experience an inability to generate high forces repeatedly due to an inadequate reserve of fast twitch fibers. Individuals with a preponderance of fast twitch fibers may be capable of providing high force exertions, but not be able to maintain sustained low forces exertions.

The wrist biomechanical model developed by Armstrong and Chaffin (1979) predicts that wrist size affects wrist loading such that greater tendon load per unit length is inversely proportional to the radius of curvature of the pulley.

Variations in work methods will result in different tissue loading due to variations in the postures, motions, and magnitude of the external forces experienced. While variations in work methods may result variation in anthropometric properties and strength differences, variations in skill levels, work habits, underlying tissue tolerances, pain sensitivity, and response to work organization characteristics (productivity standards, incentive programs).

6.   Discussion

Given the diverse measurement methodologies available to researchers, the framework for quantifying physical stresses and properties described in Section 3 makes it possible to compare studies that are based on seemingly different variables. The studies listed in Table 5 demonstrate how data from a wide variety of methods available for quantifying physical stress exposure can be grouped into corresponding physical stress and property categories. For example, the wrist posture classification and time study approach used by Armstrong, et al. (1979) may be comparable with the wrist electrogoniometer methods described by Marras and Schoenmarklin (1993) since both studies quantify motion magnitude. There are however marked differences between the two methodologies.

Different instruments have different qualities of *accuracy* and *precision*. Accuracy is the difference between the quantity being measured and its true value. All measurements have varying levels of accuracy. For example, a measure of the weight of an object handled using a spring scale is less accurate for evaluating the internal stress of muscle loading than using electromyography for directly measuring muscle electrical activity. Although one type of measurement is more accurate than another, both measurements can provide useful data within their limits of accuracy. When accuracy is diminished by random error, accuracy can often be improved by making multiple measurements and averaging. Therefore a study utilizing a measurement instrument that is inherently less accurate than another may achieve comparable accuracy by collecting a greater number of data samples.

Precision is the ability of an instrument to reproduce the same measurement. Precision affects how many levels or states that the measurement can resolve. A posture classification instrument that measures wrist flexion/extension in five levels (hyper-flexion, flexion, neutral, extension, and hyper-extension) has considerably less precision than a manual goniometer that has angles marked in five degree increments.

It is possible to have two different instruments with different levels of precision, but with the same accuracy. A manual goniometer may have the same accuracy as posture classification but better precision since both methods involve visual estimates of joint angle. Genaidy, et al. (1993) found no significant differences between observational estimates of shoulder flexion angle in three ranges (low: 1°-60°, medium: 61°-120°, and high: 121°-180°) compared with goniometer measurements both taken from a video display screen, although observers tended to slightly overestimate the true angle in the low range and to underestimate the true angle in the medium and high angle ranges. Kilbom (1994) and Kurinka and Forcier (1995) have reviewed numerous instruments for assessing physical stress exposure in relation to musculoskeletal disorders. While survey and production time data may have less accuracy and precision, the methods are more practical for observing a greater numbers of subjects over longer observation periods.

Based on the relationships between external physical stress factors and properties described, Table 6 considers selected external measurement methodologies and the physical stresses that each is capable of measuring. The relative accuracy and precision of these measurements are also compared. A plot of estimated accuracy and precision for each of the measurement methodologies discussed appears in Figure 2.

7. Summary

The aim of this paper was to explore the relationships between work and tissue loading. First we reviewed the means by which the key tissues involved in the development of work-related musculoskeletal disorders (i.e. bone, ligament, tendon, muscle, disc, and nerve) are loaded during the performance of work tasks. Second we examined the relationship between external physical stresses and internal tissue loading. Furthermore we describe a system for characterizing external physical stresses. Third we describe various ways that physical stress in manual work can be measured, and how these measurement techniques relate to tissue loading. Fourth we examined the relationship between workplace design factors and physical stress exposure, and showed how individual differences can mitigate tissue loads for a given work place design. Finally we briefly considered the relationship between work organizational factors and external loads. After considering the instruments used to characterize physical stress exposure, it is clear that there is substantial variation in their accuracy and precision, yet they address similar underlying factors. Clearly the relationships between work and tissue loading are complex, however we believe there is a sufficient body of research that supports the link between the physical characteristics of work and the resulting tissue loads.

8. References

1. Adams, M.A., Hutton, W.C. (1982). Prolapsed intervertebral disc: A hyperflexion injury. *Spine*, 7, 184-191.
2. Adams, M.A., Hutton, W.C. (1985). Gradual disc prolapse. <u>*Spine*</u>, 10, 524-531.
3. Adams, M.A., Hutton, W.C., Stott, J.R.R. (1980). The resistance to flexion of the lumbar intervertebral joint. *Spine*, 5, 245-253.
4. American Academy of Orthopaedic Surgeons (1965.) <u>*Joint Moiton - Method of Measuring and Recording*</u>. American Academy of Orthopaedic Surgeons, Chicago, IL.
5. Anderson, J.J., Felson, D.T. (1988). Factors associated with osteoarthritis of the knee in the first national health and nutrition examination survey (HANES I). American J. of Epidemiology, 128, 179-189.
6. Anderson, E.G. (1990). Fatigue fractures of the foot. *Injury*, 21, 275-279.
7. Andersson, B.J.G., Ortengren, R., Nachemson, A., Elfstrom, G. (1974). Lumbar disc pressure and myelectric back muscle activity during sitting: IV. Studies on car driver's seat. *Scand. J. of Rehab Med.*, 6, 128-133.
8. Armstrong, T. J., Chaffin, D. B., and Foulke, J. A. (1979). A methodology for documenting hand positions and forces during manual work, *Journal of Biomechanics*, 12, 131-133.
9. Armstrong, T. J., Foulke, J. A., Joseph, B. A., and Goldstein, S. A. (1982) Investigation of cumulative trauma disorders in a poultry processing plant, *American Industrial Hygiene Association Journal*, 43(1), 103-116.
10. Armstrong, T. J., Werner, R. A., Waring, W. P., and Foulke, J. A. (1991). Intra-carpal canal pressure in selected hand tasks: a pilot study, *Designing for Everyone, Proceedings of the Eleventh Congress of the International Ergonomics Association*, Taylor & Francis, London, 156-158/.

11. Armstrong, T.J., Radwin, R. G., Hansen, D. J., and Kennedy, K. W. (1986). Repetitive trauma disorders: Job evaluation and design, *Human Factors*, 28(3), 325-336.

12. Armstrong, TJ, Buckle, P, Fine, LJ, Hagberg, M, Jonsson, B, Kilbom, A, Kuorinka, IA, Silverstein, BA, Sjogaard, G, Viikari-Juntura, ER. (1993). A conceptual model for work-related neck and upper-limb musculoskeletal disorders. *Scand J Work Environ Health*, 19, 73-84.

13. Armstrong, T. J. (1986). Ergonomics and Cumulative Trauma Disorders. *Occupational Injuries*, 2(3), 553-565.

14. Armstrong. T. J. and Chaffin, D. B. (1979). Some biomechanical Aspects of the carpal tunnel, *Journal of Biomechanics,* 12, 567-570.

15. Arndt, R. (1987). Work pace, stress, and cumulative trauma disorders. *The Journal of Hand Surgery,* 12A(5), 866-869.

16. Bernard, B, Sauter, S, Fine, L, Peterson, M, Hales T. (1994). Job task and psychosocial risk factors for work-related musculoskeletal disorders among newspaper employees. *Scand J Work Environ Health*, 20, 417-26.

17. Bovenzi, M, Zadini, A, Franzinelli, A, Borgogni, F. (1991). Occupational musculoskeletal disorders in the neck and upper limbs of forestry workers exposed to hand-arm vibration. *Ergonomics*, 34:5, 547-562.

18. Buseck, M.D., Schipplein, O.D., Andersson, G.B.J., Andriacchi, T.P. (1988). Influence of dynamic factors and external loads on the moment at the lumbar spine in lifting. *Spine*, 13, 918-921.

19. Bush-Joseph, C., Schipplein, O., Andersson, G.B.J., Andriacchi, T.P. (1988). Influence of dynamic factors on the lumbar spine moment in lifting. *Ergonomics*, 31, 211-216.

20. Ceron, R. J., Radwin, R. G ., Henderson, C. J. (1995). Hand skin temperature variations for work in moderately cold environments and the effectiveness of periodic rewarming. *American Industrial Hygiene Association Journal*, 56, 558-567.

21. Chaffin, D. B. and Andersson, G. B. J. (1991). *Occupational Biomechanics* (Second Edition), John Wiley & Sons, New York.

22. Chaffin, D. B., Baker, W.H. (1970). A biomechanical model for analysis of symmetric sagittal plane lifting. *AIIE Transactions*, 2, 16-27.

23. Chaffin, D. B., Herrin, G.D., Keyserling, W.M., Garg, A. (1977). A method for evaluating the biomechanical stresses resulting from manual materials handling jobs. *Amer. Ind. Hygiene Assoc. J.*, 38, 662-675.

24. Chaffin, D. B. (1969). A computerized biomechanical model –Development of and use in studying gross body actions. *J. of Biomechanics*, 2, 429-441.

25. Chao, E. Y. (1976). Experimental methods for biomechanical measurments of joint kinematics. *CRC Handbook of Engineering in Medicine and Biology*, CRC Press, Cleveland, OH, 385-411.

26. Chiang, H. C., Chen, S. S, Yu, H. S., Ko, Y. C. (1990). The occurrence of carpal tunnel syndrome in frozen food factory employees. *J Med Sci*, 6, 73-80.

27. Cholewicki, J., McGill, S. M. (1991). Lumbar posterior ligament involvement during extremely heavy lifts estimated from fluoroscopic measurements. *Journal of Biomechanics*, 25, 17-28.

28. Cowan, D. N., Jones, B. H., Frykman, P. N., Polly, D. W., Harman, E.A., Rosenstein, R. M.,

Rosenstein, M. T. (1996). Lower limb morphology and risk of overuse injury among male infantry trainees. *Medicine and Science in Sports and Exercise*, 28, 945-952.

29. De Looze, M .P., Kingma, I., Thunnissen, W., Van Wijk, M. J., Toussaint, H. M. (1994). The evaluation of a practical biomechanical model estimating lumbar moments in occupational activities. *Ergonomics*, 37, 1495-1502.

30. De Looze, M. P., Toussaint, H. M., Van Dieen, J. H., and Kemper, H. C. G. (1993). Joint moments and muscle activity in the lower extremities and lower back in lifting and lowering tasks. *J. of Biomechanics*, 26, 1067-1076.

31. Derksen, J. C. M., Van Riel, M. P. J. M., Wingerden, J. P., Snijders, C. J. (1994). A comparison of working postures of parcel sorters using three different working methods. *Ergonomics*, 37:2, 299-309.

32. Dolan, P., Mannion, A. F., Adams, M. A. (1994a). Passive tissues help the back muscles to generate extensor moments during lifting. *Journal of Biomechanics*, 27, 1077-1085.

33. Dolan, P., Earley, M., Adams, M. A. (1994b). Bending and compressive stresses acting on the lumbar spine during lifting activities. *J. of Biomechanics*, 27, 1237-1248.

34. Doormaal, M. T. A. J., Driessen, A. P. A., Landeweerd, J. A., and Drost, M. R. (1995). Physical workload of ambulance assistants. *Ergonomics*, 38, 361-376.

35. Drury, C.G., Deeb, J.M., Hartman, B., Woolley, S., Drury, C.E., Gallagher, S. (1989a). symmetric and saymmetric manual materials handling part 1: physiology and psychophysics. *Ergonomics*, 467-489.

36. Drury, C.G., Deeb, J.M., Hartman, B., Woolley, S., Drury, C.E., Gallagher, S. (1989b). symmetric and saymmetric manual materials handling part 2: biomechanics. *Ergonomics*, 565-583.

37. Feuerstein, M, Fitzgerald, T. E. (1992). Biomechanical factors affecting upper extremity cumulative trauma disorders in sign language interpreters. *Journal of Occupational Medicine*, 34(3), 257-264.

38. Floyd W.F., Silver P.H.S. (1955). The function of the erectores spinae muscles in certain movements and postures in man. *Journal of Physiology* (London) 129, 184-203.

39. Freivalds, A., Chaffin, D.B., Garg, A., Lee, K.S. (1984). A dynamic biomechanical evaluation of lifting acceptable loads. *J. of Biomechanics*, 17, 251-262.

40. Gagnon, D., Gagnon, M. (1992). The influence of dynamic factors on triaxial net muscular moments at the L5/S1 joint during asymmetrical lifting and lowering. *J. of Biomechanics*, 25, 891-901.

41. Gagnon, M., Plamondon, A., Gravel, D. (1993). Pivoting with the load: An alternative for protecting the back in asymmetrical lifting. *Spine*, 18, 1515-1524.

42. Garg, A., Saxena, U. (1980). Container characteristics and maximum acceptable weight of lift. *Human Factors*, 22, 487-495.

43. Genaidy, A. M., Simmons, R. J., Guo, L., and Hidalgo, J. A. (1993). Can visual perception be used to estimate body part angles?, *Ergonomics*, 36(4), 323-329.

44. Giladi, M., Ahronson, Z., Stein, M., Danon, Y.L., Milgrom, C. (1985). Unusual distribution and onset of stress fractures in soldiers. *Clinical Orthopaedics & Related Research*, 192, 142-146.

45. Giladi, M., Milgrom, C., Simkin, A., Danon, Y. (1991). Stress fractures. Identifiable risk factors. *American Journal of Sports Medicine*, 19, 647-652.

46. Golding, J.S.R. (1952). Electromyography of the erector spinae in low back pain. *Postgrad Medical Journal_28*, 401-406.

47. Goldstein, S.A., Armstrong, T.J., Chaffin, D.B., Matthews, L.S. (1987). Analysis of cumulative strain in tendons and tendon sheaths. *Journal of Biomechanics*, 29, 1-6.

48. Hutton, W.C., Adams, M.A. (1982). Can the lumbar spine be crushed in heavy lifting. *Spine*, 7, 586-590.

49. Hymovich, L, Lindholm, M. (1966). Hand, wrist, and forearm injuries. *Journal of Occupational Medicine*, 8(11), 573-577.

50. Jordaan, G., Schwellnus, M.P. (1994). The incidence of overuse injuries in military recruits during basic military training. *Military Medicine*, 159, 421-426.

51. Karhu, O, Harkonen, R, Vepsalainen, P. (1981). Observing working postures in industry: Examples of OWAS application. *Applied Ergonomics*, 13-17.

52. Karhu, O, Kansi, P, Kuorinka, I. (1977). Correcting working postures in industry: A practical method for analysis. *Applied Ergonomics*, 199-201.

53. Keyserling, M. W., Stetson, D. S., Silverstein, B. A., Brouwer, M. L. (1993). A checklist for evaluation ergonomic risk factors associated with upper extremity cumulative trauma disorders. *Ergonomics*, 36(7), 807-831.

54. Keyserling, M. W. (1986). A computer-aided system to evaluate postural stress in the workplace. *Am. Ind. Hyg. Assoc. J.*, 47, 641-649.

55. Kilbom, Å, (1994). Assessment of physical exposure in relation to work-related musculoskeletal disorders - what information can be obtained from systematic observations?, *Scandinavian Journal of Work, Environment Health*, 20 (Special Issue), 30-45.

56. Kippers, V., Parker, A.W. (1984). Posture related to myoelectric silence of erectores spinae during trunk flexion. *Spine*, 9, 740-745.

57. Kohatsu, N.D., Schurman, D.J. (1990). Risk factors for the development of ostearthrosis of the knee. Clinical Orthopaedics and Related Research, 261, 242-246.

58. Kromodihardjo, S. and Mital, A. (1987). Biomechanical analysis of manual lifting tasks. *Transactions of the ASME*, 109, 132-138.

59. Lavender, S. A., Li, Y. C., Andersson, G. B. J., Natarajan, R. N. (1998). The effects of lifting speed on the peak external forward bending, lateral bending, and twisting spine moments, *Ergonomics*, 41, in press.

60. Lee, Y. H., Chiou, W. K. (1995). Ergonomic analysis of working posture in nursing personnel: Example of modified Ovako Working Analysis System application. *Research in Nursing and Health*, 18, 67-75.

61. Leskinen, T. P. J., Stalhammar, H. R., Rautanen, M. T. (1992). Biomechanically and electromyograpically assessed load on the spine in self-paced and force-paced lifting work. *Ergonomics*, 35, 881-888.

62. Linenger, J. M., Shwayhat, A. F. (1992). Epidemiology of podiatric injuries in US Marine recruits undergoing basic training. *Journal of the American Podiatric Medical Association*, 82, 269-271.

63. Lindberg, H., Axmacher, B. (1988). Coxarthrosis in farmers. Acta Orthop. Scand., 59, 607.

64. Lindberg, H., Montgomery, F. (1987). Heavy labor and the occurrence of gonarthrosis. Clinical Orthopaedics and Related Research, 214, 235-236.

65. Magnusson, M., Granqvist, M., Jonson, R., Lindell, V., Lundberg, U., Wallin, L., and Hansson, T. (1990). The loads on the lumbar spine during work at an assembly line: The risks for fatigue injuries of vertebral bodies. *Spine*, 15, 774-779.

66. Malchaire, J. B., Cock, N. A., Robert, A. R. (1996). Prevalence of musculoskeletal disorders at the wrist as a function of angles, forces, repetitiveness and movement velocities. *Scand J Work Environ Health*, 22, 176-181.

67. Marras, W. S., Granata, K. P. (1997a). Spine loading during trunk lateral bending motions, *J. of Biomechanics*, 30, 697-703.

68. Marras W. S., Granata K. P. (1997b). Changes in trunk dynamics and spine loading during repeated trunk exertions. *Spine*, 22, 2564-70.

69. Marras, W. S. and Schoenmarklin, R. W. (1993). Wrist motions in industry, *Ergonomics*, 36(4), 341-351.

70. Marras, W. S., Fathallah, F. A., Miller, R. J., Davis, S. W., and Mirka, G. A. (1992). Accuaracy of a three-dimensional lumbar motion monitor for recording dynamic trunk motion characteristics. *Int. J. Ind. Ergonomics*, 9, 75-87.

71. Marras, W.S., Granata, K.P. (1995). A biomechanical assessment and model of axial twisting in the thoracolumbar spine. *Spine*, 20, 1440-1451.

72. Marras, W. S., Lavender, S. A., Leurgans, S. E., Rajulu, S. L., Allread, W. G., Fathallah, R. A., and Ferguson, S. A. (1993). The role of dynamic three-dimensional trunk motion in occupationally-related low back disorders. *Spine*, 617-628.

73. Marras, W. S., Sommerich, C. M. (1991). A three-dimensional motion model of loads on the lumbar spine: II Model Validation. *Human Factors*, 33, 139-150.

74. Marras, W. S. (1993). Wrist motions in industry. *Ergonomics*, 36:4, 341-351.

75. McAtamney, L. and Corlett, E. N. (1993). RULA: a survey method for the investigation of work-related upper limb disorders. *Applied Ergonomics*, 24, 91-99.

76. McGill, S. M. (1992). A myoelectrically based dynamic three-dimensional model to predict loads on lumbar spine tissues during lateral bending. *J. of Biomechanics*, 25, 395-414.

77. McGill, S. M., Norman, R. W. (1985). Dynamically and statically determined low back moments during lifting. *J. of Biomechanics*, 18, 877-885.

78. McGill, S. M., Norman, R. W. (1986). Partitioning of the L4-L5 dynamic moment into disc, ligamentous, and muscular components during lifting. *Spine*, 11, 666-678.

79. McGill, S. M., Norman, R. W., Cholewicki, J. (1996). A simple polynomial that predicts low-back compression during complex 3-D tasks. *Ergonomics*, 39, 1107-1118.

80. Moore, A., Wells, R. and Ranney, D. (1991). Quantifying exposure in occupational manual tasks with cumulative trauma disorder potential, *Ergonomics*, 24(12), 1433-1453.

81. Morris, J. M., Lucas, D. B., and Bresler, B. (1961). Role of the trunk in stability of the spine. The *Journal of Bone and Joint Surgery*, 43-A, 327-351.

82. Murthy, G., Kahan, N. J., Hargens, A. R., and Rempel, D. M. (1997). Forearm muscle oxygenation decreases with low levels of voluntary contraction. *J. of Orthopaedic Research*, 15, 507-511.

83. Nachemson, A., and Morris, J. M. (1964). In vivo measurements of intradiscal pressure. *The J. of Bone and Joint Surgery*, 46-A, 1077-1092.

84. Nordin, M., Ortengren, R., and Andersson, G. B. J. (1984). Measurement of trunk movements during work. *Spine*, 9, 465-469

85. Novak, G. J., Schipplein, O. D., Trafimow, J. H., and Andersson, G. B. J. (1993). Influence of erector spinae muscle fatigue on the lumbo-sacral moment during lifting. *European J. Exp. Musculoskeletal Research*, 2, 39-44.

86. Parnianpous, M., Nordin, M., Kahanovitz, N., and Frankel, V. (1988). The triaxial coupling of torque generation of trunk muscles during isometric exertions and the effect of fatiguing isoinertial movements on the motor output and movement patterns. *Spine*, 13, 982-992.

87. Potvin, J. R., Norman, R. W, McGill, S. M. (1991). Reduction in anterior shear forces on the L4/L5 disc by the lumbar musculature. *Clinical Biomechanics*, 6, 88-96.

88. Punnett, L., Fine, L. J., Keyserling, W. M., Herrin, G. D., and Chaffin, D. B. (1991). Back disorders and nonneutral trunk postures of automobile assembly workers. *Scan. J. Work Env. Health*, 17, 337-346.

89. Radwin, R. G., Armstrong, T. J., and D. B. Chaffin. (1987). Power hand tool vibration effects on grip exertions, *Ergonomics*, 30 (5), 833-855.

90. Radwin, R. G., Lin, M. L., and T. Y. Yen. (1994). Exposure assessment of biomechanical stress in repetitive manual work using frequency-weighted filters, *Ergonomics*, 37(12), 1984-1998.

91. Radwin, R. G. and Lin, M. L. (1993). An analytical method for characterizing repetitive motion and postural stress using spectral analysis. *Ergonomics*, 36(4), 379-389.

92. Rempel, D. (1995). Musculoskeletal loading and carpal tunnel pressure, Repetitive Motion Disorders of the Upper Extremity, *American Academy of Orthopedic Surgeons*, Rosemont, IL, 123-132.

93. Schipplein, O. D., Reinsel, T. E., Andersson, G. B. J., and Lavender, S. A. (1995). The influence of initial horizontal weight placement on the loads at the lumbar spine while lifting. *Spine*, 20, 1895-1898.

94. Schipplein, O. D., Trafimow, J. H., Andersson, G. B. J., Andriacchi, T. P. (1990). Relationship between moments at the L5/S1 level, hip and knee joint when lifting. *J. of Biomechanics*, 23, 907-912.

95. Schultz, A., Andersson, G., Haderspeck, K, Nachemson, A., (1982a). Loads on the lumbar spine: Validation of a biomechanical analysis by measurements of intradiscal pressures and myoelectric signals. *The J. of Bone and Joint Surgery*, 64-A, 713-720.

96. Schultz, A., Andersson, G. B. J., Ortengren, R., Bjork, R., Nordin, M. (1982b). Analysis and quantitative myoelectric measurements of loads on the lumbar spine when holding weights in standing postures. *Spine*, 7, 390-396.

97. Schultz, A. B., Andersson, G. B. J., Haderspeck, K. H., Ortengren, R., Nordin, M., Bjork, R. (1982c). Analysis and measurement of lumbar trunk loads in task involving bends and twists. *J. of Biomechanics*, 15, 669-675.

98. Silverstein, B. A., Fine L. J., and Armstrong, T. J. (1986). Hand wrist cumulative trauma disorders in industry. *British Journal of Industrial Medicine*, 43, 779-784.

99. Sjogaard, G. (1996). The significance of sustained muscle loading versus dynamic muscle loading at low forces in workplace design. In D. Rempel and T. Armstrong (eds.) *Marconi Computer Input Device Research Conference Proceedings*, University of California at Berkley, 19.

100. Snijders, C .J., Van Riel, M. P. J. M., and Nordin, M. 1987. Continuous measurements of spine movements in normal working situations over periods of 8 hours or more. *Ergonomics*, 30, 639-653.

101. Tanzer, R. C. 1959. The carpal-tunnel syndrome. *The J. Bone and Joint Surgery*, 41-A, 626-634.

102. Toussaint, H. M, de Winter, A. F., de Looze, Y. H. M. P, Van Dieen, JH, Kingma, I (1995). Flexion relaxation during lifting: implications for torque production by muscle activity and tissue strain at the lumbo-sacral joint. *J. of Biomechanics*, 28, 199-210.

103. Trafimow, J. H., Schipplein, O. D., Novak, G. J., Andersson, G. B. J. (1993). The effects of quadriceps fatigue on the technique of lifting. *Spine*, 18, 364-367.

104. Tsuang, Y. H., Schipplein, O. D., Trophema, J. H., Andersson, G. B. J. (1992). Influence of body segment dynamics on loads at the lumbar spine during lifting. *Ergonomics*, 35, 437-444.

105. Tveit, P., Daggfeldt, K., Hetland, S., and Thorstensson, A. 1994. Erector spinae lever arm length variations with changes in spinal posture. *Spine,* 19, 199-204.

106. Vingard, E., Alfredsson, L., Goldie, I., Hogstedt, C. (1991). Occupation and osteoarthrosis of the hip and knee: A register-based cohort study. International J. of Epidemiology, 20, 1025-1031.

107. White, A. A., Panjabi, M. M. (1990). *Clinical Biomechanics of the Spine*: Second Edition. J.B. Lippincott Company: Philadelphia.

108. Wieslander, G., Norback, D., Gothe C. J., Juhlin, L. (1989). Carpal tunnel syndrome (CTS) and exposure to vibration, repetitive wrist movements, and heavy manual work: a case-referent study. *British Journal of Industrial Medicine*, 46, 43-47.

109. Winkel, J. and Mathiassen, S. E., (1994). Assessment of physical work load in epidemiological studies: concepts, issues and operational considerations, *Ergonomics*, 37(6), 979-988.

Table 1: Examples of Physical Stress Factors Cited in The Literature

Reference	Factors Considered
Armstrong, et al., 1981	Repeated exertions with certain postures Stressful exertions High forces
Armstrong, et al., 1986	Repetitive and sustained exertions Certain postures Vibration Low temperatures Mechanical stresses
Arndt, 1997	Work pace
Bernard, et al., 1994	Working time Time pressure Hours of computer use
Bovenzi, et al., 1991	Vibration acceleration Vibration exposure
Chiang, et al., 1990	Local exposure to cold
Derksen, et al., 1994	Poor working postures
Feuerstein and Fitzgerald, 1992	Rest-break frequency Deviations from neutral Work envelope excursions High-impact hand contacts Pace of movements Intensity of muscular tension Smoothness of movements
Keyserling, 1986	Awkward working postures
Keyserling, et al., 1993	Repetitiveness Local mechanical contact stress Forceful manual exertions Awkward posture Hand tool use
Marras and Schoenmarklin, 1993	Angular velocity Angular acceleration
McAtamney, and Corlett, 1993	Posture Muscle use (repetitive or static) Force or load
Silverstein, et al., 1986	Repetitive motion Forceful exertions
Wieslander, et al., 1989	Exposure to vibration Heavy loads on the wrist

Table 2. Theoretical Framework for the Relationship Between External Physical Stress Factors

and Properties as Typically Described in the Scientific Literature

Physical Stress	Property		
	Magnitude	Repetition Rate	Duration
Force	Forceful Exertions	Repetitive Exertions	Sustained Exertions
Motion	Extreme Postures and Motions	Repetitive Motions	Sustained Postures
Vibration	High Vibration Level	Repeated Vibration Exposure	Long Vibration Exposure
Cold	Cold Temperatures	Repeated Cold Exposure	Long Cold Exposure

Table 3. Relationship Between External Physical Stress Factors and their Properties as

They are Typically Measured

Physical Stress	Property		
	Magnitude	Repetition Rate	Duration
Force	Force generated or Applied	Frequency that Force is Applied	Time that Force is Applied
Motion	Joint Angle, Velocity, Acceleration	Frequency of Motion	Time to Compete Motion.
Vibration	Acceleration	Frequency that Vibration Occurs	Time of Vibration Exposure
Cold	Temperature	Frequency of Cold Exposure	Time of Cold Exposure

Table 4. Relationships Between External and Internal Physical Stress

Physical Stress	Property		
	Magnitude	Repetition	Duration
Force	• Tissue loads and stress • Muscle tension and contraction • Muscle fiber recruitment • Energy expenditure, fatigue, and metabolite production • Joint loads • Adjacent anatomical structure loads and compartment pressure • Transmission of vibrational energy	• Tissue loading rate and energy storage • Tissue strain recovery • Muscle fiber recruitment and muscle fatigue rate • Energy expenditure, fatigue and elimination of metabolites • Cartilage or disc rehydration	• Cumulative tissue loads • Muscle fiber recruitment and muscle fatigue rate • Energy expenditure, fatigue and metabolite production
Motion	• Tissue loads and stress • Adjacent anatomical structure loads and compartment pressure • Transmission of vibrational energy*	• Tissue loading rate and energy storage • Tissue strain recovery	• Cumulative tissue loads
Vibration	• Transmission of vibrational energy to musculoskeletal system • Transmission of vibrational energy to somatic and autonomic sensory receptors and nerves • Transmission of energy to muscle spindles*	• Recovery from vibrational energy exposure	• Cumulative vibrational energy exposure
Cold	• Thermal energy loss from the extremities • Cooling of tissues and bodily fluids • Somatic and autonomic receptor stimulus	• Recovery from thermal energy loss	• Cumulative thermal energy loss

Table 5: Examples of External Physical Stress Measurements Cited in the Literature

Reference	Method	Physical Stress Measured				Body Region	Application	Individual Factors
		Force	Motion	Vibration	Cold			
Wieslander, et al., 1988	Survey of job classification questionnaire	Duration	Duration	Duration		Wrist	CTS cases and other surgical referents	
Chiang, et al., 1990	Survey of job activities		Repetition		Magnitude	Wrist	Frozen food factory	
Bernard, et al., 1994	Survey of job activities and work organization condition questionnaires	Duration	Duration			Neck Shoulders Wrist Hand	Newspaper employees	
Armstrong, Chaffin & Foulke, 1979	Electromyography / Posture classification / Time study from motion picture film	Magnitude Duration	Magnitude Duration			Hand	Garment workers	
Armstrong, et al., 1982	Posture Classification / Elemental analysis from video tape	Magnitude Repetition Duration	Magnitude Repetition Duration			Shoulder Elbow Wrist Hand	Poultry processing	
Silverstein, Fine and Armstrong, 1986	Time study & production rates from video tape / Weight of objects handled and electromyography	Magnitude Repetition				Wrist Hand	Electronics, appliance, investment casting, apparel sewing, iron foundry and bearing manufacturing	
Keyserling, 1986	Posture Classification / Time and motion study in real-time off video tapes / Time spent in each posture		Magnitude Repetition Duration			Trunk Shoulder	Automobile assembly	
Keyserling, et al., 1993	Risk factor checklist / No. Occurrences per cycle / Cycle Time	Magnitude Repetition Duration	Magnitude Repetition Duration	Magnitude Repetition Duration		Shoulder Elbow Wrist Hand	Engine plant, metal stamping plant, part distribution center	
Bovenzi, et al., 1991	Manual goniometer / Observation checklist / ISO 5349 frequency-weighted vibration / Survey of personal attributes		Magnitude	Magnitude Duration		Neck Shoulder Elbow Forearm Wrist Hand	Chainsaw operators, mechanics, electricians and painters	
Marras & Schoenmarklin, 1993	Electrogoniometer / Angle, velocity and	Magnitude	Magnitude			Wrist	Automotive parts & building products	

Table 5 (Continued)

Reference	Method	Physical Stress Measured				Body Region	Application	Individual Factors
		Force	Motion	Vibration	Cold			
	acceleration						manufacturing	
Moore, Wells & Ranney, 1991	Electrogoniometer Electromyography	Magnitude Repetition	Magnitude Repetition			Wrist Hand	Simulated pistol grip tool operation	
Latco, et al.,	Observer ratings		Repetition					
Derksen, et al., 1994	Electrogoniometer		Magnitude Duration			Trunk	Parcel shipping	
Radwin & Lin, 1993	Electrogoniometer Spectral analysis		Magnitude Frequency			Wrist	Laboratory simulation	
Radwin, et al., 1994	Electrogoniometer Local discomfort frequency-weighted filters		Magnitude Repetition Duration			Wrist	Laboratory simulation	
Cernon, Radwin and Henderson, 1995	Thermistors				Magnitude Frequency Duration	Hand	Poultry processing	
Marras et al., 1993	Electrogoniometer	Magnitude Repetition	Magnitude Repetition			Back	Industrial Workers	Anthropometry
Punnett et al., 1991	Observer ratings	Magnitude	Magnitude Duration			Back	Automotive Workers	Age. Back Injury history
Andersson et al., 1974	Intra-discal Pressure	Magnitude	Magnitude			Back	Sitting in a Vehicle Seat	
Doormaal et al., 1995	Posture Coding, Biomechanical Model	Magnitude	Magnitude Duration			Back, Shoulder Hip, Neck Knees	Ambulance Assistants	
Lee and Chiou	Postural Coding	Magnitude	Magnitude Repetition			Back	Nursing Personnel	

Table 6. Selected External Measurement Methodologies and Their Relationship to Internal Stress

External Measure	Physical Stresses That Can Be Assessed	Accuracy of Estimate	Precision of Estimate
Job or Task Title	Indeterminate		
Task Descriptions	Force (Magnitude, Repetition, Duration) Motion (Magnitude, Repetition, Duration) Vibration (Magnitude, Repetition, Duration) Cold (Magnitude, Repetition, Duration)	Low	Low
Employee Self-Reports	Force (Magnitude, Repetition, Duration) Motion (Magnitude, Repetition, Duration) Vibration (Magnitude, Repetition, Duration) Cold (Magnitude, Repetition, Duration)	Low	Low
Tools, Materials and Equipment Handled or Operated	Force (Magnitude) Motion (Magnitude) Vibration (Magnitude) Cold (Magnitude)	Low	Medium
Observation	Force (Magnitude, Repetition, Duration) Motion (Magnitude, Repetition, Duration) Vibration (Magnitude, Repetition, Duration) Cold (Magnitude, Repetition, Duration)	Medium	Low
Production Rates	Force (Repetition) Motion (Repetition) Vibration (Repetition)	Low	High
Time Standards	Force (Duration) Motion (Duration) Vibration (Duration) Cold (Duration)	Low	High
Measured Cycle Times	Force (Duration) Motion (Duration) Vibration (Duration) Cold (Duration)	Medium	High
Time and Motion Study (elemental times)	Force (Repetition, Duration) Motion (Repetition, Duration) Vibration (Repetition, Duration) Cold (Repetition, Duration)	High	High
Loads Handled (mass)	Force (Magnitude)	Medium	Medium
Forces Opposed (force gages, load cells, force sensors)	Force (Magnitude)	Medium	High
Electromyography	Force (Magnitude, Repetition, Duration)	High	Medium
Internal Compartmental Pressure	Force (Magnitude, Repetition, Duration)	High	High
Posture Classification	Motion (Magnitude)	Medium	Medium
Reach Distances and Workstation Layout	Motion (Magnitude)	Low	High
Manual Goniometer	Motion (Magnitude)	Medium	High
Electrogoniometer	Motion (Magnitude, Repetition, Duration)	High	High
Motion Analysis (video, optical, electromagnetic)	Motion (Magnitude, Repetition, Duration)	High	High
Biomechanical Models Using Reach Distances, Loads Handled and Time	Force (Magnitude)	High	Medium

Table 6. Continued

External Measure	Physical Stresses That Can Be Assessed	Accuracy of Estimate	Precision of Estimate
Study			
Biomechanical Models Using Electrogoniometers/Motion Analysis and Forces Opposed	Force (Magnitude)	High	High
Accelerometers Attached to Objects Contacted	Vibration (Magnitude, Repetition, Duration)	Medium	High
Ambient Temperature	Cold (Magnitude)	Low	Medium
Temperature of Extremities	Cold (Magnitude)	Medium	High
Continuous Monitoring of Extremity Temperature	Cold (Magnitude, Repetition, Duration)	High	High

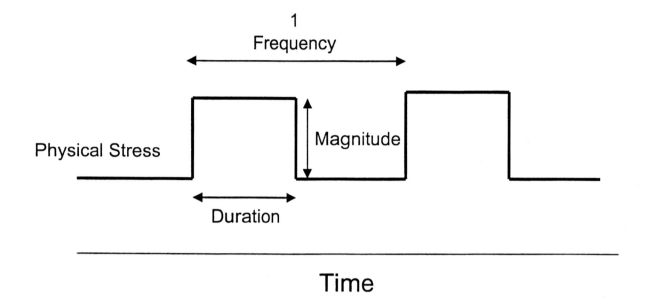

Figure 1: Representation of Magnitude, Duration and Repetition for Physical Stress-Time Record.

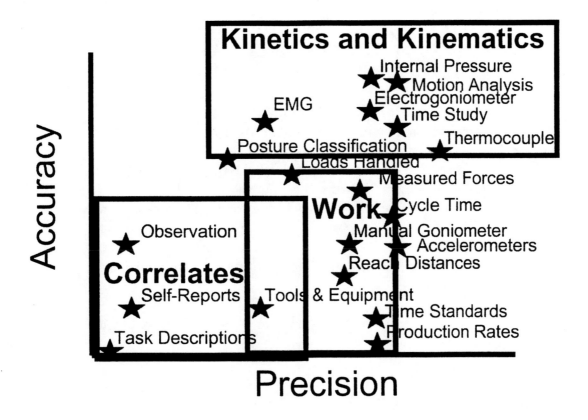

Figure 2: Relationship between accuracy and precision for different measurement methodololgies

WORK-RELATED MUSCULOSKELETAL DISORDERS: EXAMINING THE RESEARCH BASE
EPIDEMIOLOGY: PHYSICAL FACTORS

Bradley Evanoff, MD, MPH
Washington University School of Medicine, St. Louis, MO

This abstract will address four questions concerning the NIOSH document "Musculoskeletal Disorders and Workplace Factors," as requested by the conference organizers. In my review of this document, I focused on the studies of elbow disorders, carpal tunnel syndrome (CTS), and hand/wrist tendinitis.

1. Has NIOSH missed or overlooked any important body of epidemiological evidence in its review?

The NIOSH review was comprehensive and inclusive; important epidemiological evidence was not overlooked.

NIOSH conducted a series of wide-ranging literature searches of appropriate databases, using suitable search terms. Articles were selected for detailed review if they pertained to the epidemiology of work-relatedness of musculoskeletal disorders, and contained explicit descriptions of the studied populations and assessments of health outcomes and exposures. Of the more than 2000 articles identified, NIOSH chose over 600 for detailed review. NIOSH did not provide a listing of which articles had been identified but rejected for detailed review; such a list would be helpful in evaluating their search and review strategy. I am unaware of any important articles omitted by NIOSH; their selection was generally more extensive and inclusive than that of previous published reviews.

2. Describe the study methods of the studies that have been heavily weighted in the NIOSH assessment. What is the general quality of these studies?

The general quality of these studies is good; a major drawback is the small number of longitudinal studies.

The design of most reviewed studies was cross-sectional. Many cross-sectional studies included temporal data on exposures and health outcomes, and can thus address the issue of whether the exposures preceded the health effects. More longitudinal studies would be helpful; these studies face a host of logistical hurdles including high turn-over of workers in many high-exposure jobs. In general, the weighted studies had appropriate and well-characterized referent groups.

The weighted studies chose appropriate epidemiological case definitions, which required both symptoms of a MSD as well as physical examination (PE) findings. For epicondylitis and hand / arm tendinitis, these case definitions were analogous to commonly used clinical diagnostic criteria, and included PE maneuvers such as tenderness to palpation and pain on resisted movement, as well as examination for other causes of upper extremity symptoms.

For carpal tunnel syndrome, the use of case definitions based on symptoms and physical examination alone is more controversial. The most accurate definition of CTS would include electrodiagnostic studies (EDS) as well as symptoms (and possibly PE). This definition was used in some of the studies reviewed by NIOSH. EDS alone should not be used as a case definition. Several studies have evaluated the performance of case definitions based on symptoms and physical examination alone; although there is some misclassification of disease using this case definition, it is appropriate for studies where the disadvantage of misclassification can be offset by other factors, such as a larger sample size.

The weighted studies did not use self-report or job titles as a measure of exposure, but used directly observed and measured data on specific exposures.

The weighted studies controlled for potential biases and confounders through a variety of mechanisms. Individual risk factors such as age, gender, pre-existing disease, non-occupational activities, and metabolic diseases were controlled to some extent in all the weighted studies. Measurements of health and exposure status were done in a blinded manner. Weighted studies all had participation rates of $\geq$70%, decreasing the chance of respondent bias.

3. Would either the inclusion of any omitted studies or the assessment of the quality of those reviewed substantially alter the interpretation of the epidemiological evidence that certain physical stressors in the workplace increase risk of acquiring certain MSDs?

Addition of omitted studies would not alter the interpretation of the evidence. More stringent requirements for study quality could change the conclusions only by excluding most or all current studies.

The literature review and study weighting process adopted by NIOSH included most or all important evidence. Other authors, using different criteria for literature selection, have also concluded that certain physical stressors in the workplace increase the risks of acquiring certain MSDs. Authors who conclude that there is insufficient evidence to permit this interpretation have excluded most or all of the current epidemiological evidence, citing the lack of longitudinal data and questions about the significance of health outcomes measured in these studies.

The well-designed cross sectional studies weighted by NIOSH provide data useful for causal inference. These studies took steps to avoid bias in the measurement of exposures and health outcomes. Data on the temporality of exposure and symptom or disease onset were available to ensure that the putative exposures occurred before symptom onset. These studies thus offer more than a "snapshot in time." Other potential causes of the observed associations were sought. To discount these studies, one must assume that measurements were significantly biased, or that persons prone to developing MSDs were preferentially placed into jobs with high physical demands. In cross-sectional studies, survivor effects will typically decrease the observed associations between symptomatic disorders and physically demanding jobs.

Another question has been whether epidemiological case definitions represent "real" clinical disorders. Many MSDs are self-limited or cause minimal disability, while others are more severe. Case definitions can be designed to capture a broad or a narrow spectrum of illness; it is probably not true that only the most severe cases are clinically "real." Case definitions used in the weighted studies required both symptoms and physical examination findings by an experienced clinician, and were analogous to common clinical diagnostic practices. For CTS, the issue of diagnosis without EDS is controversial as noted above. Many clinicians make the working diagnoses of CTS, and start therapy in individual patients, based on the same symptom and physical examination criteria used in those weighted studies which did not use EDS.

4. What does the evidence tell us about incidence in the general population versus specific groups of workers?

MSDs are common in the general population. Epidemiological studies of occupational risk factors must include appropriate referent groups for valid comparisons. Many studies show much higher than expected rates of MSDs among workers with high exposures to physical risk factors. The prevalence and incidence of MSDs is highly dependent on the reporting mechanisms and case definitions adopted.

Summary:

The current best evidence shows consistent, strong associations between certain physical factors and MSDs. The quality of evidence is adequate but not perfect. It seems unlikely that future longitudinal studies will invalidate causal inferences drawn from current studies.

THE EPIDEMIOLOGY OF WORKPLACE FACTORS AND MUSCULOSKELETAL DISORDERS: AN ASSESSMENT OF THE NIOSH REVIEW

Alfred Franzblau, MD

Associate Professor of Occupational Medicine, University of Michigan School of Public Health

A relationship between workplace factors and musculoskeletal disorders has been noted for hundreds of years, however, scientific (including epidemiological) study of the potential contribution of workplace factors to musculoskeletal disorders was only initiated in the early and middle decades of the current century. At present, a considerable body of work has accrued, and a critical review of the accumulated data represents a worthwhile effort. In 1997 the National Institute for Occupational Safety and Health published a review of the epidemiological literature pertaining to workplace factors and musculoskeletal disorders of the neck, upper extremity, and low back (U.S. Department of Health and Human Services, 1997). My comments will focus on this document, primarily those portions pertaining to the upper extremity since I am most familiar with this literature, and will be structured to address the four issues suggested by the workshop organizers.

1. Has NIOSH missed or overlooked any important body of epidemiological evidence in its review?

The sole focus of the NIOSH document is epidemiological investigations. This is clearly stated, along with criteria for evaluating the quality of individual studies. I don't believe that the NIOSH document has overlooked any important body of epidemiological evidence pertaining to workplace factors and musculoskeletal disorders. Overall, I am impressed with the thoroughness of what was a massive and unprecedented review of literature. However, there are other categories of scientific evidence that contribute to the key questions of concern, such as biomechanical studies, engineering studies, and laboratory and/or psychophysical studies. Scientific knowledge and understanding is not derived solely from one type of study technique. In the current instance inclusion of information from these other types of studies would have, in my opinion, corroborated the conclusions of the NIOSH review of epidemiological literature.

2. Describe the study methods of the studies that have been heavily weighted in the NIOSH assessment. What is the general quality of these studies?

There are many issues related to study methodology that one could comment on, however, I wish to focus my comments on one particular area that has received considerable attention. One of the major criticisms of epidemiological studies of workplace factors and musculoskeletal disorders is that most of the studies are cross-sectional, rather than prospective or longitudinal Although there is some basis to this criticism, and good prospective studies are of great value, in my opinion it is usually overblown in the present instance.

While, in theory, prospective studies have certain advantages, there are a number of practical reasons why they have been utilized so rarely to investigate relationships between workplace factors and musculoskeletal disorders. Aside from being far more expensive, such studies require on-going interaction between the research team and study site(s) over a prolonged period of time. Such interaction is usually time-consuming to the employer, and study procedures (especially screening medical examinations of workers) can interfere with production processes. Few employers are willing to extend this level of cooperation over a prolonged period of time, particularly when it interferes with production and thus may impact the 'bottom line'. Furthermore, when companies are bought, sold, or taken over (as has often been the case in the last 15 years), the new managers may not be committed to the study, which can lead to disruption or termination of a study. Additional complicating factors are that workers change jobs, and jobs also change. Obviously, such changes are not scheduled or designed for the convenience of the researcher. Thus, the 'exposures' are likely to be unstable over time, and tracking the 'exposure' of individual workers becomes very complicated and expensive, and, even if done, such information may be difficult to interpret.

What some researchers have done is to perform cross-sectional studies among workers (and jobs) that are known to have been stable for some minimum period of time (e.g., six months or one year). This type of cross-sectional study design overcomes some of the shortcomings of cross-sectional studies relative to prospective studies, and serves to greatly strengthen the confidence one can have in the conclusions. Many of the studies that were most heavily weighted in the NIOSH assessment fall into this category.

Finally, one needs to remember that although one of the weaknesses of cross-sectional studies relative to prospective studies is the greater potential for misclassification of exposures and outcomes, the effect of such misclassification is usually to reduce the apparent strength of association. Random misclassification almost always leads to a reduction in the apparent strength of the relationship between exposures and outcomes. Furthermore, one of the most common non-random effects on a cross-sectional study of workers is a survivor bias: study of a stable worker population is frequently biased by the 'healthy worker effect' since those workers with the worst 'effect' will have left the jobs in question. Thus, whatever statistical measure of risk is employed in analyses, if a positive (and statistically significant) relationship is found in a cross-sectional study, then one can assume that the true risk is probably even greater than what was found. Thus much of the criticism of the reliance on cross-sectional versus prospective studies is without foundation. A great deal that is useful has been learned from cross-sectional studies. And, in terms of utilization of resources, they are almost always cheaper and faster to complete than prospective studies. I believe that the studies most heavily relied on by NIOSH in its assessment of workplace factors and musculoskeletal disorders are of good quality.

3. Would either the inclusion of any omitted studies or the assessment of the quality of those reviewed substantially alter the interpretation of the epidemiological evidence that certain physical stressors in the workplace increase risk of acquiring certain MSDs?

No.

4. What does the evidence tell us about incidence in the general population versus specific groups of workers?

Overall, there have been very few studies of the incidence or prevalence of specific musculoskeletal disorders in the general population. This is certainly a weakness in our overall understanding of these conditions, and it would be very helpful if such studies were performed. Even among those studies of musculoskeletal disorders in the general population which do exist, there is reason to believe that the published estimates may substantially miss the mark. For example, the best study we have of the incidence of carpal tunnel syndrome in the general population was published by Stevens et al., in 1988. This study was based on data collected from 1961 through 1980. It is notable that the incidence rates for carpal tunnel syndrome in this study increased substantially over this 20 year period, probably reflecting better diagnosis, and greater attention paid to this condition by both clinicians and patients. However, the data on which this study is based were collected prior to the massive increase in work-related carpal tunnel syndrome that began in the early 1980's and peaked in about 1994 or 1995 (Brogmus, 1995; Hanrahan, 1991; Bureau of Labor Statistics, 1989). With increased attention focused on this condition during the 1980's and 1990's, there is strong reason to believe that the true incidence of carpal tunnel syndrome in the general population may be substantially greater that the estimates provided by Stevens et al. There is even empirical evidence to support this contention (DeKrom et al., 1992).

Despite the absence of a substantial body of data concerning the incidence or prevalence of specific musculoskeletal disorders in the general population, this does not detract materially from our understanding of the potential contribution of workplace factors to the development of such disorders. Almost all of the best studies of musculoskeletal disorders among workers have employed internal control groups (usually defined on the basis of ergonomic exposures) from the same company or a similar company in the same geographic location. Such internal comparison populations usually provide for better control of potential confounders since they are more likely to be better matched sociodemographically to the exposed population than would be the general population.

References:

Brogmus GE. Reporting of Cumulative Trauma Disorders of the Upper Extremities May be Leveling Off in the U.S. Proceedings of the Human Factors and Ergonomics Society 39th Annual Meeting - 1995. pp.591-595.

Bureau of Labor Statistics. Occupational Injuries and Illnesses in the United States by Industry, 1989: U.S. Department of Labor, Bulletin 2379. Washington, D.C.: U.S. Government Printing Office, 1991.

DeKrom MCTFM, Knipschild PG, Kester ADM, Thijs CT, Boekkooi PF, Spaans F. Carpal tunnel syndrome: prevalence in the general population. J Clinical Epidemiology. 1992;45(4):373-376.

Hanrahan LP, Higgins D, Anderson H, Haskins L, Tai S. Project SENSOR: Wisconsin Surveillance of Occupational Carpal Tunnel Syndrome. Wis Med J. 1991;90(2):80,82-83.

Stevens JC, Sun MD, Beard CM, O'Fallon WM, Kurland LT. Carpal tunnel syndrome in Rochester, Minnesota, 1961 to 1980. Neurology. 1988;38:134-138.

U.S. Department of Health and Human Services/National Institute for Occupational Safety and Health. <u>Musculoskeletal Disorders and Workplace Factors: A critical review of epidemiologic evidence for work-related musculoskeletal disorders of the neck, upper extremity, and low back</u>. DHHS (NIOSH) Publication No. 97-141. July, 1997.

WORKSHOP ON WORK-RELATED MUSCULOSKELETAL INJURIES: EXAMINING THE RESEARCH BASE

PANEL ON EPIDEMIOLOGY: RISK FACTORS

Fredric Gerr, MD
Associate Professor, Rollins School of Public Health, Emory University, Atlanta, GA

1. Has NIOSH missed or overlooked any important body of epidemiological evidence in its review?

No. NIOSH has been thorough in its collection of epidemiological evidence for inclusion in its review (NIOSH [Bernard, B., Ed.]. Musculoskeletal disorders and workplace factors. US Department of Health and Human Services, Washington, DC., 1997).

2. Describe the study methods of the studies that have been heavily weighted in the NIOSH assessment. What is the general quality of these studies?

Prior to addressing this question, it may be useful to review the NIOSH methods for identifying studies for inclusion and its scheme for weighting more heavily those of greater methodological rigor.

The authors of the NIOSH assessment described the strategy used for selection and inclusion of studies. They required that included studies 1) have well defined exposed and referent populations, 2) use well defined explicit criteria for identification of health outcomes, 3) evaluated exposure so that inferences could be made about specific ergonomic exposures, and 4) use the following designs: population based study, case control study, cross-sectional study, longitudinal cohort study, and case series. These guidelines, in general, are reasonable and appropriate.

The majority of studies included by NIOSH in its assessment were cross-sectional in design. The specific methods varied considerably across studies, in particular with regard to the rigor of exposure assessment, health outcome assessment, control of confounding, and minimization of sample distortion occurring as a result of poor participation. NIOSH made efforts to addressed the methodological heterogeneity of the studies it reviewed by establishing a set of criteria for weighting studies' relative methodological quality. Specifically, NIOSH considered studies to be more influential if 1) participation was >=70%; 2) the health outcome of interest was defined by symptoms and physical examination, 3) the investigators were blinded to health or exposure status when assessing health or exposure status, and 4) the joint under consideration "was subjected to an independent exposure assessment, with characterization of the independent variable [i.e., exposure] of interest". These criteria for identifying studies of relatively greater methodological rigor are reasonable and appropriate.

Before examining the literature as a whole, NIOSH examined statistical significance and control of confounding and other biases present in each study. Finally, NIOSH applied well established criteria to the literature reviewed to determine whether "strong evidence", "evidence", "insufficient evidence" or "evidence of no effect" suggestive of a causal association was present.

As described, the system NIOSH used to identify studies for inclusion in its review, its methods of assessing their methodological rigor, and its process for evaluating the literature as a whole were reasonable and appropriate. In terms of application, however, NIOSH was, at times, less rigorous than its multi-level system of identifying and considering studies of high epidemiological quality might otherwise suggest. Two examples are provided for illustration:

NIOSH included numerous studies of neck and neck/shoulder MSDs in which the exposure variable was a measure of ergonomic exposure of the *hand and/or wrist* in which no measures of force, repetition, or posture directly applicable to the neck or neck/shoulders were obtained. NIOSH acknowledged that such studies were more prone to exposure "misclassification" and indicated that they were given lesser weighting because of it (p. 2-2). The utility of including such studies at all, however, is unclear as they add little or nothing to the clarification of the relationship between ergonomic exposure to the neck or neck and shoulders and disorders of these regions.

NIOSH indicated that only 2 of the 27 studies of the relationship between repetition and neck or neck/shoulder MSDs met all four "evaluation criteria" (indicators of methodological rigor) and that only one of those reported odds ratios for the exposure (p. 2-4). Despite this relatively low number of studies meeting criteria for epidemiologic rigor, NIOSH reported in its *Conclusions Regarding Repetition* that 27 studies found ORs greater than one and that statistically significant increases in risk were found in 19 studies (p.2-12). Basing such summary statements on a body of literature that includes at least some studies of questionable methodological quality may overstate the actual strength of inference that can be made from the limited number of high quality studies available.

Other examples similar to those provided here can be found in other sections of the NIOSH report.

The body of literature describing the association between work and musculoskeletal disorders is of heterogeneous quality. This has been acknowledged by many investigators and authors, and has been the subjects of numerous published reviews. It appears that NIOSH has included many studies of questionable quality in its comprehensive review although it did make efforts to identify studies of higher and lower quality and to weight those of higher quality in its assessments. NIOSH may have been insufficiently rigorous, however, in its efforts to consider only those studies of sufficiently high methodological quality to render their results useful and to eliminate from consideration those so flawed that their results add little to the resolution of the issue of work-relatedness. In doing so, NIOSH may have weaken the case that it hoped to make from its literature review.

3. Would either the inclusion of any omitted studies or the assessment of the quality of those reviewed substantially alter the interpretation of the epidemiological evidence that certain physical stressors in the workplace increase risk of acquiring certain MSDs?

More rigorous elimination of those studies that failed to meet criteria for methodological rigor would substantially reduce the number of studies available for review for each of the body locations (i.e., neck, shoulder, elbow, etc.) considered. Review of this smaller, but more rigorous body of literature, would not, in my opinion, substantively change the conclusions drawn from the literature regarding work and musculoskeletal disorders. Because of a relative paucity of high quality investigations, some specific associations, such as that between repetition and neck disorders or force and epicondylitis might be considerably less firm than currently reported if weak studies were excluded from consideration. The conclusion that the literature supports an association between work characterized by forceful and repeated use of the hands and arms and a range of painful musculoskeletal disorders of the upper extremities would still be justifiable, however.

4. What does the evidence tell us about incidence in the general population versus specific groups of workers?

No studies of which I am aware have applied identical criteria for identification of MSDs to specific working groups and to the "general population". Some studies have attempted to examine the relationship between work and musculoskeletal disorders in the general population. Virtually were cross-sectional and few, if any, such population based studies used objective assessment of both health and ergonomic exposure, however. As a result, such studies are subject to reporting bias in which those with a painful MSD may be more likely to report exposure than those without such a condition.

EPIDEMIOLOGIC STUDIES OF PHYSICAL ERGONOMIC STRESSORS AND MUSCULOSKELETAL DISORDERS

Laura Punnett, Sc.D.
Department of Work Environment, University of Massachusetts Lowell

The extensive literature review edited by Bernard and colleagues at NIOSH (1997) was rigorous in its methodology. The four review criteria applied to the literature (page 1-10) reflected well-accepted, important principles of epidemiology. They gave greatest emphasis to studies in which selection bias and information bias were unlikely to have exerted a large influence on the results. Almost all of the studies judged to be of highest quality (Armstrong 1987a; Bovenzi 1995; Chatterjee 1982; Chiang 1990, 1993: Jonsson 1988; Kilbom 1986; Juopajärvi 1979; Ohlsson 1994, 1995; Osorio 1994; Punnett 1991; Silverstein 1987), and many of the other papers as well, employed standard epidemiologic and statistical techniques to control for multiple covariates, making confounding also an unlikely explanation for the reported associations. Thus, the most heavily weighted investigations were rigorously conducted according to standard scientific principles and are highly appropriate for NIOSH and OSHA to rely upon. A number of them also followed quasi-experimental procedures in selecting study subjects, in order to obtain good contrast between exposure levels, and thereby were particularly informative with regard to good contrast between exposure levels, and thereby were particularly informative with regard to exposure-response relationships. In addition, some of the papers that NIOSH judged not to meet all 4 criteria could have been evaluated in a more positive light if they had been read as part of a body of work, rather than as stand-alone studies (e.g., Punnett 1985; Riihimäki 1989b). In sum, this group of 13 (or more) high quality papers represents a larger body of epidemiologic evidence than OSHA has been able to rely upon for almost any prior rule-making in the agency's history.

Although it is always possible to overlook some papers, despite one's best efforts, there were few omissions proportionate to the volume of literature reviewed. I have not found any body of evidence relevant to the stated scope of the review was systematically overlooked. I have noticed the apparent omission of a few studies, although some of them at least may have been excluded intentionally because they examined health outcomes that did not fit the specific body part categories designated for the review. Most of the omitted studies that I have noted were investigations of changes in health status following reductions in exposure, either from intentional ergonomic interventions in the workplace or from evolving production processes, equipment, and work environments. The documentation of such health benefits speaks directly to the question of temporal relationship and is often held to provide very strong evidence of a causal relationship. Thus, if these studies had been included, they would likely have strengthened NIOSH's conclusions. Some of them were in fact reviewed, but the fact that they provided evidence of health benefits following reduction in occupational exposure was not highlighted as much as it might have been. Since the intervention literature will be reviewed in a later session, I will only mention here a sample, such as a large cohort of visual display unit (VDU) operators, in which the use of new keyboards led to the recovery of some neck, shoulder and upper arm problems over a 7-year follow-up period (Bergqvist 1995). Among other groups of VDU operators, multifaceted ergonomics programs produced benefits such as decreased frequency of symptoms, physical findings, and diagnosed cases (Kamwendo 1991; Ong 1984; Oxanburgh 1985). In a study of electronics manufacturing, employees moved to a less repetitive job assignment experienced fewer new disorders as well as remission in affected individuals (Jonsson 1988).

The conclusions of the NIOSH report also rely somewhat on the large number of studies that met at least one, but not all four, of the specified criteria. This it is appropriate to address some features of these papers, as well. In particular, I will comment briefly on the information that can be obtained from workers' self-reports of exposure and of musculoskeletal health status.

Observing or measuring physical ergonomic stressors in the workplace would seem to be preferable to asking workers for their estimates of exposure, but both have potential disadvantages. For example, work postures are often observed on only a single occasion, for a brief period (e.g., ten minutes) per subject. As WMK mentioned earlier, these limited observations raise the possibility of misclassification (probably non-differential) if the workers' postures are not constant over time, and they cannot be used to estimate past exposures at all. A number of papers have addressed the validity and reproducibility of physical ergonomic exposure measures derived from questionnaire data, demonstrating that self-reported exposure intensity, frequency and duration are moderately, although not perfectly, correlated with the corresponding objectively measure variables (Armstrong 1989; Gamberale 1985; Punnett 1988; Torgén 1996; Viikari-Juntura 1996; Wiktorin 1993). For example, Nathan et al. (1993) found very high agreement between observed and self-reported measures for a wide range of ergonomic exposures in a large occupational cohort. In several studies of VDU operators, duration of keyboard use was described consistently by people in the same jobs (Bernard 1993) and the differences between self-reported and observed keying times were nondifferential with respect to case status (Bernard 1993; Faucett 1996; Hales 1992; Silverstein 1990).

The use of self-reported symptoms to determine health status is not unique to the study of musculoskeletal disorders (MSDs); a standardized questionnaire for the assessment of chronic obstructive pulmonary disease has been widely used for years. Misclassification of health outcome is a potential concern; since individuals differ in their experience of and threshold for pain, responses might vary among study subjects with similar symptoms. On the other hand, the use of multiple items to construct a composite outcome variable, as was done in many of these studies, improves its precision and validity compared with the use of a single symptom question (Stellman 1987). It has been shown repeatedly that symptom reports with appropriately high thresholds have a strong relationship with MSDs as determined by physical examination (e.g., Baron 1996; Hünting 1981), and that cases defined by symptoms and by physical findings show extremely similar associations with the ergonomic characteristics of subjects' jobs (e.g., Bernard 1993; Silverstein 1986, 1987; Punnett 1991; Punnett 1998). Symptom prevalences have also been highly correlated with the frequency of workers' compensation claims and work-related repetitive trauma disorders recorded by employers in the same occupations (Fine 1986) and were predictive of seeking medical services for MSD conditions (Westgaard 1992). With reference to carpal tunnel syndrome (CTS), Bernard et al. (1993) found that a subject meeting a case definition based on symptoms was 43 times more likely to have abnormal median nerve latency than one who was not a case. Nathan and colleagues found a strong association between the prevalence of symptoms ("probable CTS") and the severity of slowed median nerve conduction velocity (p<0.001 for both 1984 and 1989 data)(1992a).

In addition, it has been argued that clinical medicine does not yet provide the necessary diagnostic techniques for all of the soft tissue disorders, especially in their early stages, and that self-reported symptoms or functional impairments may often be more useful indicators than the available physical examination maneuvers and objective tests (e.g., Mackinnon 1994).

Both the NIOSH document itself and several panelists here today have addressed the fact that a large majority of the reviewed studies were cross-sectional in design. Rather than repeat those points, I would simply like to note that – once a study has found a positive association between exposure and outcome – the final question is whether there are reasonable alternative explanations for that finding, or whether the most plausible explanation is a causal relationship. Although the ambiguous temporal direction is often cited as a weakness of cross-sectional studies, it is highly unlikely that workers who have already developed musculoskeletal pain would preferentially transfer into jobs with higher physical exposures. On the contrary, it has been shown that workers tend to leave or transfer to lower exposure jobs after MSD onset (Östlin 1988; Punnett 1996; Silverstein 1987), which would bias toward, rather than away from the null hypothesis. Thus, positive bias by this mechanism is not a plausible alternative explanation for the findings of these studies.

There is very little direct evidence as to incidence rates in the general population versus specific groups of workers, both because so few longitudinal studies have been published to date and because in the United States and many other countries there are no (reliable) registries that can provide data on population incidence of MSDs. However, the literature reviewed by NIOSH clearly demonstrates that people occupationally exposed to physical ergonomic stressors, especially at the extremes of magnitude, duration and frequency, have higher prevalences of many MSDs than people without or with lower exposures. In fact, it is impressive that a group of over one dozen studies, utilizing different study designs and data collection protocols and carried out on several continents, have all produced findings consistent with the hypothesis that occupational exposure to physical stressors increases the risk of MSDs. An issue sometimes raised is that these disorders are so common in the general population, because of the many non-occupational risk factors, that occupational factors cannot account for a large proportion of the musculoskeletal disease burden in general. This is irrelevant to the question at hand. Numerous studies have shown that, after accounting for age, gender, body mass index, smoking, recreational activities, systemic disease, and other individual characteristics, there are still impressive associations between MDSs and occupational exposure to physical stressors. The question of whether or not these factors account for few or many MSDs in the general population has no bearing on the question of whether or not people at work can be protected from preventable risks in their workplaces. If physical ergonomic stressors are shown to increase the risks in their workplaces. If physical ergonomic stressors are shown to increase the risk for otherwise generally healthy working people – as I believe the literature shows – then OSHA has a responsibility to consider formally how it can most effectively pursue primary prevention of these often-disabling disorders.

In closing, I would like to refer to Adrian Renton's article, "Epidemiology and Causation," in the *J Epi Comm Health*. She pointed out that – because we define disease in terms of abnormal variation in structure or function – a cause must be understood as a factor that influences a biological process or mechanism to evolve toward that abnormal state. In other words, the search for causation is not merely at the level of biological induction from repeated observations, but for factors that are directly involved in biological mechanisms. We should not overemphasize problems of inferential logic at the expense of understanding the material causes of disease. Epidemiology must be integrated with other basic medical sciences in order to inform rational public health decision-making as it relates to disease prevention.

To quote,

> "The consistent association between a factor and a disease occurring in correct time order in observational studies, where bias has been minimized, suggests a causal or confounded relationship. A strong relationship which persists in the face of strenuous attempts to control confounding in observational studies and through intervention studies shifts the balance towards causation. A knowledge of the mechanisms of pathogenesis of the disease, and the demonstration that a factor will materially influence these mechanisms through the material laws which govern them, adds further to our confidence in causation. Hill's criteria of biological gradient, plausibility, and coherence shift the epidemiologist's attention towards the real material basis of disease causation. Where there is evidence, either from basic medical science or epidemiology of causation, policy makers will consider whether the use of public health technology to modify the distribution of the factor or to identify those exposed might be possible and appropriate. Where there is both of these, properly designed public health programmes might certainly be expected to yield some success and controlled trials, where ethical, are likely to be the best way to assess their effectiveness."

I congratulate the Academy for its wisdom in bringing together these multiple disciplines, all of which contribute insights into the biological mechanisms involved in the etiology of work-related musculoskeletal disorders. It is precisely through the convergence of these approaches and knowledge bases that we will be able to arrive at an appropriate public health solution to this pressing problem.

REFERENCES

Note: Citations are listed below only if they did not appear in the NIOSH review itself.

Bergqvist U. (1995). Visual display terminal work - a perspective on long-term changes and discomforts. Inter J Industr Ergonomics 16: 201-209.

Bernard B. (1997). Musculoskeletal disorders and workplace factors: A critical review of epidemiologic evidence for work-related musculoskeletal disorders of the neck, upper extremity, and low back. *97-141*, Department of Health and Human Services, National Institute of Occupational Safety and Health, Cincinnati, OH.

Faucett J, Rempel D. (1996). Musculoskeletal symptoms related to video display terminal use: An analysis of objective and subjective exposure estimates. <u>AAOHN Journal</u> 44(1): 33-39.

Fine LJ, Silverstein BA, Armstrong TJ, Anderson CA, Sugano DS. (1986). Detection of cumulative trauma disorders of upper extremities in the workplace. <u>J Occ Med</u> 28: 674-678.

Gamberale F. (1985). The perception of exertion. <u>Ergonomics</u> 28: 299-308.

Kamwendo K, Linton SJ. (1991). A controlled study of the effect of neck school in medical secretaries. <u>Scand J Rehab Med</u> 23: 143-152.

Mackinnon SE, Novak CB. (1994). Clinical commentary: Pathogenesis of cumulative trauma disorders. <u>J Hand Surg</u> 19A: 873-883.

Ong CN. (1984). VDT work place design and physical fatigue: a case study in Singapore. <u>Ergonomics and Health in Modern Offices</u>, E Grandjean, ed., Taylor & Francis, London.

Oxenburgh MS, Rowe SA, Douglas DB. (1985). Repetition strain injury in keyboard operators: Successful management over a two year period. <u>J Occ Health Safety-Aust NZ</u> 1:106-112.

Punnett L. (1998). Ergonomic stressors and upper extremity disorders in vehicle manufacturing: Cross-sectional exposure- response trends. <u>Occup Environ Med</u> 55(6): 414-420.

Silverstein BA, Armstrong TJ, Flaschner D, Woodland D, Burt S, Fine LJ. (1990). Upper limb ergonomic stressors in selected newspaper jobs: A pilot study. National Institute for Occupational Safety and Health and The University of Michigan, Cincinnati OH.

Stellman J, Klitzman S, Gordon GC, Snow BR. (1987). Work environment and the well-being of clerical and VDT workers. <u>J Occ Behav</u> 8: 95-114.

Torgén M, Alfredsson L, Köster M, Wiktorin C, Kilbom Å. Reproducibility of a questionnaire for assessment of present and past physical work loads. *25th International Congress on Occupational Health*, Stockholm, Sweden, 140.

Westgaard RH, Jansen T. (1992). Individual and work related factors associated with symptoms of musculoskeletal complaints: I. A quantitative registration system. <u>Brit J Industr Med</u> 49: 147-153.

ANALYSIS OF THE SCIENTIFIC APPROACH IN ASSESSING EPIDEMIOLOGICAL EVIDENCE FOR THE RELATIONSHIP BETWEEN WORK AND MUSCULOSKELETAL DISORDERS

Howard M. Sandler, M.D.
Richard S. Blume, M.D., M.P.H.
Occupational and Environmental Medicine

INTRODUCTION

Musculoskeletal injuries, disorders and/or symptoms affect virtually everyone at various points in their lives. There are various known and suspected causes including trauma, genetics, metabolic disorders, psychogenic factors, lifestyle factors, body habitus and occupational as well as non-occupational activities. Workers with MSDs and MSD symptoms suffer significant morbidity and generate costs in billions of dollars annually in workers compensation and lost productivity.

Increasing interest about the relationship between work and musculoskeletal disorders or injuries (MSDs) over the past few decades has generated significant research in biomechanics, ergonomics and the epidemiology of MSDs. Numerous studies have been published examining the potential work - MSDs relationship as well as non-work factors. Several reviews of the epidemiologic data, including those employing meta-analytic techniques have yielded conflicting conclusions about the work - MSD association for specific disorders, e.g., carpal tunnel syndrome and low back pain.

The NAS workshop session on physical factor epidemiology will endeavor to assess the overall contribution of published epidemiological studies associating physical stressors with musculoskeletal disorders. Specifically, the "quality of the science" will be examined. A focus of the session will involve assessment of the National Institute for Occupational Safety and Health (NIOSH) review of work-related MSD epidemiologic evidence, released by the Institute in July, 1997 including methods for evidence weighting, completeness of the literature base, MSD incidence in working and general populations and quality of the literature base.

METHODOLOGY FOR CAUSAL DETERMINATION OF WORK AND MSDs

Causal association from an epidemiological standpoint as described by Hill, Rothman and others, requires careful critical analysis of individual studies comprising the body of literature, determination of "causal criteria", and development and utilization of a weighting scheme to objectively assess the evidence for associating exposure and effect. The NIOSH document has identified, assembled, and critiqued the epidemiological literature base regarding work, specifically physical factors and MSDs. And given the constraints of the literature as acknowledged by NIOSH, the document did not assess specific dose-relationships, relative contributions of work versus non-work factors, and thresholds (e.g., "triggers") among other items of considerable import. These important issues may or may not be able to be evaluated given the state of the present epidemiological database. The NIOSH document also examined a limited number of specific MSDs in certain anatomical locations, e.g., the back, hands/wrists, elbows and neck; carpal tunnel syndrome, epicondylitis, shoulder tendonitis, low back pain, etc.

Study Critique

NIOSH chose four criteria to qualitatively critique each study: participation rate, health outcome definition, blinding, and exposure status. Each criterion was further specified but limited in their characterization and requirements, e.g., health outcome was limited to symptoms and physical examination. MSDs such as carpal tunnel syndrome may require additional evidence such as electrodiagnostic studies for diagnosis. The exclusion of electrodiagnostic results from assessment of health outcome in screening studies may therefore significantly limit the reliability of associations. This has been demonstrated in recent studies and the potential impact of overstated health outcome presence may be substantial. Other important factors in study methodology such as confounding were not systematically addressed in the NIOSH document. The selection of criteria for determining study inclusion and weighting in a formal assessment is a key element and one which requires validation. The NIOSH document does not provide a basis for the limited critique approach or describe epidemiologic sources validating the approach.

The NIOSH document states that it applied the greatest qualitative weight to those studies which met the four criteria considered in the NIOSH document. The methodology used to perform this weighting is not specified in the NIOSH document. In addition, application of the four critique criteria demonstrated significant deficiencies in the body of literature cited in the NIOSH document. This significant observation deserves discussion beyond that provided in the document. Despite the known limitations of certain epidemiologic study designs in causal analysis, e.g., cross-sectional, such studies were included. The importance of using a tested and validated critique methodology cannot be underscored. For example, would the criteria approach in the NIOSH document yield expected results if applied to a more well-recognized exposure-effect relationship, e.g., smoking and chronic obstructive lung disease? Without such confirmation, the validity of the methodology remains to be established. Furthermore, the actual weighting process used in applying the criteria to derive causal associations needs to be fully defined. It is important to note that other scientific investigators utilizing comprehensive critique criteria, e.g., Stock, could as a result employ but a few studies in the epidemiologic assessment of work and carpal tunnel syndrome while the NIOSH document employed a much greater number of studies.

Weight of Evidence Approach

Based upon available information provided in the document, it appears that the NIOSH document's overall approach in weighting the causal evidence is as follows:

- Selected studies are critiqued using a limited quality criteria scheme;
- Using undefined methods, the selected studies are weighted for quality based upon the critique;

- Selected causal criteria are then applied to the cited literature and studies meeting the criteria are identified; again, the weighting system used to apply the results of the causal criteria is undefined;
- Finally, exposure - effect, evidence or "strength" is classified according to a rating scheme apparently unique to the NIOSH document, with scores including "– ,"" 0/+," "++, " and "+++."

The NIOSH document employed two components in assessing the work physical factors - MSD relationship once the studies were critiqued and selected: causal criteria and "evidence classification categories". Six causal criteria were employed by NIOSH. The criteria chosen are consistent with published criteria and employ the areas principally discussed throughout the scientific literature on causal association. Limitations are noted in the NIOSH document's utilization of these criteria. For example under temporality, the one criterion which absolutely has to be met to establish causation, i.e., the exposure must precede the effect, the NIOSH document recognizes that cross-sectional studies cannot satisfy this criteria. However, the MSD epidemiological literature employed by the NIOSH document primarily consists of cross-sectional studies. Nonetheless, the NIOSH document states that from such studies "reasonable assumptions" regarding temporality can be made and specifically cites two authors who have published studies which are said to support the document's assumption.

For example, Rothman (1996) was reported to state that some assumptions about timing for exposure and disease must be made. However, there is no indication that worker interviews or work histories are reliable in terms of predicting presence or absence of pre-existing conditions or symptoms. Disorders such as tendonitis do come and go. Recall of prior medical history is variable as has been noted in a variety of other health issues, such as recall of spontaneous abortion, which is undoubtedly a more significant health event. Citing Kleinbaum (1991), the NIOSH document states that with additional information such as biomechanical findings, temporality can be established. Unfortunately there is no scientific evidence offered to evaluate the proposal that individuals with underlying hand/wrist tendonitis will not seek work which may require significant use of the hand and wrist. This assumption may or may not be operative. Workers with certain skill sets can also be assumed to be qualified in, and primarily gain entry to the same type of job/industry.

A critical consideration which affects the basis for any conclusions derived in the NIOSH document is its use of a four-point category scheme to classify "evidence". To our knowledge this approach has not been previously published, defined or validated in other scientific settings. Unfortunately, the NIOSH document does not define the methodology it employed to classify each physical factor or physical factor combination and associated health outcomes. Without a clearly defined epidemiologic basis for this approach and a defined methodology for applying the critique and causal criteria to derive the ratings, it is not possible to determine whether the ratings are appropriate and scientifically supported. As in all scientific endeavors, replication of the results using the same methodology is crucial to assure that the conclusions are indeed well-founded. It is not possible to replicate the findings of the NIOSH document as the methods used in the document are not fully defined. It is critical to the discussion at hand to be able to replicate the NIOSH document's evidence determination for work - MSD causation. However, without such stated methodology, the process becomes merely a "black box" from which certain data goes in and a classification rating emerges from the other end.

The use of a four-point scale is to some extent quantitative. Interestingly, the NIOSH document had referred earlier in the analysis to qualitative weighting, but does not offer any additional explanation. Further, in describing the ratings, the NIOSH document employs the terms "very likely," "convincing," "insufficient" and "adequate." Again, an epidemiologic basis for applying these terms to the ratings is not provided. No definitions or triggers are supplied to describe when those terms apply, nor how those terms satisfy the rating structure. To draw an analogy, similar rating schemes are used in medicine, for example, to grade reflexes or muscle strength. There is significant variability between examiners when evaluating reflexes and muscle strength, as a result of the lack of well-established definitions and validation that the system indeed is accurate. Various validated tools are now increasingly employed in such evaluations. Other well-defined rating systems such as the ILO system for describing and rating pneumoconiosis, the latter also using a proficiency testing program have nevertheless been shown to be subject to significant inter-reader variability. These observations beg the question, what would be the reproducibility of the approach employed in the NIOSH document, even if it was fully described and therefore could be independently replicated?

Work-Related and Non-work-Related MSD Incidence

One question posed to this workshop session concerns the incidence of MSDs in workers versus that in the general population. Incidence generally cannot be derived from cross-sectional studies. The overwhelming number of studies use in the NIOSH document's assessment are cross-sectional in design. Additionally, there is a dearth of data in the scientific literature from which to determine the incidence of MSDs in the general population. Various studies cited in the NIOSH document employed workers with different exposures such as clerical workers to serve as controls. Lastly, confounding variables were not consistently considered in the cited studies to assure that other factors would not account for any differences found. Thus, determination of incidence and incidence differences is hampered by such factors.

SUMMARY

It is imperative that specific relationships between work physical factors and potentially other factors, and the development and aggravation of MSDs and related symptoms be determined. Such information is vital to the effective protection of worker health and safety. The question is not just, are MSDs and/or their symptoms related to work? But, more importantly, how are work physical factors, psychosocial factors and other nonwork factors related to MSDs development and aggravation? This includes dose-response, specific factor or factor combination relationships and safe levels, as well as other areas of inquiry.

An assessment of the NIOSH document's approach to the weight of the epidemiologic evidence to determine the causal associations between various work factors and MSDs is a key element in this scientific undertaking. We have been provided a valuable exercise in assessing the NIOSH document's findings regarding specific MSDs including those of the back, neck and upper extremity. Aspects of the approach described in the NIOSH document and concerns regarding the resulting weight of evidence findings inhibit use of the document in causal determination. Fully defined and validated scientific methodology for epidemiologic literature critique, classification and weighting should provide a valid assessment of the present state of the art for various physical work factors and MSD development. Additionally, NIOSH, NIOSH-funded, and various other studies currently underway by a vast array of academic, government, labor and business researchers should start to provide answers to specific causal and prevention questions which are so vital in establishing scientifically-based regulatory and enforcement approaches.

We are pleased to have had the opportunity to participate in this scientific process to attempt to analyze the relationships between work and MSDs. Establishing and understanding the potential causal associations in this area is essential in the process to prevent and manage work-related musculoskeletal disorders.

SUMMARY COMMENTS

David H. Wegman, MD, MSc

Professor and Chair, Department of Work Environment, University of Massachusetts Lowell, Lowell, MA 01854

NIOSH staff accepted an important charge and a sizeable task when they undertook a comprehensive review of musculoskeletal disorders and workplace factors. They appear to have spent substantial effort in determining an appropriate approach and carrying out that approach in a transparent, public manner with continuous internal and external review. As a member of today's panel I have been asked to evaluate several central aspects of the process and the final product.

1. Regarding whether NIOSH has missed or overlooked any important body of epidemiological evidence in its review, this will inevitably be a matter of opinion. Their approach to gathering information was systematic and comprehensive using electronic literature searches supplemented by suggestions from a large number of subject-matter experts. I am not aware of any omissions. In an effort to evaluate comprehensiveness I compared the NIOSH report with a literature review I co-authored some years ago [1]. Articles not included by NIOSH that we considered had been appropriately excluded and the risk factor approach undertaken by NIOSH was superior to the exposure considerations used in our review.

2. Since study methodology was not the sole criterion used to select studies to be given greatest weight in determining work-relatedness, there is no way to identify the study "methods" that have been heavily weighted in the NIOSH assessment. To select studies, NIOSH developed a comprehensive approach that combined several factors to serve as the basis for judgements about work-relatedness. The quality of the studies that were most heavily weighted was generally quite high because they met the multiple criteria set out by NIOSH for weighting: high participation rates, appropriate "blinding" of investigators, health outcomes defined by symptoms and physical exam and independent exposure measures. Those that met all criteria were weighted most heavily, but thankfully, NIOSH did not eliminate all other studies. Rather studies that met a minimum threshold were still considered, with appropriate lesser weighting. In its weighting, NIOSH paid attention to explicit criteria for causality applying a standard definition of causality for epidemiologic studies. Possibly unique in such an effort, and a substantial contribution to any review of work and musculoskeletal disorders are the extensive tables in the body and the appendix. These tables summarize each study's adherence to the four criteria as well as provide a comprehensive, readable summary of many detailed aspects of each study, thus allowing the reader to develop independent judgements. Furthermore, the authors have developed an excellent graphical presentation format that permits rapid review of the large number of studies.

3. It is unlikely that any reasonable reassessment of the quality of the studies reviewed would substantially alter the interpretation of the epidemiological evidence that certain physical stressors in the workplace increase risk of acquiring certain musculoskeletal disorders. While it

is clear that judgement is involved, the demands made of each study are quite severe and the summary evaluations that are presented are quite conservative. Serious disagreements in how these data should be interpreted may come from those who question the legitimate use of epidemiology in any forum such as this, but epidemiologists can be expected to see these judgements as soundly based and determined on reasonable and well articulated criteria. The scheme developed to evaluate strength of evidence is clear and consistent with similar efforts by agencies such as the International Agency for Research on Cancer or organizations such as the American Conference of Governmental Industrial Hygienists.

4. NIOSH appropriately does not directly address the question of *incidence* in the general population versus specific groups of workers. There are a variety of data sources that might be used to estimate population *prevalence* (for example, NHIS, NHANES, and other surveys from NCHS, SSA Disability Reports, data accumulated as byproducts from health insurance) but none provide incidence data and none serve as a useful comparison for NIOSH's evaluation. NIOSH is careful to provide explicit information on the comparison populations (for example no or low exposure groups in cohort studies, unaffected controls in case control studies). Since the assessment examined specific physical factors, several of which may have been included in a particular study, the reviewers take care to determine that a proper unexposed or low exposed group is defined in terms of the specific exposure factor studied in cohort or cross-sectional studies. In case control studies the assessments made of both cases and controls are with regard to the specific factor under study.

5. I want to answer a question not asked: Is the approach taken by NIOSH to evaluate and summarize the epidemiologic literature on work-related musculoskeletal disorders of the neck, upper extremity, and low back appropriate and the most desirable? One might ask why NIOSH did not attempt several meta-analyses rather than use their more qualitative review? Meta-analysis is not appropriate when the question under study is as broad as the one NIOSH addressed. In my judgement Shapiro provides the answer which, in his words is: "I question whether quantitative methods can ever be as thoroughgoing, probing and informative as qualitative methods."[2]. In addition, in his final comments from a symposium on "Meta-analysis of Observational Studies" he summarizes apparent agreement with two other leading epidemiologists that synthetic meta-analyses (efforts to arrive at a single risk estimate by combining multiple studies) are of questionable validity and more likely to be misleading than helpful. One might also ask why did NIOSH not exclude case series from their review? The answer is provided by Checkoway, et al. in their classic textbook [3]. In discussing causal inference, he says: "Attempts to codify guidelines for assessing research quality are invariably detrimental to the practice and application of epidemiologic methods." He goes on to illustrate, through a hypothetical example, how a case series can easily provide information at least as important as a well-designed epidemiologic study. There is no "correct" way to carry out a literature review particularly with as large a scope as the one undertaken by NIOSH. The authors of the NIOSH report are to be commended for developing a methodology that is reasonable, understandable, clearly presented, open and conservative. It is hard to imagine a more effective way to summarize this literature.

Notes:

Hagberg M, Wegman DH. Prevalence Rates and Odds Ratios of Shoulder Neck Diseases in Different Occupational Groups. British Journal of Industrial Medicine, 44:602-610, 1987.

Shapiro S. Is there is or is there ain't no baby?: Dr. Shapiro replies to Drs. Pettiti and Greenland. Amer J Epid (1994) 14:788-791 (see also preceding three articles by Shapiro, Pettiti and Greenland in the same issue)

Checkoway H, Pearce NE, Crawford-Brown DJ. Research Methods in Occupational Epidemiology. Oxford University Press, New York, 1989 (pp 13-14).

NON-BIOMECHANICAL FACTORS POTENTIALLY AFFECTING MUSCULOSKELETAL DISORDERS

Julia Faucett, RN, PhD
UC Northern California Center for Occupational and Environmental Health, and School of Nursing, University of California, San Francisco CA 94143-0608

and

Robert A. Werner, MD
University of Michigan, and Veterans Administration Medical Center, Ann Arbor, MI 48105

Multiple occupational risk factors have been proposed for common musculoskeletal disorders. Chief among them are biomechanical factors such as repetition and force. In growing numbers, however, investigators in Europe, Japan, and the United States are reporting associations between non-biomechanical aspects of work and musculoskeletal disorders. Factors related to the way work tasks are organized, integrated, and controlled; the psychological demands of the job as well as demands for production speed and quality; and the structural and social aspects of supervision and coworker relationships are examples. Several measures for evaluating the worksite, the job, and worker perceptions about the job have been developed and are gaining in use. Furthermore, increasing evidence linking these factors with musculoskeletal outcomes has stimulated investigators to propose theoretical models to explain potential causal effects and guide additional research in the field (Bongers et al. 1993; Sauter & Swanson 1996; Armstrong et al. 1993; Smith & Sainfort 1989).

To fully understand the etiology of musculoskeletal disorders, however, it is important to examine physical and health-related factors intrinsic to the individual worker in addition to work-related biomechanical and non-biomechanical factors. Factors such as age, obesity, chronic illness, and anatomical variation for example have been studied to evaluate their contribution to the development of musculoskeletal disease. This paper on non-biomechanical factors thus reviews personal characteristics of the worker in addition to characteristics of the job and work environment. Literature searches were conducted separately to identify studies that investigated key personal and work-related variables for their associations with musculoskeletal disease and related symptoms. Following the request of the Academy, each section includes a discussion of the search strategies and inclusion criteria, summary of relevant research findings, critical examination of research methods that have been used in key or exemplary studies, and an overview of the investigators' conclusions and their plausibility.

Section One: Personal Factors (Author: *Robert Werner*)

Articles included in this focused review were selected based upon the following criteria:

- The study represents a scientific inquiry, not simply commentary or opinion (cross-sectional, longitudinal or experimental design).

- The study had a minimum of 30 subjects included.
- Appropriate statistical analysis, emphasis on including logistic regression or multilinear regression in an attempt to control for other factors
- The study was published in English.

Medical Conditions: diabetes, rheumatoid arthritis, thyroid disease, connective tissue disorders, vitamin B6 deficiency, pregnancy

Body Mass Index (BMI): Weight, Stature

- Gender

Wrist dimension / Anatomical size and shape of the carpal canal

Age

General conditioning: strength, aerobic conditioning

Genetics

Table 1: Non-Biomechanical Risk Factors for CTDs

The search strategy included a MEDLINE search using the qualifier, 'etiology,' or 'epidemiology' with the medical subject headings of: carpal tunnel syndrome (CTS), median nerve injury, cumulative trauma disorders (CTDs), low back pain and repetitive strain disorders. If the study focused on age, gender, medical status, obesity, physical condition, anatomical variation or genetics, it was screened for the above criteria based upon the abstract. The articles selected are not meant to represent an exhaustive list but simply the studies with an adequate scientific basis.

There are many personal co-factors that have been related to the development of CTS and to a lesser extent all CTDs. Obesity (body mass index), square wrist configuration, small carpal canal area, diabetes as well as several other connective tissue disorders and poor general fitness have all been associated with higher prevalence of CTS. The ultimate mechanism of injury is probably ischemia so anything that influences the health of the vascular system may compromise the soft tissues, i.e. nerve, muscle and tendon. Several investigators have suggested that CTDs and specifically CTS are primarily a result of health habits and lifestyle and secondarily to the biomechanical stress. Of the numerous personal co-factors that have been reported, few have been quantified as to the strength of the association. In the instances where the relative risk has been determined, attempts at modeling disease based upon these factors have only explained a small percentage of the variance.

Systemic Disorders

Many systemic disorders place an individual at higher risk for the development of soft tissue injuries. Diabetes and rheumatoid arthritis are the most obvious risk factors affecting the development of overuse syndromes (Stevens et al. 1992; Albers et al. 1996; Atcheson et al. 1998). Rheumatoid arthritis patients as well as those with other connective tissue disorders are at higher risk for development of joint abnormalities as well as muscle and nerve injuries (Stevens

1992). Diabetes is well known to be a risk factor for CTS and other compression mononeuropathies (Albers et al. 1996). Stevens et al. (1992) calculated a standardized morbidity ratio for rheumatoid arthritis (3.6), for diabetes (2.3) and for pregnancy (2.5). Thyroid disease and kidney disease also have many connective tissue side effects placing the individual at higher risk for nerve injuries; thyroid disease may also lead to muscle disease. Systemic disease causes the nerves to be more susceptible to compression and ischemia. The biologic plausibility of this association is high and the association is very strong, but these disorders affect a small percentage of active workers. Atcheson et al. (1998) suggest that these disorders are more common among workers diagnosed with CTS compared to other CTDs and may be under recognized in the industrial setting. The studies reviewed in this area use a methodology based upon population based data or large cross-sectional data. There is little bias associated with sample selection and the statistics are appropriate for the sample.

Vitamin B6

In 1973, Ellis and Presley suggested an association between vitamin B6 deficiency and CTS. Over the next 2 decades, several additional reports appeared which suggest that this association is causal in many cases. The impact of these studies on physician understanding and treatment of CTS is substantial. Vitamin deficiency is mentioned in a major textbook of occupational medicine (Keyserling & Armstrong 1992) as a possible CTS risk factor, implying that such deficiency contributes to CTS among workers.

Unfortunately, the studies which demonstrate an association between vitamin B6 status and CTS usually include small numbers of non-randomly selected subjects, frequently rely on non-standard or entirely subjective measures of outcome, and occasionally suffer from serious design flaws. Recent prospective and population based studies have not borne out this relationship (Folker et al. 1978; McCann & Davis 1978; Ellis et al. 1979, 1981, 1982; Amadio 1985; Franzblau et al. 1996). The recent population based studies and large cross-sectional studies are without the selection bias of earlier studies and use appropriate statistical analysis. The recent study by Kensinton et al. (1998) suggesting a relationship between vitamin B6 deficiency, vitamin C, and CTS (among women but not men) has methodological as well as statistical flaws (Franzblau et al. 1998).

The biologic plausibility is moderate. However, the strength of the relationship is weak except in severely vitamin B6 deficiency (and a severe B6 deficiency is rare). The cross-sectional studies of active workers and population based studies are sound enough to say that there is not a significant relationship between B6 levels and carpal tunnel syndrome.

Pregnancy / Gynecologic History

Pregnancy is considered an independent risk factor (estimated RR of 2.5) for the development of CTS due to increased vasculature and interstitial fluids (Soferman et al. 1964; Gould & Wissinger 1978; Masey et al. 1978; Stevens et al. 1992). These studies have adequate sample size and statistical analysis. This is a strong association with strong biologic plausibility. Fortunately this condition is a time limited and there is usually resolution of symptoms at the end of the pregnancy or shortly thereafter.

Both the use of oral contraceptives and gynecologic surgery have been hypothesized as risk factors for CTS based on epidemiological data, but this has not been consistently identified as a risk factor. (Saborur & Fadel 1970; Jorkquist et al. 1977; Cannon et al. 1981; DeKrom et al. 1990). The biological significance and rational for this is not well established although increased interstitial fluid as a result of hormonal changes is a suggested mechanism. This is a weak association with modest biologic plausibility. These studies are large cross-sectional studies with statistically significant findings in some of the studies but the clinical significance is low.

Body Mass Index (BMI)

Several investigators have reported that individuals with CTS were heavier and shorter than the general population. Cannon et al. (1982) noted that 27% of individuals (8 of 30) with CTS were obese compared to 12% (11 of 90) in a control population; this difference did not reach statistical significance. Dieck and Kelsey (1985) found an increased prevalence of CTS, within an adult female population, among individuals with short stature, greater weight and recent weight gain. The BMI was significantly higher in the CTS group (27 kg/m^2 versus 25 kg/m^2, p=0.01). Vessey et al. (1990) found that the risk for CTS among obese women was double that of slender women.

Within an industrial population, Nathan et al. (1992) demonstrated that a higher BMI was associated with a higher prevalence of median mononeuropathy. They found a relative risk of 4.1 for obese individuals compared to slender individuals. This relationship was more pronounced in men (RR=5.1) than in women (RR=2.7). This study did have a number of methodological flaws of which the most prominent was an analysis by hand instead of by person. The findings of Werner et al. (1994) support the hypothesis that individuals with a higher BMI are at increased risk for CTS.

In terms of obesity, the pathophysiology that would explain this relationship is not well understood. Letz and Gerr (1994) found the same relationship between obesity and slow conduction of the median nerve across the wrist in a large population based study, but an inverse relationship was found between obesity and other peripheral nerve measures. The conduction velocity of the peroneal, sural and ulnar nerves all tended to improve among subjects who were more obese whereas only the median sensory nerve across the wrist demonstrated slowing. The finding that BMI is correlated with the median but not ulnar sensory distal latencies suggest that the condition of obesity affects the nerves differently. The additional finding that the difference in the latencies is more strongly correlated with BMI than the median latency alone further supports this contention. This was a large cross-sectional study of Vietnam veterans. Its strength lies in the large sample size (>6,000) and the uniform electrodiagnostic testing.

If a causal relationship between obesity and a slowing of median conduction across the wrist exists, it may relate to increased fatty tissue within the carpal canal or to increased hydrostatic pressure throughout the carpal canal in obese individuals compared to normal or slender individuals. The median nerve at the wrist is more compartmentalized than the ulnar, peroneal or sural nerves and may be subjected to compression due to fatty build up within the carpal canal among obese individuals. Conversely, heavier individuals may simply place more mechanical stress on their hands and wrists and thus place the median nerve at higher risk as opposed to some intrinsic change within the carpal canal. The possible association between obesity and the development of early type II diabetes may be a confounder but is not related to the workers' report of diabetes. Alternatively, thinner subjects may be a surrogate of a person's overall conditioning which may in term influence the performance of the median nerve. This is a very strong association and appears to have a dose response relationship. The studies are either case control or large cross-sectional studies with sound statistical analysis. The biologic plausibility is still under question. Whether this is based upon biomechanical or metabolic factors is not known. The pathophysiology that would explain this relationship is not well understood. Although this is a strong relationship with an apparent dose response effect, this factor at best, explains only a small portion of the variance (less than 8%) related to the diagnosis of CTS or electrodiagnostic abnormalities involving the median nerve (Nathan et al. 1994; Werner et al. 1997)

Obesity is also associated with higher prevalence of lumbar back pain and leg symptoms but not thoracic or cervical back pain (Westgaard et al.1992; Milgrom et al. 1993) These are based upon cross-sectional studies with adequate sample sizes but the population studied by Milgrom et al. was military recruits as opposed to active workers studied by Westgaard et al. Other large, cross-sectional studies of industrial workers did not demonstrate a relationship between low back pain and obesity (Battie et al. 1989; Bigos et al. 1991; Daltroy et al. 1991) A study by Ryden et al. (1989) demonstrated the reverse relationship, women with low body mass were 50% more likely to have back injuries but the 95% confidence interval included 1.0 so it does not reach statistical significance. The strengthen of the association between obesity and other CTDs is weak and the larger studies have not demonstrated a consistent association.

Gender

Gender has been suggested as an independent risk factor for the development of CTS as well as repetitive strain injuries (Tanzer et al. 1959; Kendall et al. 1960; Phillips et al. 1967; Phalen 1972; Stevens et al. 1988). This risk factor is not well explained although historically women had a higher use of the health care system in this may represent another spectrum of higher use. Ashbury (1995) demonstrated an average relative risk for reporting of repetitive strain disorders of 1.5 for women compared to men across all occupations but it was much higher in some occupations: material handling (RR=6.0), construction (RR=4.0), processing (RR=3.5). Female postal workers had twice the relative risk for occupation injuries comapred to male postal workers (Zwerling et al. 1993) Bigos et al. (1991) did not demonstrate a relationship between gender and reported low back pain among Boeing workers.

The finding that women were more likely to have a higher prevalence of CTS than men is supported by population-based studies (Stevens et al. 1980, 1992) but differs from the worker compensation based data on CTS reported by Franklin. In the work place, the risk for women is only 10-20% higher than men as opposed to 300% reported in population based studies (Franklin et al. 1991; Werner et al. 1997). It was felt that the carpal canal was smaller in women thus exposing them to more compression of the median nerve. Further investigation of carpal canal dimension among women has not demonstrated any relationship between CTS and canal dimensions (see discussion of carpal canal size below).

Wrist size/dimension and CTS

A narrow carpal canal, a squarer shape of the wrist and a smaller sized hand have all been associated with a higher prevalence of CTS. Dekel et al. (1980) and Papaioannou et al. (1992) demonstrated that there was an association between a narrow carpal canal, particularly proximally, and the finding of CTS. This is a moderately strong association with high biologic plausibility.

Several studies have demonstrated a relationship between a more square shaped wrist and a finding of median mononeuropathy at the wrist (Johnson et al. 1983; Radecki 1994) but this was not confirmed by other studies (Werner et al. 1997, 1998). The relationship described by Radecki was in a clinic population of referred patients while the population studied by Werner et al. was a random selection of active workers, regardless of symptoms. The pathophysiology of this association, if it exists, has not been demonstrated. A squarer wrist has not been associated with a smaller cross-sectional area although this mechanism has been proposed. This is a relatively weak association with poor biologic plausibility.

Anomalous muscles extending into the carpal canal have been reported as etiologies for carpal tunnel syndrome (Neviaser 1974; Backhouse & Churchill-Davidson 1975; Brown et al. 1984; Cobb et al. 1984; Bauer & Trusell 1992). Muscle variants implicated include the muscle bellies of the flexor superficialis, palmaris longus, lumbrical muscles, abductor digiti quinti and the accessory palmaris longus muscle. These are rare occurrences and do not account for the typical person with CTS. Likewise, there are other space occupying lesions such as lipoma, haemangioma, synovial sarcoma, tendon sheath fibroma, ganglion or calcified mass that have been reported as etiologies of CTS, but these are also rare occurrences. This is a strong association with high biologic plausibility but again represents a rare anatomical variant (Neviaser 1974, Backhouse & Churchill-Davidson 1975).

Aging and CTDs

Increasing age has consistently been associated with slowing of the median nerve across the wrist and with CTS (Nathan et al. 1992; Stetson et al. 1992; Letz & Gerr 1994; Werner et al. 1994; Dyck et al. 1995). These studies have consistently demonstrated a strong association with high biologic plausibility. Tissue repair declines with aging and may be the basis for this relationship.

The association between aging and symptom reporting is not as strong. It is stronger for CTS than for other upper extremity cumulative trauma disorders or low back pain. Burton et al. (1989) demonstrated that a history of chronic low back pain was associated with increasing age. This study looked at prevalence or reported history as opposed to incident cases. Age did not factor into any of the models of limb or back symptoms reported by Westgaard et al. (1992). Many researchers did not find age a significant factor associated with self-reported back pain prevalence or incidence (Riesbold & Greenland 1985; Bigos et al. 1991). Daltroy et al. (1991) demonstrated that younger postal workers were at a higher risk (OR=3.0, p=0.0001) for back injuries. The association between aging and low back pain and other CTDs is weak. Greater emphasis should be placed upon the larger prospective, longitudinal studies, i.e. Boeing Study, which do not demonstrate an association.

General Fitness

Several studies have demonstrated an association between low aerobic fitness and higher musculoskeletal injury rates (mostly among military personnel) (Milgrom et al.1993; Shwayhat et al. 1994). There has also been an association between lower exercise levels and a higher prevalence of CTS as well as slowing of the median nerve across the carpal canal (Nathan & Keniston 1993). Most studies demonstrate a close correlation of poor general fitness with higher BMI, alcohol/tobacco use, and older age. Even when general fitness is identified as a significant independent factor (as is the case with CTS) it accounts for a very small component of the variance (3% or less) (Nathan & Keniston 1993). There are conflicting studies that do not demonstrate a relationship between general fitness/exercise level and higher musculoskeletal injuries. (Battie 1989; Franzblau et al. 1996; Milgrom et al. 1986; Westgaard et al. 1993). Battie et al. (1989) demonstrated that active workers (Boeing Study) with greater strength (isometric testing) were at higher risk for reporting low back pain. Also in the Boeing Study, Battie et al. demonstrated that cardiovascular fitness did not predict reporting of low back pain. The association between general fitness and CTS is modest, while the association with low back pain and other CTDs is poor. Due to the numerous co-variates that are associated to general fitness, the strength of the relationship varies. The biologic plausibility is reasonable, although the exact mechanism is unclear. The largest, prospective study (Boeing Study) does not demonstrate a relationship between better fitness and reduced low back pain; it does suggests that stronger individuals are at higher risk. These results should be more heavily weight than some of the smaller cross-sectional studies.

Genetics

There are a limited number of studies that explore the relationship between specific genetic markers and the incidence of CTDs. It is clear that genetics plays a role in the risks associated with gender, obesity, carpal canal size and several connective tissue disorders, but apart from these relationships, the role of genetics in the etiology of CTDs is not well established. There are a few studies suggesting a familial component to the incidence back pain and radiculopathy. Battie et al. (1995), for example, determined that the risk for degenerative disk disease was explained more by genetics and similarities among 115 identical twins than by documentation of physical loads. Richardson (1997) demonstrated that discogenic pain was more common in family members of subjects with discogenic pain than found among families of the subjects without such pain.

Radecki (1994) demonstrated a higher prevalence of carpal canal surgery or clinical history of CTS among family members with a documented slowing of the median nerve at the wrist compared to the families of other patients without slowing of the median nerve. Twenty seven percent of subjects with a documented median mononeuropathy had a positive family history of CTS compared to 13% without evidence median mononeuropathy (p<0.001). The familial occurrence of CTS has usually been reported as a single family or two involving two or three generations. An autosomal dominant inheritance has been postulated. The mechanism for a hereditary etiology for CTS is unclear but may relate to a thicker carpal tunnel ligament, smaller carpal canal or altered geometry or it may be related to obesity. Although the sample sizes in these studies are relatively small, the relationship is robust and suggests a strong association but more study is necessary to establish the strength of the relationship.

Section Two: Work-related Factors (Author: *Julia Faucett*)

Smith and Carayon hypothesized that the organizational, technological, environmental and task-related features of work systems influence workers' responses to their jobs, including their perceptions and performance of work (Smith & Sainfort 1989; Smith & Carayon 1996). Work system factors include organizational job characteristics that may be temporal (e.g. work-rest schedules, shift work); content-related (e.g. job complexity or monotony); social (e.g. solitary work, team work); financial (e.g. piecework, incentive pay); bureaucratic (e.g. multiple middle management levels); or more global (e.g. organizational climate, culture) (Sauter & Swanson 1996). The work stress paradigm suggests that workers' perceptions about work system factors, particularly perceptions that personal attributes and resources are not adequate to cope with work stressors, may result in work strain or detrimental emotional and physical outcomes (Sauter & Swanson 1996). Others have also suggested that the effects of work strain may be buffered by job-related decision control or social support (Johnson 1989; e.g. Karasek et al. 1981). Thus, for example, the worker's perception that the job is characterized by high psychological job demands, low perceived job control, and poor support from supervisors and coworkers increases the risk for job strain and poor health outcomes.

The impact of work system factors, and workers' psychological perceptions about those factors, on musculoskeletal outcomes theoretically arises from alterations they produce along multiple pathways: increases in biomechanical strain, physiological vulnerability, or symptom attribution and reporting (Bongers et al. 1993; Sauter & Swanson 1996). Feuerstein et al. (1996,1997) proposed that workers respond to work system factors, and their appraisals of them, with unique behavioral, cognitive, and physiological reactions. In turn, these reactions, jointly termed "work style," contribute to the development of musculoskeletal symptoms and disorders. Thus, a managerial decision to increase production demands among data processors may evoke fear in an individual worker that the task may not be completed on time, and lead to faster and harder keying, increased levels of catecholamines and cortisol, and detrimental delays in the awareness of musculoskeletal discomfort.

Search Strategy and Selection Criteria

Research literature was identified for this review using computer assisted searches of the MEDLINE PLUS and PsycINFO databases from 1988 through the first half of 1998. The time constraints set by the Academy did not allow searching for reports through other literature data bases or that were published only in conference proceedings or books. Reports in English that focused on musculoskeletal diseases, cumulative trauma disorders, repetitive strain injury, nerve entrapment or compression syndromes, carpal tunnel syndrome, tendinitis or tenosynovitis, sprains and strains as well as hand, arm, neck, shoulder or back symptoms were initially identified. This set was subsequently searched using keywords related to psychosocial workload, job stress, job demand, mental demand, job control, decision control or latitude, job satisfaction, job security or insecurity, job clarity, social support, work organization, supervision, shiftwork, overload, underload, monotonous work, work pace, work rest breaks, rest breaks, machine pacing, and electronic performance monitoring. After a review of abstracts, over 100 studies that investigated the etiology of musculoskeletal disorders using pertinent non-biomechanical work factors were identified. Seventy studies that could be located were then scored based on the criteria in Table 2. The scoring system led to ties among the highest scoring studies. Twelve studies were finally chosen from among the highest scoring studies as exemplars for review. These twelve were selected to represent a variety of industries. Ten were either cross-sectional or case control studies, two were prospective studies.

.Study design : longitudinal (2) vs. cross-sectional or case control (1) vs. other types of reports (0)

Sampling: more than one (1) vs. one worksite represented (0);

Sampling: more than (1) vs. less than 60% response rate (0);

Measurement: reliability and/or validity were (1) or were not (0) investigated for work factors survey;

Measurement: did (1) or did not (0) include measures of physical work load;

Measurement: did (1) or did not (0) include measures of personal factors or non-work activities;

Multimethod approaches: did (1) or did not (0) include multiple techniques to evaluate work setting;

Outcomes: included physical examinations (2) vs. evaluation of specific symptom features (1) vs. general incidence of musculoskeletal symptoms (0);

Outcomes: did (1) or did not (0) evaluate symptoms based on body location (e.g. hand/arm pain, back pain, neck/shoulder pain); and

Outcomes: did (1) or did not (0) blind clinicians doing physicals from data on independent variables.

Table 2: Evaluation criteria for selecting exemplar studies for review.

Summary of Results

The twelve exemplar studies are listed in Table 3 along with significant findings related to selected non-biomechanical work factors. In the main, the findings are drawn from multivariate analyses that controlled for selected physical job demands and workers' personal characteristics. To summarize the results from these studies, non-biomechanical work-related predictors were first placed into six categories based on the name of the factor. Then, studies evaluating factors in each category were reviewed together. The categories were: (1) *job demand* (included such factors as psychological work load, work pace, deadlines, and fluctuations in work load in addition to job demand), (2) *job content* (included such factors as requirements for attention and stimulation from the job in addition to job content, (3) *job control* (included such factors as influence, task flexibility, and control over rest breaks in addition to job control), (4) *social relationships at work* (included such factors as social support, contact or relationships with coworkers, solitary work, supervisor climate, and supervisor support in addition to social relationships), (5) *work role ambiguity,* and (6) *job satisfaction* (included job task enjoyment). Although it may be argued that a factor could be placed into more than one category, this system allowed some comparison among studies that utilized different measures and alternative names for key factors.

The above method identified nine studies that investigated *job demand* or related variables. Seven of these studies (including three that investigated physical examination findings) found significant associations with musculoskeletal outcomes. The eighth study found a significant association for overstrain in a cross-sectional design, but not on follow up ten years later (Leino & Hänninen 1995). Bergqvist et al. (1995b) did not find a significant relationship for work demand. Similarly, five studies (including two that evaluated clinical findings) out of eight that investigated *job content* or similar variables found significant associations with musculoskeletal outcomes. The sixth study found a significant association for attention demands, but not for job content (Ekberg et al. 1994). Leino and Hänninen (1995) found a significant association in a cross-sectional design, but again not on follow up after ten years. Work content failed to attain significance in the eighth study (Ohlsson et al. 1994). Five studies (including two that evaluated clinical findings) out of nine that investigated *job control* or related factors found significant associations with musculoskeletal outcomes. The sixth and seventh studies found significant associations for control specifically over temporal aspects of the job, but no associations for general job control or influence (Bergqvist et al. 1995b; Skov et al. 1996). The eighth and ninth studies also found no associations for job control (Ohlsson et al. 1994; Leino & Hänninen 1995). Five studies (including two that evaluated clinical findings) out of seven found significant associations in the expected direction between *social relationships* and musculoskeletal outcomes. The sixth study found that very high levels of contact with peers were significantly detrimental (Bergqvist et al. 1995b). Skov et al. (1996) did not find a significant relationship between supervisor support and musculoskeletal outcomes. *Work role ambiguity* was found to be associated with musculoskeletal disorders in two studies. Skov et al. (1996), on the other hand, did not find that musculoskeletal outcomes were significantly associated with role ambiguity or role conflict, but did find a significant association for job insecurity. Additionally, a significant association between *job satisfaction* and musculoskeletal disorders was found in the Bigos et al.(1991) study of worker compensation claims for back injury, but not in the Leclerc et al. (1998) study of CTS outcomes.

Review of Methods

The exemplars chosen for review were selected from among the most carefully designed studies in this field of research. They included workers from a wide diversity of industries: fish processing, construction, manufacturing, sales, newspaper and office work. Community wide studies were also represented. Sample sizes tended to be substantial and adequately representative, outcome measures often included findings from blinded physical examinations in addition to self reported symptoms, and predictor variables were generally assessed using questionnaires with previously investigated psychometrics. Furthermore, for the majority of the studies, potential confounders including the physical aspects of the job and workers' personal characteristics were concomitantly investigated. Additionally, all of the studies included comparisons with subjects who did not have the outcome of interest.

The limitations of these studies are related primarily to design and to measurement. Longitudinal studies of non-biomechanical work factors are sparse in number, yet only prospective studies will allow investigation of temporal relationships between cause and effect. Prospective studies, however, are not without their own pitfalls (Frese & Zapf 1988). The vast majority of studies surveyed workers to collect data on non-biomechanical work factors because they are likely to have the most immediate information about their jobs, and survey techniques are relatively efficient and inexpensive. Additionally, data on workers' perceptions may only be gathered using self reports. Such surveys, however, introduce potential recall bias for the workers who have developed persistent musculoskeletal symptoms or related clinical diagnoses. Observer assessments are thought to offer more objective, if not unbiased, evaluations of the work system. For these reasons, the use of multiple methods to assess the work environment was considered a strength in this review. Multiple survey measures of predictor variables may also be used to strengthen study designs. None of the cross-sectional studies in this set of exemplars, however, fully utilized the multitrait-multimethod approaches that have been recommended (Campbell & Fiske 1959; Frese & Zapf 1988).

Overall, where there were significant associations between the six categories of work factors and musculoskeletal outcomes, they typically indicated modest to moderate increases in risk for the worker with a poorer work environment. Additionally, the strength of the associations varied from study to study, often depending upon whether the outcome measure was symptoms or clinical findings. The method for determining the physical job stresses also varied from study to study and this may account for some of the variation in findings for the non-biomechanical work factors. It is of interest that Johansson and Rubenowitz (1994) added a control variable based on whether the worker thought the symptoms were job-related or not, on the grounds that non-occupational musculoskeletal symptoms are common. This added control measure resulted in an increase in the risk for occupational musculoskeletal symptoms attributed to non-biomechanical work factors. The increased risk was comparable to that obtained for the association of physical work factors with musculoskeletal symptoms.

Investigators tended to use diverse survey questionnaires to assess non-biomechanical work factors. This diversity of measures makes comparisons across studies difficult and suggests a basis for the conflicts in findings reported above. Scales purportedly measuring the same key factors were occasionally based on differing items. The work control scale, for example, in the Leino and Hänninen (1995) study was based on items about access to information, influence over changes, and satisfaction with management attitudes. By contrast, the job control scale in the LeClerc et al. (1998) study was based on items about work breaks, work pace, and control over work quantity. Similarly , Bigos et al. (1991) obtained their most significant results for a single item, enjoyment of job tasks, that was taken from a scale focusing largely on relationships with coworkers and supervisors. Although most measures had been used in previous studies and investigated for their psychometric qualities, few investigators reported psychometric information about the use of the questionnaire in their current study. In the Holmstr m et al. (1992) studies, for example, Cronbach's alpha for the psychosocial scales ranged from 0.72 to 0.45 – thus from adequate to unacceptably low values. Additionally, although a few studies addressed dose response relationships, overall there were few data to inform us about critical gradations of the non-biomechanical work factors that displayed significant relationships with musculoskeletal outcomes. Several studies addressed unique work factors in addition to the more commonly studied six categories above. Findings related to these unique factors often lack replication in subsequent studies even though they are intriguing. Examples include working against different types of deadlines (Bernard et al. 1993, 1994) or the notion of "just in time" production (LeClerc et al. 1998).

Outcome in addition to predictor measures in the study examples demonstrated a lack of consensus among researchers in the field. Not all studies included clinical findings, although it is important to investigate predictors of both self reports of symptoms and clinical diagnoses because of the implications for related suffering, impairment, and disability. For the studies that employed physical examinations, clinical criteria were often standardized but they differed from study to study, making comparisons difficult. Some studies established scores for clinical findings (e.g. Leino and Hänninen 1995), for example, while others focused on establishing clinical diagnoses (e.g. Hales et al. 1992, 1994).

Finally, there is likely to be a synergistic effect among the non-biomechanical factors and between those factors and the biomechanical factors. Few of the studies above investigated interactions among factors other than for the traditional divisions between genders, age groups, or blue and white collar workers. Although it has been suggested that one pathway by which psychosocial factors may influence musculoskeletal outcomes is through increases in biomechanical load, there is a lack of studies which attempt to specify relationships along this pathway (e.g. Feuerstein et al. 1997; Waerstad et al. 1991). Studies are also needed that link psychosocial work stressors with musculoskeletal outcomes via physiological mechanisms (e.g.Theorell et al. 1991; Lundberg et al. 1989); and via social or individual influences on symptom reporting.

Additional Non-Biomechanical Factors

This review has considered the non-biomechanical work factors most commonly addressed in the occupational health literature. Additional factors considered by individual researchers bear further investigation, but have not been as widely studied nor was there time to fully review these studies. Furthermore, occupational health literature focusing on work stress and general health conditions suggests other risk factors that may be associated with musculoskeletal disorders. The work system paradigm offered by Smith and Carayon (1996) provides a useful scheme to organize some of the topics that have received attention from researchers: (1) *Work task*: work rest breaks (e.g. Sauter, Swanson, Conway, & Galinsky 1998; Bergqvist et al. 1995a; Kopardekar & Mital 1994; Wood 1997; Henning et al. 1989), task complexity (e.g.Waerstad et al. 1991), and job enrichment; (2) *Organization*: piecework or incentive pay systems (e.g. Brisson et al. 1992; Vinet et al. 1989; Schleifer 1986), quality improvement teams, and bureaucratic structures (e.g. Billette et al. 1989; Murphy et al. 1997): (3) *Technology*: the increasing computerization of work (e.g. Amick & Celentano 1991 and multiple investigations of VDT use), machine or otherwise externally driven work pace, and electronic monitoring (e.g. Smith, Carayon, Sanders, Lim & LeGrande 1992; Hales et al. 1994); (4) *Work environment*: work climate or work culture (e.g. DeJoy et al. 1995; MacIntosh & Gough 1998). There are also *extra-organizational* factors with the potential to influence reports, diagnoses, and treatment of work-related musculoskeletal symptoms and related disability that initial studies suggest are important to consider. These include regional and other differences in clinical practice (Hadler, 1992; Atcheson et al. 1998) and flutuations in local economies and job availability (Volinn et al. 1991).

Conclusion

This review has considered research on non-biomechanical factors that may influence the development of occupational musculoskeletal symptoms and disorders. Over time there has been considerable improvement in study design and implementation as these topics have drawn the attention of researchers and policy makers. Furthermore, findings from well-designed studies demonstrate increasing consistency. The findings from this review suggest that some personal factors may play a role, albeit a modest one, in the development of CTS. In terms of the broader category of musculoskeletal disorders, non-biomechanical occupational factors appear to have significant associations with health outcomes, even after controlling for personal factors and biomechanical work factors. Although the time to produce this report was limited, it is doubtful that these overall conculsions would have differed in a more extensive review. The findings about exposure to non-biomechanical in addition to biomechanical factors in the work setting, affirm that these disorders are complex and multifactorial.

References

Systemic Disease and CTS

Atcheson, S.G., Ward, J.R., & Lowe, W. (1998). Concurrent medical disease in work-related carpal tunnel syndrome. *Arch Intern Med, 158*, 1506-1512.
Albers, J.W., Brown, M.B., Sima, A.A.F., & Greene, D.A.(1996). Frequency of median mononeuropathy in patients with mild diabetic neuropathy in the early diabetes intervention trial. *Muscle Nerve, 19*, 140-146.
Stevens, J.C., Beard, C.M., O'Fallon,W.M., & Kurland, L.T.(1992). Conditions associated with carpal tunnel syndrome. *Mayo Clin Proc, 67*, 541-548.

Vitamin B6 and CTS

Amadio, P.C.(1985). Pyridoxine as an adjunct in the treatment of carpal tunnel syndrome. *J Hand Surg, 10*, 237-241.
Atisook, R., Benjapibal, M., Sunsaneevithayakul, P., & Roongpisuthipong, A.(1995). Carpal tunnel syndrome during pregnancy: prevalence and blood level of pyridoxine. *J Med. Assoc Thailand, 78*, 410-414.
Ellis, J., Folkers, K., Levy, M., et al.(1982). Response to vitamin B6 deficiency and the carpal tunnel syndrome to pyridoxine. *Proc Natl Acad Sci USA, 79*, 7494-7498.
Ellis, J., Folkers, K., Levy, M., et al.(1981). Therapy with vitamin B6 with and without surgery for treatment of patients having idiopathic carpal tunnel syndrome. *Res Immun Pathol Pharmacol, 33*, 331-334.
Ellis, J., Folkers, K., & Watanabe, T., et al.(1979). Clinical results of a cross-over treatment with pyridoxine and placebo of the carpal tunnel syndrome. *J Clin Nutr*, 2046-2070.
Folkers, K., Ellis, S., & Watanbe, T.(1978). Biomechanical evidence for a deficiency of vitamin B6 in the carpal tunnel syndrome based on a crossover clinical study. *Proc Natl Acad Sci USA, 75*, 3410-3412.
Folkers, K., Willis, R., & Takemura, K.(1985). Biochemical correlations of a deficiency in

vitamin B6, the carpal tunnel syndrome and the Chinese restaurant syndrome. *Int Commun Sys J Med, 9,* 441.

Franzblau, A., Rock, C.L., Werner, R.A., Albers, J.W., Kelly, M.P., & Johnston,E.(1996). The relationship of vitamin B6 to median nerve function and carpal tunnel syndrome among active industrial workers. *J Occup Env Med, 38,* 485-491.

Franzblau, A., Rock, C.L., Werner, R.A., & Albers, J.W.(1998). Vitamin B6, vitamin C, and carpal tunnel syndrome [letter]. *J Occup Environ Med, 40,* 305-309.

Keniston, R.C., Nathan, P.A,, Leklem, J.E., & Lockwood, R.S.(1997). Vitamin B6, vitamin C, and carpal tunnel syndrome. A cross-sectional study of 441 adults. *J Occ Environ Med, 39,* 949-959.

Keyserling,W.M. & Armstrong, T.J.(1992). Ergonomics. In Rom WN, ed. *Environmental and Occupational Medicine.* 2nd. ed. Boston: Little, Brown.

McCann, J. & Davis, R.(1978). Carpal tunnel syndrome, diabetes and pyridoxal. *Aust J Med, 8,* 638-640.

Pregnancy/Gynecologic History and CTS

Bjorkquist, S.E., Lang, A.H., Punnunen, R., et al.(1977). Carpal tunnel syndrome in ovariectomized women. *Acta Obstet Gynecol Scand, 56,*127-130.

deKrom, M.C.T.F.M., Kester, A.D.M., Knipschild, P.G., & Spaans, F.(1990). Risk factors for carpal tunnel syndrome. *Am J Epid, 132,* 1102-1110.

Gould, J.S. & Wissinger, A.(1978). Carpal tunnel syndrome in pregnancy. *South Med J, 71,* 144-145.

Masey, E.W.(1978). Carpal tunnel syndrome in pregnancy. *Obstet Gynecol Surg, 33,*145-147.

Sabour, M. & Fadel, H.(1970). The carpal tunnel syndrome: a new complication ascribed to the pill. *Am J Obstet Gynecol, 107,*1265-1267.

Soferman, N., Weissman, S.L., & Haimou, M.(1964). Acroparesthesias in pregnancy. *Am J Obstet Gynecol, 89,* 528-31.

Obesity

Bigos, S.J., Battie, M.C., Spengler, D.M., et al.(1991). A prospective study of work perceptions and psychosocial factors affecting the report of back injury. *Spine, 16,* 1-6 .

Cannon, L.J., Bernacki, E.J., & Walter, D.S.(1982). Personal and occupational factors associated with carpal tunnel syndrome. *J Occup Med, 23,* 255-258.

de Krom, M.C., Kester, A.D., Knipschild, P.G., & Spanns, F.(1990). Risk factors for carpal tunnel syndrome. *Am J Epidemiol, 132,* 1102-1110.

Dieck, G.S. & Kelsey, J.L.(1995). An epidemiologic study of the carpal tunnel syndrome in an adult female population. *Prev Med, 14,* 63-69.

Gerr, F. & Letz, R.(1992). Risk factors for carpal tunnel syndrome in industry: Blaming the victim? *Occup Med, 34,* 1117-1118.

Letz, R. & Gerr, F. (1994). Covariates of human peripheral nerve function: I. nerve conduction velocity and amplitude. *Neurotoxicology and Teratology, 16,* 95-104.

Nathan, P.A., Keniston, R.C., Myers, L.D., & Meadows, K.D.(1992). Obesity as a risk factor for slowing of sensory conduction of the median nerve in industry: A cross-sectional and longitudinal study involving 429 workers. *J Medicine, 34,* 379-383.

Ryden, L.A., Molgaard, C.A., Bobbitt, S., & Conway, J.(1989). Occupational low-back injury in a hospital employee population: an epidemiologic analysis of multiple risk factors of a high-risk occupational group. *Spine, 14,* 315-20.

Vessey, M.P., Villard-Mackintosh, L., & Yeates, D.(1990). Epidemiology of carpal tunnel syndrome in women of childbearing age. Findings in a large cohort study. *Int J Epidemiol, 19,* 655-659.

Werner, R.A., Albers, J.W., Franzblau, A., & Armstrong, T.J.(1997). The influence of body mass index and work activity in determining the prevalence of median mononeuropathy at the wrist. *J Occ Env Med, 54,* 268-271.

Werner RA, Albers JW, Franzblau A, & Armstrong TJ.(1994). The relationship between body mass index and the diagnosis of carpal tunnel syndrome. *Muscle Nerve, 17,* 632-636

Zwerling, C., Ryan, J., & Schootman, M.(1993). A case-control study of risk factors for industrial low back injury. The utility of preplacement screening in defining high-risk groups. *Spine, 18,* 1242-7.

Zwerling, C., Sprince, N.L., Wallace, R.B., Davis, C.S., Whitten, P.S., & Heeringa, S.G.(1996). Risk factors for occupational injuries among older workers: an analysis of the health and retirement study. *AJPH, 86,* 1306-9.

Gender and CTS

Ashbury, F.D.(1995). Occupational repetitive strain injuries and gender in Ontario, 1986 to 1991. *J Occup Env Med, 37,* 479-85.

Bigos, S.J., Battie, M.C., Spengler, D.M., et al.(1991). A prospective study of work perceptions and psychosocial factors affecting the report of back injury. *Spine, 16,* 1-6.

Franklin, G.M., Haug, J., Heyer, N., Checkoway, H., & Peck, N.(1991). Occupational carpal tunnel syndrome in Washington state, 1984-1988. *AJPH, 81,*741-6.

Kendall D. (1960) Aetiology, diagnosis, and treatment of paraesthesia in the hands. *British Med J 3*:1633-1640.

Phalen G. (1972) The carpal tunnel syndrome: clinical evaluation of 598 hands. *Clin Orthop Relat Res; 83*:29-40.

Phillips R. (1967) Carpal tunnel syndrome as a manifestation of systemic disease. *Ann Rheum Dis 26(1):* 59-63.

Stevens, J.C., Sun, S., Beard, C.M., O'Fallon, W.M., & Kurland, L.T.(1988). Carpal tunnel syndrome in Rochester, Minnesota, 1961-1980. *Neurology, 38,*134-138.

Tanzer R. (1959). The carpal tunnel syndrome. *J Bone Joint Surg [Am], 41*:626-634.

Werner, R.A., Albers, J.W., Franzblau, A., & Armstrong, T.J.(1997). The influence of body mass index and work activity in determining the prevalence of median mononeuropathy at the wrist. *J Occup Env Med, 54,* 268-271.

Zwerling,C., Sprince, N.L., Ryan, J., & Jones, M.P.(1993). Occupational injuries: comparing the rates of male and female postal workers. *Am J Epid, 138,* 46-55.

Carpal Canal Size/ Wrist shape

Backhouse, K.M. & Churchill-Davidson, D.(1975). Anomalous palmaris longus muscle producing carpal tunnel-like compression. *Hand, 7,* 22-24

Bauer, J.M. & Trusell, J.J.(1992). Palmaris profundus causing carpal tunnel syndrome. *Orthopaedics, 15,* 1348-50.

Bleecker, M.L., Bihlman, M., Moreland, R., & Tipton, A.(1985). Carpal tunnel syndrome: role of carpal canal size. *Neurology, 35,* 1599-1604.

Brown, F.E., Morgan, G.J., Taylor, T., et al.(1984). Coexistence of muscle anomalies and rheumatoid arthritis in patients with carpal tunnel syndrome. *Clin Exp Rheumatol 2,* 297-302.

Cobb, T.K., An.K.N., Cooney, W.P. et al. (1984). Lumbrical muscle incursion into the carpal tunnel during finger flexion. *J Hand Surg, 4,* 434-438.

Gelmers, H.(1981). Primary carpal tunnel stenosis as a cause of entrapment of the median nerve. *Acta Neurochir, 55, 317*-320.

Johnson, E.W., Gatens, T., Poindexter, D. et al.(1983). Wrist dimensions: correlation with median sensory latencies. *Arch Phys Med Rehabil, 64,* 556-557.

Masgaradeh, M., Schneck, C.D., Bonakdarpour, A,, Mitra, A., & Conaway, D.(1989). Carpal Tunnel: MR Imaging Part II. Carpal tunnel syndrome. *Radiology 171,* 749-754.

Nakamichi, K. & Tachibana, S.(1995). Small hand as a risk factor for idiopathic carpal tunnel syndrome. *Muscle Nerve, 18,* 664-666.

Neviaser, R.J.(1974). Flexor digitorum superficialis indicis and carpal tunnel syndrome. *Hand, 6,*155-156.

Radecki, P.(1994). A gender specific wrist ratio and the likelihood of a median nerve abnormality at the carpal tunnel. *Am J Phys Med Rehabil, 73,* 157-162.

Werner, R.A., Albers, J.W., Franzblau, A., & Armstrong, T.J.(1997). The influence of body mass index and work activity in determining the prevalence of median mononeuropathy at the wrist. *J Occup Env Med, 54,* 268-271.

Winn, F.J. & Habes, D.J.(1990). Carpal tunnel area as a risk factor for carpal tunnel syndrome. *Muscle Nerve, 13,* 254-258.

Aging and CTDs

Bigos, S.J., Battie, M.C., Spengler, D.M., Fisher, L.D., Fordyce,W,E., Hansson, T., Nachemson, A.L., & Zeh, J.(1992). A longitudinal, prospective study of industrial back injury reporting. *Clinical Orthopaedics & Related Research,* 21-34.

Bigos, S.J., Battie, M.C., Spengler, D.M., et al.(1991). A prospective study of work perceptions and psychosocial factors affecting the report of back injury. *Spine, 16,* 1-6.

Burton, A.K., Tillotson, K.M., & Troup, J.D.(1989). Prediction of low-back trouble frequency in a working population. *Spine, 14,* 939-946.

Cannon, L.J., Bernacki, E.J., & Walter, D.S.(1982). Personal and occupational factors associated with carpal tunnel syndrome. *J Occup Med, 23,* 255-258.

Daltroy, L.H., Larson, M.G., Wright, E.A., Malspeis, S., Fossel, A.H., Ryan, J., Zwerling, C., & Liang, M.H.(1991). A case-control study of risk factors for industrial low back injury: implications for primary and secondary prevention programs. *Am J Ind Med, 20,* 505-15.

deKrom, M.C.T.F.M., Kester, A.D.M., Knipschild, P.G., & Spaans, F.(1990). Risk factors for carpal tunnel syndrome. *Am J Epid, 132,* 1102-1110.

Dieck, G.S. & Kelsey, J.L.(1985). An epidemiologic study of the carpal tunnel syndrome in an adult female population. *Prev Med, 14,* 63-69.

Dyck, P.J., Litchy,W.J., Lehman, K.A. et al.(1995). Variables influencing neuropathic endpoints: the Rochester diabetic neuropathy study of healthy subjects. *Neurology, 45,* 1115-1121.

Letz, R. & Gerr, F.(1994). Covariates of human peripheral nerve function: I. nerve conduction velocity and amplitude. *Neurotoxicology and Teratology, 16*, 95-104.

Reisbord, L.S. & Greenland, S.(1985). Factors associated with self-reported back-pain prevalence: a population-based study. *J Chr Dis, 38,* 691-702.

Stetson, D.S., Albers, J.W., Silverstein, B.A., et al.(1992). Effects of age, sex, and anthropometric factors on nerve conduction measures. *Muscle Nerve, 15,* 1095-1104.

Stevens, J.C., Beard, C.M., O'Fallon, W.M., & Kurland, L.T.(1992). Conditions associated with carpal tunnel syndrome. *Mayo Clin Proc, 67,* 541-548.

Stevens, J.C., Sun, S., Beard, C.M., O'Fallon,W.M., & Kurland, L.T.(1988). Carpal tunnel syndrome in Rochester, Minnesota, 1961-1980. *Neurology, 38,* 134-138.

Vessey, M.P., Villard-Mackintosh, L., & Yeates, D.(1990). Epidemiology of carpal tunnel syndrome in women of childbearing age. Findings in a large cohort study. *Int J Epidemiol, 19,* 655-659.

Werner, R.A., Albers, J.W., Franzblau, A., & Armstrong, T.J.(1997). The influence of body mass index and work activity in determining the prevalence of median mononeuropathy at the wrist. *J Occup Env Med, 54,* 268-271.

Werner, R.A., Albers, J.W., Franzblau, A., & Armstrong, T.J. (1994). The relationship between body mass index and the diagnosis of carpal tunnel syndrome. *Muscle Nerve, 17,* 632-636.

Physical Conditioning

Battie, M.C., Bigos, S.J., Fisher, L.D. et al.(1989). Isometric lifting strength as a predictor of industrial back pain reports. *Spine,* 851-856.

Battie, M.C., Bigos, S.J., Fisher, L.D., Spengler, D.M., Hansson, T.H., Nachemson, A.L., & Wortley, M.D.(1990). Anthropometric and clinical measures as predictors of back pain complaints in industry: a prospective study. *J Spinal Disorders, 3,* 195-204.

Battie, M.C., Bigos, S.J., Fisher, L.D., Hansson, T.H., Nachemson, A.L., Spengler, D.M., Wortley, M.D., & Zeh, J.(1989). A prospective study of the role of cardiovascular risk factors and fitness in industrial back pain complaints. *Spine, 14,*141-7.

Milgrom, C., Finestone, A., Lev, B., Wiener, M., & Floman,Y.(1993). Overexertional lumbar and thoracic back pain among recruit: a prospective study of risk factors. *J Spine Disorders, 6,*187-93.

Milgrom,C., Giladi, M., Stein et al.(1986). Medial tibial pain: a prospective study of its cause among recruits. *Clin Orthop, 213,*167-71.

Nathan, P.A. & Keniston, R.C.(1993). Carpal tunnel syndrome and its relation to general physical condition. *Hand Clinics, 9,* 253-261.

Nathan, P.A., Keniston, R.C., Lockwood, R.S., & Meadows, K.D.(1996). Tobacco, caffeine, alcohol, and carpal tunnel syndrome in American industry. A cross-sectional study of 1464 workers. *J OccupEnvMed, 38,* 290-298.

Shwayhat, A.F., Linenger, J.M., Hofherr, L.K.et al.(1994). Profiles of exercise history and overuse injuries among united states navy sea, air and land recruits. *Am J Sports Med, 22,*

835-840.

Westgaard, R.H., Jensen, C., & Hansen, K.(1993). Individual and work-related risk factors associated with symptoms of musculoskeletal complaints. *Int Arch Occup Environ Health, 64*, 405-13.

Genetics and CTDs

Battie, M.C., Videman, T., Gibbons, L.E., Fisher, L.D., Manninen, H., & Gill, K.(1995). 1995 Volvo Award in clinical sciences. Determinants of lumbar disc degeneration. A study relating lifetime exposures and magnetic resonance imaging findings in identical twins. *Spine, 20*, 2601-2612.

Danta, G.(1975). Familial carpal tunnel syndrome with onset in childhood. *J Neurol Neurosurg Psychiatry, 38*, 350-355.

Radecki, P.(1994). The familial occurrence of carpal tunnel syndrome. *Muscle Nerve, 17*, 325-330.

Richardson, J.K.(1997). A familial predisposition toward lumbar disc injury. *Spine, 22*, 1487-1493.

Non-biomechanical Work Factors–Exemplar Studies

Bergqvist, U., Wolgast, E., Nilsson, B., & Voss, M. (1995b). Musculoskeletal disorders among visual display terminal workers: individual, ergonomic, and work organizational factors. *Ergonomics, 38*(4), 763-76.

Bernard, B., Sauter, S., Petersen, M., Fine, L., & Hales, T. (1993). *HETA 90-013-2277: Los Angeles Times* . Cinncinati OH: National Institute for Occupational Safety and Health.

Bernard, B., Sauter, S., Fine, L., Petersen, M., & Hales, T. (1994). Job task and psychosocial risk factors for work-related musculoskeletal disorders among newspaper employees. *Scand J Work Environ Health, 20*(6), 417-26.

Bigos, S. J., Battie, M. C., Spengler, D. M., Fisher, L. D., Fordyce, W. E., Hansson, T., Nachemson, A. L., & Zeh, J. (1992). A longitudinal, prospective study of industrial back injury reporting. *Clinical Orthopaedics and Related Research*(279), 21-34.

Ekberg, K., Bjorkqvist, B., Malm, P., Bjerre-Kiely, B., Karlsson, M., & Axelson, O. (1994). Case-control study of risk factors for disease in the neck and shoulder area. *Occup Environ Med, 51*(4), 262-6.

Hales, T. R., Sauter, S. L., Peterson, M. R., Fine, L. J., Putz-Anderson, V., Schleifer, L. R., Ochs, T. T., & Bernard, B. P. (1992). *HETA 89-299-2230: US West Communications*. Cinncinati OH: National Institute for Occupational Safety and Health.

Hales, T. R., Sauter, S. L., Peterson, M. R., Fine, L. J., Putz-Anderson, V., Schleifer, L. R., Ochs, T. T., & Bernard, B. P. (1994). Musculoskeletal disorders among visual display terminal users in a telecommunications company. *Ergonomics, 37*(10), 1603-21.

Holmström, E., Moritz, U., & Engholm, G. (1995). Musculoskeletal disorders in construction workers. *Occup Med, 10*(2), 295-312.

Holmström, E. B., Lindell, J., & Moritz, U. (1992a). Low back and neck/shoulder pain in construction workers: occupational workload and psychosocial risk factors. Part 1: Relationship to low back pain. *Spine, 17*(6), 663-71.

Holmström, E. B., Lindell, J., & Moritz, U. (1992b). Low back and neck/shoulder pain in construction workers: occupational workload and psychosocial risk factors. Part 2: Relationship to neck and shoulder pain. *Spine, 17*(6), 672-7.

Johansson, J., & Rubenowitz, S. (1994). Risk indicators in the psychosocial and physical work environment for work-related neck, shoulder, and low back symptoms: A study among blue- and white-collar workers in eight companies. *Scand J Rehab Med, 26,* 131-142.

Lagerström, M., Wenemark, M., Hagberg, M., & Hjelm, E. W. (1995). Occupational and individual factors related to musculoskeletal symptoms in five body regions among Swedish nursing personnel. *Int Arch Occup Environ Health, 68*(1), 27-35.

Leclerc, A., Franchi, P., Cristofari, M. F., Delemotte, B., Mereau, P., Teyssier-Cotte, C., & Touranchet, A. (1998). Carpal tunnel syndrome and work organisation in repetitive work: a cross sectional study in France. Study Group on Repetitive Work. *Occup Environ Med, 55*(3), 180-7.

Leino, P. I., & Hänninen, V. (1995). Psychosocial factors at work in relation to back and limb disorders. *Scand J Work Environ Health, 21*(2), 134-42.

Ohlsson, K., Hansson, G. A., Balogh, I., Stromberg, U., Palsson, B., Nordander, C., Rylander, L., & Skerfving, S. (1994). Disorders of the neck and upper limbs in women in the fish processing industry. *Occup Environ Med, 51*(12), 826-32.

Skov, T., Borg, V., & Ørhede, E. (1996). Psychosocial and physical risk factors for musculoskeletal disorders of the neck, shoulders, and lower back in salespeople. *Occup Environ Med, 53*(5), 351-6.

Non-biomechanical Work Factors - Other References

Amick III, B. C., & Celentano, D. D. (1991). Structural determinants of the psychosocial work environment: Introducing technology in the work stress framework. *Ergonomics, 34,* 625-646.

Armstrong, T. J., Buckle, P., Fine, L. J., Hagberg, M., Jonsson, B., Kilbom, A., Kuorinka, I. A. A., Silverstein, B. A., Sjogaard, G., & Viikari-Juntura, E. R. (1993). A conceptual model for work-related neck and upper-limb musculoskeletal disorders. *Scand J Work Environ. Health, 19,* 73-84.

Bergqvist, U., Wolgast, E., Nilsson, B., & Voss, M. (1995). The influence of VDT work on musculoskeletal disorders. *Ergonomics, 38,* 754-762.

Billette, A., Carrier, M., & Bernier, M. (1990). The social organization of work and health problems: A study of word processing secretaries in large bureaucracies. *Work With Display Units, 89,* 257-271.

Bongers, P. M., De Winter, C. R., Kompier, M. A., & Hildebrandt, V. H. (1993). Psychosocial factors at work and musculoskeletal disease. *Scand J Work Environ. Health, 19,* 297-312.

Brisson, C., Vezina, M., & Vinet, A.(1992). Health problems of women employed in jobs involving psychological and ergonomic stressors: The case of garment workers in Quebec. *Women and Health, 18,* 49-65.

DeJoy, D., Murphy, L. R., & Gershon, R. M. (1995). Safety climate in health care setting. *Advances in Industrial Ergonomics and Safety, 7,* 923-929.

Feuerstein, M. (1996). Workstyle: Definition, empirical support, and implications for prevention, evaluation, and rehabilitation of occupational upper extremity disorders. In S.D. Moon and S.L. Sauter (Eds.). *Beyond Biomechanics: Psychosocial Aspects of Musculoskeletal Disorders in Office Work*. London: Taylor & Francis.

Feuerstein, M., Carosella, A.M., Burrell, L.M., Marshall, L., & DeCaro, J. (1997). Occupational upper extremity symptoms in sign language interpreters: prevalence and correlates of pain, function, and work disability. *J Occup Rehab, 7*, 187-205.

Frese, M., & Zapf, D. (1988). Methodological issues in the study of work stress: Objective vs subjective measurement of work stress and the question of longitudinal studies. In C. L. Cooper and R. Payne (Eds.), *Causes, Coping and Consequences of Stress at Work*, Chichester, New York: John Wiley.

Hadler, N. M. (1992). Arm pain in the workplace: A small area analysis. *Journal of Medicine. 34*, 113-119.

Henning, R. A., Sauter, S. L., Salvendy, G., & Krieg Jr, E. F. (1989). Microbreak length, performance, and stress in a data entry task. *Ergonomics, 32*, 855-864.

Johnson, J. V. (1989). Control, collectivity and the psychosocial work environment. In S. K. Sauter, J. J. Hurrell, Jr. and C. L. Cooper (Eds.), *Job Control and Worker Health*. New York: John Wiley and Sons.

Karasek, R., Baker, D., Marxer, F., Ahlbom, A., & Theorell, T. (1981). Job decision latitude, Job demands, and cardiovascular disease. *AJPH, 71*, 694-705.

Kopardekar, P., & Mital, A. (1994). The effect of different work-rest schedules on fatigue and performance of a simulated directory assistance operator's task. *Ergonomics, 37*, 1697-1707.

Lundberg, U., Granqvist, M., Hansson, T., Magnusson, M., & Wallin, L. (1989). Psychological and physiological stress responses during repetitive work at an assembly line. *Work & Stress, 3*, 143-153.

Macintosh, M., & Gough, R. (1998). The impact of workplace change on occupational health and safety: A study of four manufacturing plants. *Human Factors and Ergonomics in Manufacturing, 8*, 155-175.).

Murphy, L., Grosch, J., Gershon, R., & DeJoy, D. (1997). Safety climate and injuries: The case of occupational exposure to HIV. In P. Seppala, T. Luopajarvi, C-H Nygard, and M. Mattila (Eds.). *Proceedings of the 13th Triennial Congress of the International Ergonomics Association, From Experience to Innovation*, IEA'97 . Helsinki, Finland: Finnish Institute of Occupational Health.

Sauter, S., Swanson, N., Conway, F., Galinsky, T., & Lim, S.Y. (1997, April 13-16, 1997). *Redesign of rest-breaks and musculoskeletal discomfort in video display terminal work*. Paper presented at the Marconi Research Conference, Marshall, CA.

Sauter, S. L., & Swanson, N. G. (1996). An ecological model of musculoskeletal disorders in office work.. In S.D. Moon and S.L. Sauter (Eds.). *Beyond Biomechanics: Psychosocial Aspects of Musculoskeletal Disorders in Office Work*. London: Taylor & Francis.

Schleifer, L. M. (1987). An evaluation of mood disturbances and somatic discomfort under slow computer-response time and incentive-pay conditions. *Work With Display Units, 86*, 793-802.

Smith, M.J., Carayon, P., Sanders, K.J., Lim, Soo-Yee and LeGrande, D. (1992). Employee stress and health complaints in jobs with and without electronic performance monitoring. *Applied Ergonomics, 1*, 17-28.

Smith, M.J. (1997). Psychosocial aspects of working with video display terminals (VDTs) and employee physical and mental health. *Ergonomics, 40,* 1002-1015.

Smith, M.J., & Sainfort, P.C. (1989). A balance theory of job design for stress reduction. *Intl J Ind Ergo, 4,* 67-79.

Smith, M.J., & Carayon, P.C. (1996). Work organization, stress and cumulative trauma disorders. In S. Moon and S. Sauter (Eds.), *Beyond Biomechanics: Psychosocial Aspects of Cumulative Trauma Disorders.* London: Taylor & Francis.

Theorell, T., Harms-Ringdahl, K., Ahlberg-Hulten, G., & Westin, B. (1991). Psychosocial job factors and symptoms from the locomotor system - A multicausal analysis. *Scand J Rehab Med, 23,* 165-173.

Vinet, A., Vezina, M., Brisson, C., & Bernard, P. M. (1989). Piecework, repetitive work and medicine use in the clothing industry. *Social Science and Medicine, 28,* 1283-1288.

Waersted, M., & Bjorklund, R. A. (1991). Shoulder muscle tension induced by two VDU-based tasks of different complexity. *Ergonomics, 34,* 137-150.

Wood, D. D. (1997). Minimizing fatigue during repetitive jobs: Optimal work-rest schedules. *Human Factors and Ergonomics Society, 39,* 83-101.

Volinn E., Van Koevring, D., & Loeser, J.D. (1991). Back sprain in industry: The role of socio-economic factors in chronicity. *Spine, 16,* 542-8.

TABLE 3: Summary of significant findings from reviewed studies (N=12).

AUTHORS	DESIGN	SAMPLE: INDUSTRY (SIZE=STUDY TOTAL)	MS OUTCOMES	SIGNIFICANT FINDINGS FOR NON-BIOMECHANICAL WORK FACTORS	
Bergqvist et al. 1995b	Cross sectional	Office work (n=260)	Back discomfort	None	
			Neck/shoulder discomfort	Limited break opportunity	OR: 2.7 (CI:1.2-5.9)
			Intense neck/shoulder discomfort	None	
			Tension neck	Limited break opportunity	OR: 7.4 (CI:3.1-17.4)
			Cervical diagnoses	None	
			Shoulder diagnoses	Limited break opportunity	OR: 3.3 (CI:1.4-7.9)
				Low task flexibility	OR: 3.2 (CI:1.2-8.5)
			Arm/hand discomfort	Extreme peer contacts	OR: 2.1 (CI:1.1-1.4)
			Arm/hand diagnoses	Extreme peer contacts	OR: 4.5 (CI:1.3-15.5)
Bernard et al. 1993	Cross sectional	Newspaper (n=1050)	Neck symptoms	Hours on deadline	OR: 1.7 (CI:1.4-3.0)
				Work variance	OR: 1.5 (CI:1.1-1.8)
				Import. of ergon. to mgmt.	OR: 1.4 (CI:1.2-1.9)
			Shoulder symptoms	Job decision making	OR: 1.6 (CI:1.2-2.1)
				Job pressure	OR: 1.4 (CI:1.0-1.9)
			Hand/wrist symptoms	Hours on deadline	OR: 1.7 (CI:1.2-2.3)
				Supervisor support	OR: 1.4 (CI:1.1-1.6)
			Any hand/wrist diagnoses	Changes in workload	OR: 3.2 (CI:2.5-4.1)
Bigos et al. 1991	Prospective	Aircraft manufacture (n=3030)	Back diagnoses	Enjoy job	RR: 1.7 (CI:1.31-22.21)
Ekberg et al. 1994	Case control	Diverse – community (cases n=109; control A n=136, control B n=327)	Neck/shoulder diagnoses	Work pace - medium	OR: 2.5 (CI:1.0-6.2)
				- rushed	OR: 3.5 (CI:1.3-9.4)
				Work role ambiguity (high)	OR:16.5 (CI:6.0-46)
				Attention demands (high)	OR: 3.8 (CI:1.4-11)

TABLE 3 continued

AUTHORS	DESIGN	SAMPLE: INDUSTRY (SIZE=STUDY TOTAL)	MS OUTCOMES	SIGNIFICANT FINDINGS FOR NON-BIOMECHANICAL WORK FACTORS	
Hales et al. 1994	Cross sectional	Telecommunications (n=573)	Neck disorders	Job decision making	OR: 4.2 (CI: 2.1-8.6)
				Lack of production standard	OR: 3.5 (CI:1.5-8.3)
				Fear of replace. by computer	OR: 3.0 (CI: 1.5-6.1)
				Hi inform. process.demand	OR: 3.0 (CI: 1.4-6.2)
			Shoulder disorders	Task variety	OR: 2.9 (CI:1.5-5.8)
				Work pressure	OR: 2.4 (CI: 1.1-5.5)
				Fear of replace. by computer	OR: 2.7 (CI: 1.3-5.8)
			Elbow disorders	Fear of replace. by computer	OR: 2.9 (CI: 1.4-6.1)
				Job decision making	OR: 2.8 (CI: 1.4-5.7)
				Surges in workload	OR: 2.4 (CI: 1.2-5.0)
			Hand/wrist disorders	Hi inform. process.demand	OR: 2.3 (CI: 1.3-4.3)
Holmström et al. 1992	Cross sectional	Construction (n=1773)	Back symptoms	Qualitative demands	OR: 1.1 (CI: 1.0-1.4)
				Quantitative demands	OR: 1.3 (CI: 1.2-1.6)
				Solitary work	OR: 1.1 (CI: 1.0-1.2)
			Severe back symptoms	Quantitative demands	OR: 2.0 (CI: 1.2-3.2)
				Solitary work	OR: 1.5 (CI: 1.2-1.9)
				Understimulation	OR: 2.2 (CI: 1.4-3.3)
			Neck/shoulder symptoms	Qualitative demands	OR: 1.2 (CI: 1.0-1.4)
				Quantitative demands	OR: 1.4 (CI: 1.2-1.7)
				Solitary work	OR: 1.1 (CI: 1.0-1.2)
			Severe neck/shoulder symptoms	Qualitative demands	OR: 1.4 (CI: 1.0-2.0)
				Quantitative demands	OR: 3.0 (CI: 2.1-4.0)
				Solitary work	OR: 1.5 (CI: 1.2-1.8)

TABLE 3 continued

AUTHORS	DESIGN	SAMPLE: INDUSTRY (SIZE=STUDY TOTAL)	MS OUTCOMES	SIGNIFICANT FINDINGS FOR NON-BIOMECHANICAL WORK FACTORS	
Johnasson & Rubenowitz 1994	Cross sectional	Manufacturing (blue collar n=241; white collar n=209)	Work-related back symptom	Blue collar Supervisor climate Understimulation Psych. Workload	partial correl.coefficient = 0.18 partial correl.coefficient = 0.16 partial correl.coefficient = 0.35
			Work-related neck symptoms	Blue collar Supervisor climate Understimulation Psych. Workload White collar Control over work Psych. Workload	partial correl.coefficient = 0.16 partial correl.coefficient = 0.14 partial correl.coefficient = 0.25 partial correl.coefficient = 0.17 partial correl.coefficient = 0.21
			Work-related shoulder symptoms	Blue collar Control over work Supervisor climate Understimulation Psych. Workload White collar Control over work Supervisor climate Understimulation Coworker relations Psych. Workload	partial correl.coefficient = 0.18 partial correl.coefficient = 0.16 partial correl.coefficient = 0.26 partial correl.coefficient = 0.27 partial correl.coefficient = 0.17 partial correl.coefficient = 0.20 partial correl.coefficient = 0.22 partial correl.coefficient = 0.24 partial correl.coefficient = 0.21
Lagerström et al.1995	Cross sectional	Health care (n=688)	Back symptoms Severe back symptoms Neck symptoms Severe neck symptoms Shoulder symptoms Severe shoulder symptoms Hand symptoms Severe hand symptoms	Supervisor support None Supervisor support Work demand Work control Work demand Understimulation None	OR: 1.8 (CI: 1.1-2.8) OR: 2.0 (CI: 1.3-3.2) OR: 1.8 (CI: 1.1-2.9) OR: 1.7 (CI: 1.1-2.7) OR: 1.6 (CI: 1.0-2.6) OR: 1.6 (CI: 1.1-2.4)
Leclerc et al. 1998	Cross sectional with control group	Multiple (exposed to repetitive work n=1210; non-exposed controls n=337)	CTS	Job control	OR: 1.6 (CI: 1.0-2.4)

TABLE 3 continued

AUTHORS	DESIGN	SAMPLE: INDUSTRY (SIZE=STUDY TOTAL)	MS OUTCOMES	SIGNIFICANT FINDINGS FOR NON-BIOMECHANICAL WORK FACTORS	
Leino et al. 1995	Prospective	Manufacturing (n=411)	Musculoskeletal morbidity index: Cross sectional models		
			Symptoms (Model R^2=0.22)	Overstrain	Beta=0.21 (p<0.001)
				Work content	Beta=0.16 (p<0.001)
			Findings (Model R^2=0.23)	Work content	Beta=0.13 (p<0.001)
				Overstrain	Beta=0.12 (p<0.001)
			Follow up models		
			Symptoms (Model R^2=0.36)	Social relations	Beta=0.11 (p<0.01)
			Findings (Model R^2=0.31)	Social relations	Beta=0.15 (p<0.001)
Ohlsson et al. 1994	Cross sectional with control group	Fish processing (exposed to industrial work n=206; non-exposed controls n=208)	Neck/shoulder symptoms	Work strain	
				-medium exposed	OR: 2.5 (CI: 1.2-5.5)
				control	OR: ns
				-high exposed	OR:5.5 (CI: 2.4-12)
				control	OR:3.4 (CI: 1.4-7.9)
			Neck shoulder diagnoses	Fellowship	
				-high exposed	OR: ns
				control	OR: 3.3 (CI: 1.0- 10.8)
				Work strain	
				-medium exposed	OR: 2.9 (CI: 1.1-7.6)
				control	OR: ns
				-high exposed	OR: 6.6 (CI: 2.6-17)
				control	OR: 3.0 (CI: 1.1-8.7)
			Hand/elbows – not presented		
Skov et al. 1996	Cross sectional	Sales (n=1306)	Back symptoms	Social contact -next to least	OR: 1.5 (CI: 1.0-2.1)
				-least	OR: 1.8 (CI: 1.2-2.6)
				Overwork -next to most	OR: 1.4 (CI: 1.2-2.0)
				-most	OR: 2.0 (CI: 1.4-3.0)
			Neck symptoms	Work variation -lowest	OR: 1.8 (CI: 1.2-2.7)
				Control over time –low	OR: 1.4 (CI: 1.1-1.9)
				Competition -high	OR: 1.4 (CI: 1.1-1.9)
			Shoulder symptoms	Work demand –highest	OR: 1.5 (CI: 1.0-2.1)
				Uncertainty of employment	
				-next to highest	OR: 1.8 (CI: 1.3-2.5)
				-highest	OR: 1.5 (CI: 1.0-2.3)

A REVIEW OF RESEARCH ON INTERVENTIONS TO CONTROL MUSCULOSKELETAL DISORDERS

Michael J. Smith, Ben-Tzion Karsh, Francisco B. P. Moro
Dept. of Industrial Engineering, University of Wisconsin-Madison

A. Introduction

The purpose of our paper is to address the question posed by the National Academy of Sciences (NAS) - 'What is the state of available scientific evidence on interventions to control musculoskeletal disorders?' Toward this end we will also be answering the following four questions: (1) What kinds of interventions have been assessed for their effectiveness in controlling the incidence and/or severity of musculoskeletal disorders of the back and/or upper extremities? (2) What do the overall results from these studies reveal about the effectiveness of these interventions? (3) How trustworthy is the research basis for drawing conclusions on intervention effectiveness? (4) Do studies show the relative contributions of biomechanical and other factors to intervention effectiveness? We have intentionally limited the analysis in this paper to peer reviewed journal articles. Although we also reviewed proceedings documents and book chapters, in our opinion, the latter do not meet the criteria for "scientific evidence" as well. Therefore these were excluded from the analysis. We did not review trade journal articles or articles in the popular press, nor did we review the NIOSH or OSHA documents on successful ergonomic interventions.

This paper begins with a description of the model that served as our conceptual framework. We then describe the methodology used to select papers for this review. The research evidence relating to the efficacy of laboratory interventions, field interventions with healthy subjects, and field interventions with injured subjects is then presented, followed by concluding remarks about the state of the scientific knowledge on interventions to control musculoskeletal disorders.

We propose a model to examine interventions to control musculoskeletal disorders based on the balance theory of Smith & Carayon-Sainfort (1989, 1995). This model states that working conditions (and other environmental features outside of work) can produce a "stress load" on the person. That load can have biomechanical, physiological and psychological consequences such as forces on the joints, increased blood pressure and/or perceptions of pain. The load can produce a negative influence on the person which leads to "strain" if it exceeds the person's capacity. This has been called a "misfit" between the environmental demands and the personal resources. If exposure continues for a prolonged time period, then this strain can produce serious musculoskeletal disorders.

Figure 1 illustrates a system's model for conceptualizing the various elements of a work system, that is, the loads that working conditions can exert on workers. In this model these various elements interact to determine the way in which work is done and the effectiveness of the work in achieving individual and organizational needs and goals. At the center of this model is the individual with his/her physical characteristics, perceptions, personality and behaviors. The

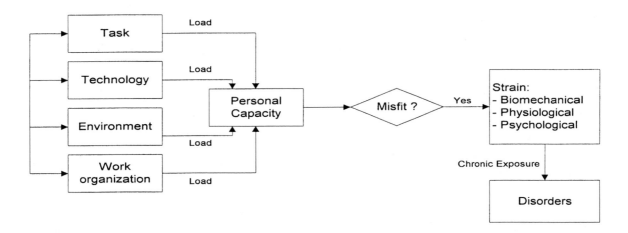

Figure 1: Balance Model of Work System Misfit

individual has technologies available to perform specific job tasks. The capabilities of the technologies affect performance and also the worker's skills and knowledge needed for its effective use. The task requirements also affect the skills and knowledge needed. Both the tasks and technologies affect the content of the job and the physical demands the job makes on the person. The tasks with their technologies are carried out in a work setting that comprises the physical and the social environment. There is also an organizational structure that defines the nature and level of individual involvement, interaction and control.

The purpose of interventions to control musculoskeletal disorders is to reduce the stress load to eliminate strain. As discussed below, this can be done by modifying the elements of the work system shown in Figure 1. Another tactic to control musculoskeletal disorders is to increase the capacity of the individual to handle greater loads, thereby reducing the possibility of a misfit.

B. The Nature of Interventions to Control Musculoskeletal Disorders

There are a variety of actions that have been applied in the workplace for eliminating or reducing the occurrence of occupational musculoskeletal disorders. These include engineering redesigns, changes in work methods, administrative controls, training, organized exercise, work hardening, personal protective equipment, and medical management to reduce exposures. Some of these have been evaluated in research studies using both laboratory and field settings. The purpose of this paper is to characterize the nature of these research studies, evaluate their methodological soundness, and determine conclusions that can be made based on their strengths and weaknesses. We will first comment on the types of actions.

Engineering redesign aims to control exposures to the biomechanical risk factors for musculoskeletal injury. Engineering redesign has three main directions: (1) redesign of machinery, (2) providing assistive devices, and (3) tool redesign. Redesign of machinery deals with reducing exposure to biomechanical risk factors through modification of the machinery or the workstation. An example would be the use of adjustable tables to improve the postures of body parts (neck, shoulders, arms, hands, wrists, and back). Another would be the realignment of controls for better access that promotes less forceful activation with better body part postures.

Assistive devices provide mechanical advantages when dealing with loads. An example would be a lifting device such as a lift table, a hoist or a patient lifter. Tool redesign could be thought of as a sub-set of machinery design, but we have separated them due to the extensive efforts in tool redesign. Examples would be a reduction in the weight of powered hand tools, improved grip designs, alternative keyboard designs, and alternative mouse designs. The primary risk factors addressed with engineering redesign are loads (forces, weights) and body part postures.

Work methods improvement is also aimed primarily at biomechanical risk factor control, but can also influence the psychosocial work environment. The improvement requires changes in employee behavior to achieve risk reduction. This approach is often accompanied by employee training to provide a basis for the behavior change. The main direction of work methods improvement is to modify the task design to reduce or eliminate risk factors. An example would be changing the techniques used in cutting meat to reduce the frequency of cutting motions, and to improve body part postures while reducing loads.

Administrative controls are aimed at reducing the time of exposure to biomechanical and psychosocial risk factors. The two main directions are rotating employees among jobs with differing exposures and the use of rest breaks. Improved medical management activities could also be considered as administrative controls although the OSHA Ergonomic Guidelines for the Red Meat Industry considers medical management as a separate category.

Training is aimed at informing employees about the risk factors of musculoskeletal injury, and/or changing behavior to reduce risk. An example would be an ergonomic education program that provides employee orientation to risk factors. Another would be providing on-the-job instruction in revised task methods. A third would be providing instruction on how to use specific capabilities of workstation adjustments such as how to properly adjust a chair or a work table.

Exercise and work hardening programs increase the capacity of the employee. That could mean increasing strength, or flexibility, or tolerance for pain, or skills to conduct tasks.

Personal protective equipment typically blocks employee contact with a hazard. For musculoskeletal injury, an example would be gloves to dissipate the energy from hand tool vibration. However, for musculoskeletal injury there is another type of personal protective device that serves as a "support" for the musculature to reduce/balance forces: the back belt (or similar devices).

C. Methods Used to Review the Literature

The methodology used to evaluate the state of intervention research for the control of musculoskeletal disorders proceeded in five phases as outlined in Table 1.

Phase 1 consisted of a comprehensive search to find any article related to musculoskeletal disorder interventions. To accomplish this, the on-line databases PsychLit (1974 – present), Engineering Index (1987 - present), and Medline (1966 – present) were searched using 21 different search terms related to musculoskeletal disorder interventions, put into various combinations. At the same time, we looked through 14 different publications which included NIOSH publications, text and reference books in Ergonomics, and National Safety Council publications. The combined efforts yielded 720 articles.

In phase 2, abstracts from all 720 articles were read. If the article was a review of many other research articles, then the entire article was read and the bibliographies were examined for additional relevant articles. This brought the total number of articles to 768.

In phase 3 all empirical studies that employed what could be liberally considered an intervention for controlling musculoskeletal disorders were obtained from the library. There were 198 such articles.

In phase 4, 186 of the 198 articles were read and categorized. Twelve of the articles were unavailable through our library or interlibrary loan services within the review time scope. The categories consisted of laboratory vs. field studies, which were further broken down by intervention type: engineering, administrative, work method, training/exercise, and personal protective equipment.

Phase 5 consisted of selecting articles from the pool of 186 that met the following criteria:

- Peer reviewed journal article
- Directly related to musculoskeletal disorder interventions
- Representative of the research
- Methodologically sound (relative to the other articles)

For an article to have been considered methodologically sound, the following characteristics were considered:

- Control condition
- Accounting for confounds
- Relevancy of measures
- Randomized trials
- Blinded evaluators

Based on the steps in this phase, we selected 43 articles for in-depth review and analysis. Not all articles selected met all the conditions for methodological soundness.

D. General Discussion of the Strengths and Limitations of Research on the Effects of Interventions on Musculoskeletal Disorders

Hersey, Collins, Gershon, and Owen (1996) described the main challenges to all intervention research: use a theoretical basis, have sensitive measures, use "sound" research design, have appropriate statistical power, and apply interventions that can provide "interpretable" results. Similar issues have also been discussed by Lipsey (1998). Whereas these challenges are present in all types of intervention research, they are tailored here to interventions for the control of musculoskeletal disorders. The first challenge is for intervention research to be based on theory. Thus there is the need to have research questions, hypotheses, and/or a conceptual idea of the issue under study. In some disciplines the observation of phenomenon is the basis for generating concepts, and naturally occurring experiments (passive interventions) are examined. In others there is the need for manipulation of the variables (active interventions).

The second challenge is to use sensitive measures. Ergonomic intervention studies can fall short of this by using measures somewhat removed from musculoskeletal injury or by using measures that are not sensitive to the intervention. An example of the former would be a laboratory study that measured posture changes as an outcome. Such posture changes may influence the risk of injury, but may represent a low probability of injury. An example of a measure that may not be sensitive to a given intervention would be using the total number of workplace injuries in a facility as the measured outcome when the intervention was only geared toward preventing back injuries. Another way ergonomic intervention studies try to accomplish the goal of sensitive measures is by using multiple related measures. While this provides redundant and even contrasting information about an issue, there is no guarantee that multiple measures will provide any better characterization or precision.

The next challenge is to use a sound research design. In traditional experimental design this includes having sufficient observations, random assignment to conditions, using control groups, controlling for confounds, and having multiple observation points for each participant. In "naturally occurring interventions" many of these conditions are not met. For instance, random assignment is unlikely, as are control groups which received no treatment.

An important issue is statistical power. Many intervention studies seem to have low power, either because of poor contrast between the intervention and control groups (i.e. the control group received a treatment not unlike the intervention group), contamination effects (i.e. the intervention and control subjects worked together making it easy for the controls to be exposed to the intervention), insensitive dependent variables, or small (often inadequate) sample sizes. These problems are most frequent in field intervention studies, but are also observed in the laboratory studies. For instance, the laboratory studies may suffer from small sample size and few repeated trials.

The fifth challenge is to use an intervention that can yield interpretable results. Studies fail this challenge when, for example, the intervention used is composed of multiple inter-related components such as training, exercise, organizational changes, and ergonomic improvements. In such cases, the contribution of any one component of the intervention cannot be assessed.

The strengths and limitations of laboratory and field methods can be best discussed in terms of threats to internal and external validity. (The scope of this paper prevents a full discussion of threats to statistical conclusion and construct validity, but see Cook and Campbell (1979) for a detailed discussion of these issues.) Internal validity concerns the ability to make causal statements, whereas external validity is the extent to which a study is generalizable. Laboratory studies are characterized by random assignment to conditions, a high degree of control over the study environment and independent variable manipulations, and very often control groups. These characteristics give laboratory studies a high degree of internal validity because in controlled settings, there is little that can influence the dependent variable except for the independent variable. On the other hand, laboratory studies are often criticized because of low external validity. Dipboye (1990) listed several reasons for this criticism. First, there is an unrealistic nature to laboratory studies. This stems from the controlled artificial environment. Second, there is a lack of representative sampling (i.e. the typical use of college students, trained athletes).

Field studies, as typically carried out, present a tradeoff in terms of threats to validity. Since field studies are carried out in real world settings, they are considered to have high external validity. This same characteristic is the reason that they also often have low internal validity. In real world settings, there are many things that are "naturally occurring" which produce changes at the same time that interventions are instituted. This produces confounds and/or unexplained variance that cannot be controlled, and may dilute, or incidentally enhance, the intervention effects. In addition, field interventions do not always use random assignment to conditions or have control groups. When "control" groups are present, they are more often than not "quasi control groups". They are often a convenient group of employees who are not getting the intervention, but for whom measures are available to contrast to the intervention group. Another tactic in field ergonomic interventions is the use of "comparison" groups which are employees who receive an alternative treatment who are then compared to the main treatment. Any of these problems can create confounding, which limits causal interpretations.

Given the tradeoffs between laboratory and field studies, it is clear that both are necessary to gain a complete picture of the effectiveness of interventions to control musculoskeletal disorders. Considering the inherent limitations discussed above, the results of any single study in isolation must be interpreted carefully. Rather, a broader view examining the entire literature as a whole provides some insight into the potential effectiveness of interventions to control musculoskeletal disorders. It must be recognized that many of the limitations and problems described above for intervention research to control musculoskeletal disorders is true for almost all types of the intervention research studies, and are not unique to musculoskeletal intervention research.

E. Review of Select Research

We selected 43 research papers to represent the intervention literature on controlling musculoskeletal disorders. The majority of studies dealt with the risks for back injuries, but there were some which dealt with upper extremity musculoskeletal disorders. These studies were put into three categories: (1) laboratory experimental studies, (2) field studies using previously injured employees as subjects, and (3) field studies using healthy employees. Each category will be discussed separately, and then the entire group will be assessed in total.

1. Conclusions from Examples of Laboratory Intervention Research:

The laboratory ergonomic intervention research can be classified into studies which examined improved procedures for carrying out tasks (lifting technique), improved equipment designs (keyboards, hand tools) and the use of personal protective equipment (back belts, gloves). We have selected fifteen studies we believe characterize the laboratory ergonomic intervention evaluations. Table 2 provides highlights of these studies.

1.1. Methodological Strengths and Weaknesses of the Laboratory Intervention Research Studies:

Strengths:

(1) There was substantial control over the exposures so that the consistency, level and frequency of exposures were constant across subjects in all of the laboratory studies. For example, Lin, Radwin and Snook (1997), using a special device, were able to ensure that each subject in their

study grasped the handle the same way, and had identical forearm-upper arm angles. Similarly, Schoenmarklin and Marras (1989) used a device to ensure that all subjects began with their right arm at a 45-degree angle to the hammering fixture. They also used a computer to pace each subject at 57 strikes/minute.

(2) The majority of the studies (12/15) had some objective response measurement, and the precision of the objective response measurements was high. The three studies that did not use "objective" measures were Lavender and Kenyeri (1995), who measured acceptable lifting weights, Smith, Karsh, Conway, Cohen, James, Morgan, Sanders and Zehel (1998), who measured perceived discomfort and did not use goniometers for the posture measures, and Swanson, Galinsky, Cole, Pan, and Sauter (1997), who measured perceived discomfort. An example of a study that used "objective" measurements is Lander, Hundley and Simonton (1992), who used a force platform, pressure transducer, and EMGs to measure some of their outcomes.

(3) The majority of the studies indicated that they randomized or counterbalanced the order of conditions. Nine of the studies randomized the order of conditions, while three counterbalanced the order presentation.

Weaknesses:

(1) The exposures were focused on a small aspect of a larger process, and their application to the "bigger picture" is debatable. For instance, Schoenmarkling and Marras (1989) examined arm angle and force when pounding nails with a hammer where the subjects had a required trunk and shoulder posture.

(2) The exposures were not representative of the "real world". They may not "generalize" or even extrapolate to the "real world". For example, Lander, Simonton and Giacobbe (1990) and Woodhouse, Heinen, Shall and Bragg (1990) both used trained athletes in their lifting technique experiments.

(3) The range and time of exposures in the laboratory studies were very limited when compared to the field studies, and most were "constrained" by the apparatus or procedures such that the subjects' responses were constrained or limited to a small range. For example, Schoenmarklin and Marras (1989) had their subjects pound nails for only three minutes per condition. Resnick and Chaffin (1997) only used 30-second trials. Lander, Simonton and Giacobbe (1990) had subjects make only six lifts.

(4) For many, the sample size was small (8/15 had ten or fewer subjects), as was the number of repeated trials (7/15 only used one repetition per condition). This may have limited the ability to detect differences in conditions, and could explain the mixed results.

(5) Except for a few studies (4 out of 15) the participants were not workers (and may not be representative of workers). In one of these studies (Oh and Radwin, 1993), where workers were

participants along with students, there were differences in the physical capacity of the workers as well as their outcomes.

(6) The outcomes examined were intermediate states or surrogates, not measures of disorder symptoms, diagnostic criteria or endstates. Some endpoints (posture, force) dealt with "risk factors", while others dealt with short-term pain, discomfort and fatigue. None dealt with diagnostic tests or disorders. The connection to the reduction of "musculoskeletal disorders" is at a distance. However, all outcomes were "theoretically" consistent with a relationship to musculoskeletal disorders. For example, Woodhouse, Heinen, Shall and Bragg (1990) measured lifting force and muscle work and power, while Swanson, Galinsky, Cole, Pan and Sauter (1997) and Smith, Karsh, Conway, Cohen, James, Morgan, Sanders and Zehel (1998) measured short term discomfort.

(7) For eleven out of fifteen (11/15) studies, the findings were mixed and thus not clear enough to serve as the basis for a recommendation about the effectiveness of an intervention. As an example, Nakaseko, Grandjean, Hunting and Gierer (1985) found that there was less ulnar wrist deviation when using an experimental keyboard (vs. a standard keyboard), but there were no differences between the keyboards in reports of pain/discomfort.

(8) Thirteen out of 15 laboratory studies used within subject designs and Anova or t-test techniques for their analyses, yet none of them mentioned that they corrected or even tested for violations of sphericity.

B. General Conclusions about the Findings from the Laboratory Intervention Research Studies:

(1) The results of studies on "proper" lifting posture and technique are unclear. It is not possible to define the "best" lifting postures and techniques. All three of the laboratory lifting technique studies found mixed results. Leskinen, Stalhammer, Kuorinka and Troup (1983) found, when comparing four different lifting styles, that the squat lift resulted in the highest peak forces in the feet, but the lowest peak L5/S1 compression forces. Hart, Stobbe and Jareidi (1987) compared three lifting postures and found that the lowest trunk flexion moments occurred in the lordotic posture. They also found that the greatest abdominal muscle activity occurred with the kyphotic lumbar posture, while the least amount was found in the straight back posture.

(2) The evidence on the effectiveness of back belt use for reducing back injury risk is inconclusive. There were no differences found between wearing and not wearing a belt for maximum acceptable weight limits, joint angles, peak lifting force, total muscle work, or average muscle power (Lavender and Kenyeri, 1995; Marley and Duggasani, 1996; Woodhouse, Heinen, Shall and Bragg, 1990). Experienced athletes doing limited weight lifting activities showed some benefits (for example increased intra-abdominal pressure - IAP), but other results were not consistent (e.g. inconsistent differences between belt and no-belt conditions for external oblique and erector spinae mean EMGs) (Lander, Simonton and Giacobbe, 1990; Lander, Hundley and Simonton, 1992).

(3) The evidence is mixed whether alternative keyboards designed to improve hand/wrist postures can provide benefits of reduced risk factors for upper extremity musculoskeletal disorders. Nakaseko, Grandjean, Hunting and Gierer (1985), Smith, Karsh, Conway, Cohen, James, Morgan, Sanders and Zehel, (1998), and Swanson, Galinsky, Cole, Pan and Sauter, (1997) found no differences in reported pain between alternative and standard keyboards. Smith, Karsh, Conway, Cohen, James, Morgan, Sanders and Zehel (1998) found that there was less pronation when using a split keyboard compared to when using a traditional keyboard.

(4) There is evidence that alternative hand tools designed to improve hand/wrist postures and/or to reduce forces on the palm/fingers can provide benefits for the reduction of risk factors for upper extremity musculoskeletal disorders. Oh and Radwin (1993) found benefits for an extended trigger on a pneumatic nutrunner and Schoenmarklin and Marras (1989) found some postural benefits for angled hammers.

(5) There is some evidence that the use of weight handling devices such as hoists can reduce the risk factors for upper extremity musculoskeletal disorders. Resnick and Chaffin (1997) found that using an articulated arm, resulted in less peak push forces compared to a hoist with an overhead rail or hoist with a fixed pivot.

2. Conclusions from Examples of Field Intervention Studies:

The field intervention studies have been classified into those studies that used injured subjects or subjects suffering from pain, and those using healthy subjects. The studies using injured subjects can be further broken down into exercise, back school, early intervention, and physical therapy interventions. The studies that used healthy subjects can be further broken down into ergonomic improvement, training, back education, exercise, and weight belt interventions.

2.1. Examples of Intervention Studies of Injured Employees:

Fifteen injured-employee intervention studies were selected as representative of the literature that used injured employees as subjects. Table 3 provides highlights of these studies.

2.1.1. Methodological Strengths and Weaknesses of the Field Studies using Injured Subjects:

Strengths:

(1) Thirteen out of 15 studies used random assignment to conditions.

(2) Eleven of the 15 studies used a control or comparison group. Six studies had control groups (i.e. groups that did not receive any treatment), and five studies had comparison groups which received the standard treatment for the disorder of interest. The four other studies had a pre-post treatment design that compared different types of interventions.

(3) Seven out of fifteen studies compared interventions. For example, Moffett, Chase, Portek and Ennis (1986) compared a back school intervention to an exercise intervention, Bergquist-Ullman and Larsson (1977) compared a back school intervention, physical therapy intervention, and a placebo intervention (heat treatment), and Bru, Mykletun, Berge and Svebàk (1994) compared a cognitive intervention, a relaxation intervention, and a combined cognitive-relaxation intervention.

(4) All of the studies had multiple outcome measures. As examples, Lindstrom, Ohlund, Eek, Wallin, Peterson, Fordyce and Nachemson (1992) measured pain, return to work rates, sick leave days, and recurrence of pain; Kellet, Kellet and Nordholm (1991) measured flexion, strength, sick leave days, and presence of symptoms; and Harkappa, Mellin, Jarvikoski and Hurri (1990) measured pain, disability, compliance with treatment, and sickness days.

(5) As compared to the laboratory studies, some of the exposures were for a long time period (several months). Donchin, Woolf, Kaplan and Floman (1990), for example, had their intervention group attend back exercise classes bi-weekly for three months, while subjects in Alaranta, Rytokoski, Rissanen, Talo, Ronnemaa, Puukka, Karppi, Videman, Kallio and Slatis (1994) received treatments for three weeks.

(6) As compared to the laboratory studies, these studies had longer-term follow-up measures. Seven out of fifteen (7/15) studies had follow-up times of one year or more, and the rest had follow-up times of less than 1 year. For example, Harma, Ilmarinen, Knauth, Rutenfranz and Hanninen (1988) conducted a follow-up assessment at 4 months; Greenwood, Wolf, Pearson, Woon, Posey and Main (1990) conducted follow-up assessment after 18 months; and Linton, Hellsing and Anderson (1993) conducted a follow-up assessments after 3 weeks, 6 months and 12 months.

(7) The studies tested interventions aimed at "real life" situations using "actual workers". Studies were not constrained to a small focus, which enhances the generalizability to the workplace.

(8) Seven out of fifteen (7/15) studies used statistical techniques that analyzed multiple independent variables simultaneously. Such techniques are advantageous because they allow for statistical control of confounders.

(9) The studies had large sample sizes. Only two of the fifteen studies had less than 100 subjects at pre-intervention. Three out of fifteen had more than 400 subjects at pre-intervention, while the majority of the studies (10/15) had sample sizes between 100 and 400 subjects at pre-intervention.

(10) Fourteen of the studies measured subjective perceptions of symptom presence or pain. Eight of the studies measured disorder endstates (such as diagnosed injury, sick days due to injury). Instances of the latter include Greenwood, Wolf, Pearson, Woon, Posey, and Main (1990), who measured days of disability and Bergquist-Ullman and Larsson (1977), who measured days absent from work.

Weaknesses:

(1) The subjects in these studies were previously injured workers. It is possible that the results would not be generalizable to healthy workers, because injured workers may behave differently than healthy workers.

(2) Ten studies reported participant attrition at follow-up assessment. The other five studies did not report whether or not subjects were lost to follow-up. For example, Kellet, Kellet and Nordholm (1991) started with 111 subjects at pre-intervention and had a final count of 85 subjects at follow-up, and Cooper, Tate, Yassi and Khokhar (1996) had 158 subjects at pre-intervention and ended up with 128 at follow-up.

(3) In eleven of the fifteen studies subjects received multiple treatments within an intervention group, and it was not possible to identify which treatments were responsible for the outcomes. For example, the intervention group in Linton, Bradley, Jenson, Spangfort and Sundell (1989) received physical therapy, training, and pain management for their intervention.

(4) With the exception of one study, none of the other fourteen adjusted the alpha level to correct for multiple testing.

B. General Conclusions about the Findings from the Field Intervention Research Studies using Injured Subjects:

(1) When evaluated as a whole, there appear to be benefits due to the interventions for reduced musculoskeletal pain and symptoms, earlier return to work, and for reduced use of sick leave. Five studies found positive results, nine found mixed results, and only one found no results.

(2) Looking solely at exercise interventions, there appear to be positive effects for greater trunk flexion, reduced risk of re-injury, earlier return to work, and reduced use of sick leave.

(3) Early intervention right after a current injury does not provide benefits over later intervention post injury for persons with a prior musculoskeletal injury.

2.2. Examples of Intervention Studies with Healthy Workers:

Thirteen intervention studies were selected as representative of the literature that used healthy employees as subjects. Table 4 provides highlights of these studies.

2.2.1. Methodological Strengths and Weaknesses of the Field Studies using Healthy Subjects.

Strengths:

(1) The subjects in all of these studies were healthy, real workers in real jobs. This provides generalizability to the "real world".

(2) The studies tested "real-life" interventions under "actual working conditions". They were not constrained by a small focus. This enhances the generalizability to the workplace.

(3) Eight out of thirteen (8/13) studies had control groups, but others had a pre-post treatment design without control groups.

(4) There were a variety of outcome measures across studies, and also several studies had multiple outcome measures. As an example, May and Schwoerer (1994) measured the number of CTDs per employee and the number of restricted work days.

(5) Compared to the laboratory studies, the exposures were for a longer period of time (several days, weeks, or months). Versloot, Rozeman, Son and Akkerveeken (1992), for example, had three back school sessions presented to the intervention group at six months intervals.

(6) Compared to the laboratory studies, these studies had extended time periods of follow-up to assess long term effectiveness of the interventions. Seven of the studies had follow-up times of one year or more, five had follow up times between one month and 48 weeks, and the remaining study was retrospective. For example, Wickstrom, Hyytiaeinen, Laine, Pentti and Selonen (1993) had a 1-year follow up, and Daltroy, Iversen, Larson, Lew, Wright, Ryan, Zwerling, Fossel and Liang (1997) had 5.5 years of follow-up.

(7) Five out of 13 studies used statistical techniques that allowed for the assessment of the effects of several independent variables simultaneously.

(8) Most studies had large sample sizes. Five studies had 500 or more subjects, five studies had between 50-499 subjects, and the remaining had less than 50 subjects.

(9) Many studies had measures of the symptoms of musculoskeletal disorder and/or disorder endstates (such as diagnosed injury, sick days due to injury). Four of the studies measured musculoskeletal symptoms or pain, and 10 studies measured endstates (the numbers add up to more than 13 because any one study may have measured both symptoms and endstates). Lanoie and Tavenas (1996) provided an example of measuring an endstate; they measured the number of back related injuries.

Weaknesses:

(1) Only four of the thirteen studies had random assignment to conditions. It is recognized, however, that in work settings random assignment can be both difficult and inappropriate since employees who work side by side could be receiving different treatments. Such a situation could create an unpleasant work atmosphere which could affect the results of the intervention.

(2) In some studies the outcome measures were not sensitive to the interventions. As an example, Versloot, Rozeman, Son and Akkerveeken (1992) measured absenteeism for all sicknesses, which may not necessarily be sensitive to a back school intervention aimed at only reducing back injuries.

(3) There were seven studies where subjects received multiple treatments within an intervention group, and it was not possible to identify which treatments were responsible for the outcomes. Examples of this type of situation include the intervention used by Orgel, Milliron, and Frederick (1992), which was composed of two different ergonomic changes and training, or the intervention used by May and Schwoerer (1994) which was composed of more than five different ergonomic changes.

(4) There was not a single study that adjusted the alpha level to account for multiple tests.

(5) Some studies may have found mixed or no intervention effects because of possible contamination effects. For example, in Daltroy, Iversen, Larson, Lew, Wright, Ryan, Zwerling, Fossel and Liang (1997), the control groups might have learned about the interventions because they worked in the same facility as the intervention group subjects. This contamination could make it difficult to find any effects of the intervention.

B. General Conclusions about the Findings from the Field Intervention Research Studies using Healthy Subjects:

Six of the studies found mixed results, while two found positive results, and five found no results. Given the limitations of the studies, it is difficult to comment on whether or not benefits exist due to the interventions examined for reduced musculoskeletal pain and symptoms, for reduced use of sick leave, or for a reduced injury incidence. Despite the methodological limitations, the findings are discussed below.

(1) Ergonomic interventions appear to have positive effects on musculoskeletal discomfort, CTD incidence, accident incidence, and body posture. These findings must be interpreted with caution, however, because the ergonomic intervention studies with health employees did not use control groups.

(2) Looking solely at exercise interventions, there appear to be positive effects for back strength, days absent from work, and days with back pain.

(3) Neither back belts nor back education (i.e. back school) appear to be effective in reducing the incidence of injuries, their severity, or the costs of injuries.

F. Global Assessment of the Literature

1. Discussion of research methods

(a) <u>Nature of subjects (who, how many)</u>: The literature provides a variety of subjects ranging from college students in laboratory studies to workers engaging in their real-life jobs. Generally speaking the field intervention studies had large sample sizes with sufficient power to detect moderate differences between interventions. Many of the laboratory studies had a small sample size and corresponding reduction in power to detect differences between interventions.

(b) <u>Use of control/comparison groups:</u> There were 38 studies where it made sense to have control groups, control conditions, or comparison groups (i.e. placebo or treatment as usual groups). The other five studies compared, for example, lifting techniques, where there could not be a control group or control condition. Of the 38, 30 did use control groups, control conditions, or comparison groups. It is recognized that in work settings it is often difficult and even disruptive to have true control groups.

(c) <u>Subject assignment to treatment(s):</u> The studies were not consistent in the random assignment of subjects to treatments. Eleven laboratory studies either randomly assigned or counterbalanced order presentation. Only half of the field studies used random assignment. Again, it is recognized that in real work settings it may be difficult and disruptive to randomly assign employees to different groups. Doing so could cause employees who work together to receive different treatments. Not only might that be impossible to implement, depending on the intervention, but it might also affect the ability to detect intervention effects due to contamination of the control subjects with the intervention subjects. There are also ethical issues concerning withholding treatment to consider.

(d) <u>Nature of measures (adequacy, accuracy, and repeatability):</u> All of the measures used in the laboratory research were "risk factors" which could be far removed from an injury. Given the theoretical model proposed by the NAS panel, most of these measures could be considered legitimate indicators of injury risk. Several of the field studies measured various aspects of injury occurrence including incidence and severity. A few measured some of the direct costs of injuries such as worker's compensation costs.

All of the field study measurements had high repeatability and were easily accessible. Some of the laboratory measurements required specialized equipment (in some cases customized) of limited availability, highly technical calibration, and special skill to make the measurements.

(e) <u>Study design (experimental, natural, repeated-measures):</u> There were a variety of study designs (pre-post, between subjects, within subjects, mixed), and most had repeated measures and multiple measures. A large number used control groups or within subjects designs (with counterbalancing of the order of presentation). Some of the field studies only examined pre-post intervention effects without a control group. However, there were enough studies with appropriate design characteristics to assess intervention effects.

(f) <u>Confounding</u>: Due to the nature of laboratory experimental descriptions, it was very difficult to know if there were confounders. They are less likely in controlled laboratory research, but experimenter effects are recognized as a potential problem.

Of the field studies, there were several that had recognized confounders which were not controlled. Twenty-one of the 28 field studies either (1) controlled for some potential confounders through stratification, or (2) showed statistical evidence that potentially relevant confounders did not differ between groups, or (3) tested whether there were differences between the intervention and control groups and subsequently controlled for those differences in the analyses. However, the extent of the confound control varied widely between the studies. For example, Bergquist-Ullman and Larsson (1977) only stratified by vocational and psychological factors, whereas Lindstrom, Ohlund, Eek, Wallin, Peterson, Fordyce and Nachemson. (1992) tested for between group differences of eight different potential confounds

(g) <u>Statistical evaluation adequacy</u>: There were very few studies that used the best statistical analysis approaches. Several used multivariate methods, but when multivariate methods were used they were poorly described leaving the reader to make assumptions about which variables were used in a specific analysis. Only one study (field investigation) adjusted their alpha level for multiple tests, and only one (a field study) reported a power calculation. Several studies used an inappropriate statistical analysis, such as failure to use a paired t-test. In general, the statistical evaluation was unsatisfactory for the laboratory studies because they did not address the assumption of sphericity, and unsatisfactory for the field studies because they did not adequately utilize statistical control for potential confounders.

2. Quality of the research

(a) <u>Strengths</u>: There is a combination of both laboratory and field research using several methods and measurements that provides a consistent picture. The laboratory studies and injured-subject field intervention research generally had sound designs (i.e. randomization with control groups). Considering the difficulties of field research, the general quality of the research reviewed was good. The outcome measures were moderate to good indicators of risk/disorder, the experimental situations provided opportunities to test the interventions, and generally the experimenters were cognizant of and sensitive to methodological and statistical concerns.

(b) <u>Weaknesses</u>: The primary weakness is the lack of a substantial body of research evidence that provides an ability to test the whole range of interventions that theoretically can influence musculoskeletal injury and risk of injury. There just is not enough completed and published research.

There is also a lack of sound research design (i.e. randomized longitudinal designs with control groups) to evaluate the effectiveness of ergonomic interventions. The current research on ergonomic interventions reported on the global effects of multiple ergonomic interventions. There is also a lack of control groups. Because of these two factors, one cannot know which one of the many ergonomic changes made in any given study led to the results. Future studies evaluating ergonomic effects should attempt to examine the effects of different ergonomic changes in isolation of other ergonomic changes. This is not to suggest that ergonomic changes should be made, for example, with and without training, in order to examine training effects. That would be both unethical and dangerous. On the other hand, researchers could attempt to limit the number of ergonomic changes made at any one time in order to isolate their effects. Also, without a control group, it is possible that any positive results are the results of a placebo effect. There is a need to quantify the changes in load or posture caused by the ergonomic interventions so that any long-term results are more interpretable. For example, if there is an ergonomic intervention such as the implementation of a new manual material handling device, the researchers should report the effect of the new device on hand forces, back compression forces, etc. This way, any long-term changes in injury rate, for example, are more interpretable.

(c) <u>Limitations for drawing conclusions:</u> There are not enough laboratory studies of interventions that examine critical risk factors for back or upper extremity disorders. There are not enough well controlled, longitudinal field studies with good measures of the effectiveness of interventions. It is just as likely that the weak healthy-subject field methodologies are diluting, as opposed to inflating, intervention effects. For example, contamination between the intervention and control groups, not using pre-treatment scores as covariates, and insensitive dependent measures are all more likely to dilute differences between intervention and control groups. If this is the general case, then stronger methodologies should help bring the positive effects of musculoskeletal disorder prevention interventions to light.

(d) <u>Do methods, findings support authors' conclusions:</u> Almost all of the authors (there were some notable exceptions) overstated their study findings in light of study limitations.

3. Discussion of the Findings from the Literature

(a) <u>Plausibility of authors' claims about findings and conclusions:</u> As stated earlier, most authors tended to overstate the strength and clarity of their results. While the laboratory studies generally had appropriate designs and reasonable statistical analysis, many did not use workers as subjects, had small sample sizes and the interventions were usually so specialized that the application to a real world settings was very questionable. Several of the field studies had design weaknesses (lack of control groups, short assessment periods, confounds, intertwined treatments), and statistical analysis weaknesses (inadequate tests, lack of confound controls, no alpha correction) that made their results difficult to interpret.

(b) <u>Implications of findings for risk and injury reduction:</u> At this point in time the research literature is very limited because there are only a few strong studies and because there are large gaps in the research areas. Based on this some scientists might feel that it is premature to conclude that interventions to control musculoskeletal disorders and their risk factors are effective. However, even with recognized study weaknesses and gaps, the intervention literature findings suggest that there are some interventions that can influence the occurrence, recurrence and severity of low back disorders, and/ or reduce the risk factors associated with increased risk for low back and upper extremity musculoskeletal disorders. The most clear findings relate to exercise and physical conditioning which show benefits for low back injury control for healthy

workers and workers with a prior back injury. In addition, hand tool design and hoist design improvements have shown benefits for reducing the forces used by the hands and back.

Several authors of intervention research studies concluded their papers with the need for more research. Based on our analysis of this literature, we agree that there is a need for substantially more research that deals with: (1) which interventions are beneficial for what circumstances, (2) what are the mechanisms through which interventions produce benefits, (3) how are various interventions related to each other and to success? In addition, the intervention research should attempt to more carefully adhere to the issues discussed by Heresy, Collins, Greaten and Owen (1996). Specifically, the important issues for musculoskeletal disorder intervention research include:

1. Random assignment to groups
2. Using control groups
3. Having clear differences between the intervention groups and controls (i.e. the interventions receive a treatment, the controls do not, and the intervention group cannot contaminate the control groups)
4. Using dependent measures that are sensitive to the goals of the intervention.
5. Checking for between group differences on a range of job, demographic, and disorder related variables and statistically controlling for differences (which can also be used in combination with stratification). Similarly, pre-treatment scores on dependent measures should be used as covariates in post-treatment group comparisons when possible.
6. Using multiple long-term assessment points to evaluate changes in intervention effectiveness over time.

G. References

Alaranta, H., Rytokoski, U., Rissanen, A., Talo, S., Ronnemaa, T., Puukka, P., Karppi, S. L., Videman, T., Kallio, V., & Slatis, P. (1994). Intensive physical and psychosocial training program for patients with chronic low back pain. A controlled clinical trial. *Spine, 19*(12), 1339-49.

Bergquist-Ullman, M., & Larsson, U. (1977). Acute low back pain in industry. A controlled prospective study with special reference to therapy and confounding factors. *Acta Orthopaedica Scandinavica*(170), 1-117.

Bru, E., Mykletun, R. J., Berge, W. T., & Svebak, S. (1994). Effects of different psychological interventions on neck, shoulder and low back pain in female hospital staff. *Psychology and Health, 9*(5), 371-382.

Cook , T. D. and Campbell D. T. (1979). *Quasi-experimentation: Design and Analysis Issues for Field Settings.* Chicago: Rand McNally.

Cooper, J. E., Tate, R. B., Yassi, A., & Khokhar, J. (1996). Effect of an early intervention program on the relationship between subjective pain and disability measures in nurses with low back injury. *Spine, 21*(20), 2329-36.

Daltroy, L. H., Iversen, M. D., Larson, M. G., Lew, R., Wright, E., Ryan, J., Zwerling, C., Fossel, A. H., & Liang, M. H. (1997). A controlled trial of an educational program to prevent low back injuries [see comments]. *New England Journal of Medicine, 337*(5), 322-8.

Dipboye, R. L. (1990). Laboratory vs. Field Research in Industrial and Organizational Psychology. *International Review of Industrial and Organizational Psychology, 5,* 1-34.

Donchin, M., Woolf, O., Kaplan, L., & Floman, Y. (1990). Secondary prevention of low-back pain. A clinical trial [see comments]. *Spine, 15*(12), 1317-20.

Feldstein, A., Valanis, B., Vollmer, W., Stevens, N., & Overton, C. (1993). The back injury prevention project pilot study: assessing the effectiveness of back attack: an injury prevention program among nurses, aides, and orderlies. *Journal of Occupational Medicine, 35,* 114-120.

Garg, A., & Owen, B. (1992). Reducing back stress to nursing personnel: an ergonomic intervention in a nursing home. *Ergonomics, 35*(11), 1353-1375.

Greenwood, J. G., Wolf, H. J., Pearson, R. J., Woon, C. L., Posey, P., & Main, C. F. (1990). Early intervention in low back disability among coal miners in West Virginia: negative findings. *Journal of Occupational Medicine, 32*(10), 1047-52.

Gundewall, B., Liljeqvist, M., & Hansson, T. (1993). Primary prevention of back symptoms and absence from work. A prospective randomized study among hospital employees. *Spine, 18*(5), 587-94.

Harkapaa, K., Jarvikoski, A., Mellin, G., & Hurri, H. (1989). A controlled study on the outcome of inpatient and outpatient treatment of low back pain. *Scandinavian Journal of Rehabilitation Medicine, 21,* 81-89.

Harkapaa, K., Mellin, G., Jarvikoski, A., & Hurri, H. (1990). A controlled study on the outcome of inpatient and outpatient treatment of low back pain. *Scandinavian Journal of Rehabilitation Medicine, 22,* 181-188.

Harma, M. I., Ilmarinen, J., Knauth, P., Rutenfranz, J., & Hanninen, O. (1988). Physical training intervention in female shift workers: I. The effects of intervention of fitness, fatigue, sleep, and psychosomatic symptoms. *Ergonomics, 31*(1), 39-50.

Hart, D. L., Stobbe, T. J., & Jareidi, M. (1987). Effect of lumbar posture on lifting. *Spine, 12,* 138-145.

Hersey, J. C., Collins, J. W., Gershon, R., and Owen, B. (1996). Methodological issues in intervention research – health care. *American Journal of Industrial Medicine, 29,* 412-417.

Kellet, K. M., Kellet, D. A., & Nordholm, L. A. (1991). Effect of an exercise program on sick leave due to back pain. *Physical Therapy, 71,* 283-291.

Keyserling, W. M., Brouwer, M., & Silverstein, B. A. (1993). Effectiveness of a joint labor-management program in controlling awkward postures of the trunk, neck, and shoulders. Results of a field study. *International Journal of Industrial Ergonomics, 11*(1), 51-65.

Lander, J. E., Simonton, R. L., & Giacobbe, J. F. K. (1990). The effectiveness of weight-belts during the squat exercise. *Medicine and Science in Sports and Exercise, 22,* 177-126.

Lander, J. E., Hundley, J. R., & Simonton, R. L. (1992). The effectiveness of weight-belts during multiple repetitions of the squat exercise. *Medicine and Science in Sports and Exercise, 24,* 603-609.

Lanoie, P., & Tavenas, S. (1996). Costs and benefits of preventing workplace accidents: The case of participatory ergonomics. *Safety Science, 24*(3), 181-196.

Lavender, S. A., & Kenyeri, R. (1995). Lifting belts: A psychophysical analysis. *Ergonomics, 38*(9), 1723-1727.

Leskinen, T. P. J., Stalhammer, H. R., Kuorinka, I. A. A., & Troup, J. D. G. (1983). A dynamic analysis of spinal compression with different lifting techniques. *Ergonomics, 26,* 595-604.

Lin, M. L., Radwin, R. G., & Snook, S. H. (1997). A single metric for quantifying biomechanical stress in repetitive motions and exertions. *Ergonomics, 40*(5), 543-558.

Lindstrom, I., Ohlund, C., Eek, C., Wallin, L., Peterson, L. E., Fordyce, W. E., & Nachemson, A. L. (1992). The effect of graded activity on patients with subacute low back pain: a randomized prospective clinical study with an operant-conditioning behavioral approach. *Physical Therapy, 72*(4), 279-90; discussion 291-3.

Linton, S. J., Bradley, L. A., Jensen, I., Spangfort, E., & Sundell, L. (1989). The secondary prevention of low back pain: a controlled study with follow-up. *Pain, 36*(2), 197-207.

Linton, S. J., Hellsing, A. L., & Andersson, D. (1993). A controlled study of the effects of an early intervention on acute musculoskeletal pain problems. *Pain, 54*(3), 353-9.

Lipsey, M. W. (1998). Design sensitivity: statistical power for applied experimental research. In L. Bickman and D. J. Rog (Eds.). *Handbook of Applied Social Research Methods*. Thousand Oaks, CA: Sage.

Marley Robert, J., & Duggasani Amarnath, R. (1996). Effects of industrial back supports on physiological demand, lifting style and perceived exertion. *International Journal of Industrial Ergonomics, 17*(6), 445-453.

May, D. R., & Schwoerer, C. E. (1994). Employee health by design: Using employee involvement teams in ergonomic job redesign. *Personnel Psychology, 47*(4), 861-876.

Mellin, G., Hurri, H., Harkapaa, K., & Jarvikoski, A. (1989). A controlled study on the outcome of inpatient and outpatient treatment of low back pain. Part II. Effects on physical measurements three months after treatment. *Scandinavian Journal of Rehabilitation Medicine, 21*(2), 91-5.

Mitchell, L. V., Lawler, F. H., Bowen, D., Mote, W., Asundi, P., & Purswell, J. (1994). Effectiveness and cost-effectiveness of employer-issued back belts in areas of high risk for back injury. *Journal of Occupational Medicine, 36*(1), 90-4.

Moffett, J. A. K., Chase, S. M., Portek, I., & Ennis, J. R. (1986). A controlled prospective study to evaluate the effectiveness of a back school in the relief of chronic low back pain. *Spine, 11*, 120-122.

Nakaseko, M., Grandjean, E., Hunting, W., & Gierer, R. (1985). Studies on ergonomically designed alphanumeric keyboards. *Human Factors, 27*(2), 175-187.

Oh, S., & Radwin, R. G. (1993). Pistol grip power tool handle and trigger size effects on grip exertions and operator preference. *Human Factors, 35*(3), 551-569.

Orgel, D. L., Milliron, M. J., & Frederick, L. J. (1992). Musculoskeletal discomfort in grocery express checkstand workers. An ergonomic intervention study. *Journal of Occupational Medicine, 34*(8), 815-8.

Parenmark, G., Engvall, B., & Malmkvist, A. K. (1988). Ergonomic on-the-job training of assembly workers: arm-neck-shoulder complaints drastically reduced amongst beginners. *Applied Ergonomics, 19*(2), 143-146.

Reddell, C. R., Congleton, J. J., Huchingson, R. D., & Montgomery, J. F. (1992). An evaluation of a weightlifting belt and back injury prevention training class for airline baggage handlers. *Applied Ergonomics, 23*(5), 319-329.

Resnick, M., & Chaffin, D. B. (1997). Ergonomic evaluation of three classes of material handling device (MHD). *International Journal of Industrial Ergonomics, 19*(3), 217-229.

Schoenmarklin, R. W., & Marras, W. S. (1989). Effects of handle angle and work orientation on hammering: I. Wrist motion and hammering performance. *Human Factors, 31*(4), 397-411.

Smith, M. J. and Carayon, P. (1995). New technology, automation, and work organization: stress problems and improved technology implementation strategies. *The International Journal of Human Factors in Manufacturing, 5(1),* 99-116.

Smith, M. J. and Sainfort, P. C. (1989). A balance theory of job design for stress reduction. *International Journal of Industrial Ergonomics, 4,* 67-79.

Smith, M. J., Karsh, B.-T., Conway, F. T., Cohen, W. J., James, C. A., Morgan, J., Sanders, K., & Zehel, D. (1998). Effects of a split keyboard design and wrist rest on performance, posture, and comfort. *Human Factors, 40*(2).

Stubbs, D. A., Buckle, P. W., Hudson, M. P., & Rivers, P. M. (1983). Back pain in the nursing profession. II. The effectiveness of training. *Ergonomics, 26*(8), 767-79.

Swanson, N. G., Galinsky, T.L., Cole, L.L., Pan, C.S. & Sauter, S.L. (1997). The impact of keyboard design on comfort and productivity in a text-entry task. *Applied Ergonomics, 28*(1), 9-16.

Versloot, J. M., Rozeman, A., Son, A. M. v., & Akkerveeken, P. F. v. (1992). The cost effectiveness of a back school program in industry: a longitudinal controlled field study. *Spine, 17,* 22-27.

Wickstrom, G., Hyytiaeinen, K., Laine, M., Pentti, J., & Selonen, R. (1993). Five-year intervention study to reduce low back disorders in the metal industry. *International Journal of Industrial Ergonomics, 12*(1-2), 25-33.

Woodhouse, M. L., Heinen, J. R., Shall, L., & Bragg, K. (1990). Selected isokinetic lifting parameters of adult male athletes utilizing lumbar/sacral supports. *J Orthop Sports Phys Ther, 11,* 467-473.

Table 1. Phases of literature review and analysis

Phase 1	• Comprehensive search yielded 720 articles.
Phase 2	• Read abstracts. • Examined review articles for additional titles. • This brought the total number of articles to 768.
Phase 3	• Obtained relevant articles from the library. • There were 198 such articles.
Phase 4	• Twelve of the articles were unavailable. • Read and categorized 186 articles.
Phase 5	• Selected 43 articles to represent the literature.

Table 2. Methodological characteristics of the laboratory intervention studies

Authors	Subjects	Intervention[1]	Random assignment (RA) or random order (RO) or counterbalancing (CB)[2]	Use of control condition[3]	Dependent measures	Statistics	Results[4]	Comments
Leskinen et al., 1983.	• 20 male subjects. • Screened for recent back trouble or spinal surgery.	Lifting technique.	Not indicated.	Not applicable.	Force at feet, spinal compression.	• Paired t-tests.	Force at feet (+), spinal compression (0)[5].	• Within-subjects design.
Stubbs et al., 1983.	• Eight female student nurses (w/ 9 month experience). Age range 19 to 23 years. • None had taken sick leave for back pain and there was no recent history of illness or abdominal operations.	Lifting technique.	RO.	Not applicable.	Intra-abdominal pressure (IAP), comfort.	• 2-way Anova.	IAP (+), comfort (0)[6].	• Within-subjects design. • Forty lifts for each procedure.
Hart et al., 1987.	• 20 male subjects (mean age = 32.9 years) currently lifting and carrying weights. • No sign or symptoms of acute low back pain. Recruited from local industries.	Lifting technique.	RO.	Not applicable.	Flexion, muscle activity (EMG).	• Mixed effects 3-way Anova. • Duncan's multiple range test used for post-hoc analysis.	Trunk flexion (>lordosis), abdominal muscles (+), external oblique (+), erector spinae (<lordosis, >kyphosis)[7].	• Within-subjects design.
Woodhouse et al., 1990.	• 10 well-conditioned male athletes aged 21-35. • Subjects could not participate if they had any one of a number of medical conditions diagnosed during a physical exam provided as part of the study.	Weight belt.	CB.	Yes.	Force, work, power.	• 1-way repeated measures Anova with Scheffe tests for post-hoc comparisons.	Force (0), work (0), power (0).	• Within-subjects design. • All lifts were squat-style lifts, at maximum contractions.
Lander et al., 1990.	• 6 skilled male adults who regularly weight lifted (mean age = 23.4).	Weight belt.	RO.	Yes.	Force, intra-abdominal pressure (IAP), muscle EMG, joint moments.	• 2-way repeated measures Anova or 2-way repeated measures Ancova, as needed.	Absolute and relative joint angles (0), IAP (+), L5/S1 moment (-), rectus abdominus (0), external obliques(+), erector spinae (+).	• Within-subjects design. • The results of the mean EMG values in the proceeding column were divided by the L5/S1 moment.
Lander et al., 1992.	• 5 skilled male adults who regularly weight lifted (mean age = 23.4).	Weight belt.	RO.	Yes.	Force, intra-abdominal pressure (IAP), muscle EMG.	• 2-way repeated measures Anova with planned comparisons.	Force platform (0), joint angles (0), IAP (+), back extensor (0), abdominal constrictor (0), knee extensor (-), hip extensor (-).	• Within-subjects design. • Lifts done at maximum effort.
Lavender and Kenyeri, 1995.	• 11 males and 5 females (age 18-33).	Weight belt.	CB.	Yes.	Maximum acceptable weight.	• Repeated measures Anova.	Maximum acceptable weight (0).	• Within-subjects design. • 2 lifts/minute for 40 minutes/condition.

Table 2 continued.

Authors	Subjects	Intervention[1]	Random assignment (RA) or random order (RO) or counter-balancing (CB)[2]	Use of control condition[3]	Dependent measures	Statistics	Results[1]	Comments
Marley and Duggasani, 1996.	• 8 college-aged males in good health (age 22-39).	Weight belt.	RO.	Yes.	Seventeen physiological, kinematic, and psychological variables.	• Full factorial Anova.	Blood pressure (greater with belt), no difference (0) on all other variables.	• Within-subjects design. • Lifting style allowed to vary.
Nakaseko et al., 1985.	• 30 female and 1 male trained typist (age 17-52) typing at least 100 strokes/min.	Alternative keyboard and wrist rest.	RO.	Yes.	Pain, force, body posture.	• Anova and t-tests.	Smaller wrist rest = up right posture, lower elbow position. Split keyboard + large wrist rest = greater inclination, arm elevation, elbow angle. Shoulder flexion and abduction: large wrist rest > small wrist rest. Ulnar abduction: traditional keyboard > split keyboard. Neck/Shoulder (0), Arm/Hand (0).	• Within-subjects design. • 30 minutes of typing per trial. • Subjects used their preferred workstation settings.
Swanson et al., 1997.	• 50 female clerical workers (age 18-38) in good health with a minimum of 6 months experience with keyboard work and typing a rate of 40-55 words/min.	Alternative keyboard.	Not indicated.	Yes.	Discomfort.	• Anova.	Overall musculoskeletal discomfort (0), fatigue (0).	• Keyboard conditions were between-subjects. • Typed 300 minutes per day for 2 days. • Workstations adjusted so that all subject body postures were equivalent.
Smith et al., 1998.	• 18 professional touch typists from a temporary agency who typed at least 55-words/ min with five or fewer typing errors in a 5-min. test. • Subjects were screened for any history of musculoskeletal cumulative trauma disorders (age 18-49, typing experience 6-32 years).	Alternative keyboard and wrist rest.	CB.	Yes.	Posture, discomfort.	• Wilcoxon signed rank test for repeated measures variables. • Mann-Whitney for between-subject variables.	Musculoskeletal pain (0), hand pronation (traditional keyboard > split keyboard), shoulder and elbow pain (without wrist rest > with wrist rest).	• Mixed design. • Typed 2 days with the alternative keyboard (8 hours) and 1 day with the standard keyboard (4 hours). • Workstations adjusted so that all subject body postures were equivalent.
Schoenmarklin and Marras, 1989.	• 8 healthy right-handed men who were novice hammer users and had no hand or wrist injuries (age 23-29).	Hammer handle angles.	Not indicated.	Yes.	Wrist angle deviations.	• Manova. • Follow-up Anova if the Manova was significant. • Used Duncan's test for mean comparisons.	Ulnar deviation less with angled hammers, radial deviation less with straight hammer, driving force (0).	• Within-subjects design. • 57 hammer strikes per minute for 3 minutes per condition.

Table 2 continued.

Authors	Subjects	Intervention[1]	Random assignment (RA) or random order (RO) or counter-balancing (CB)[2]	Use of control condition[3]	Dependent measures	Statistics	Results[4]	Comments
Oh and Radwin, 1993.	• 7 male, 11 female students and 8 male, 3 female factory workers. • The factory workers were experienced hand tool users.	Trigger and handle spans of pneumatic power hand nut runners.	RO.	Not applicable.	Finger/hand forces.	• Regression, Anova with Tukey post-hoc.	Grip strength affected by handle span. Peak finger and palmar forces increased as handle span increased. Finger and palmar holding exertions (extended trigger < conventional trigger).	• Within-subjects design.
Lin and Radwin, 1997.	• 6 male, 1 female.	Pace, force, angle.	RO.	Not applicable.	Perceived discomfort.	• Anova.	Discomfort ratings increased with increased pace, force, and angle.	• Within-subjects design. • All subjects used the same arm/hand positioning.
Resnick and Chaffin, 1997.	• 5 young healthy males and 5 young healthy females who did not report any musculoskeletal problems (mean age =20).	Manual material handling devices.	RO.	Not applicable.	Push and pull forces.	• Repeated measures Anova.	Peak pull force (0). Peak push force: articulated arm < hoist with overhead rail < hoist with fixed pivot.	• Within-subjects design. • 30 second trials.

[1]If the interventions listed are separated by an "or", that means there were more than one intervention group. If several interventions are separated by commas, it means that a single intervention group received all of those treatments.

[2]Some of the studies used random assignment after stratification.

[3]A group that received no treatment, whether randomly assigned or not. This column may contain a description of the control condition.

[4](+) means that the intervention had better scores on the DV, compared to the control/placebo/treatment as usual. (-) means that the intervention had worse scores on the DV, compared to the control. (0) means that the intervention and control did not differ.

[5]Squat lifting technique compared to the other lifting techniques.

[6]Australian (shoulder) lifting technique compared to the other lifting techniques.

[7]Straight back compared to lifting with a lumbar lordosis or kyphosis.

224

Table 3. Methodological characteristics of the injured-subject field intervention studies

Authors	Subjects	Intervention[1]	Random assignment[2]	Use of control group[3]	Dependent measures	Statistics	Results[3]	Comments
Lindstrom et al., 1992.	• 103 (pre-intervention) blue-collar workers from a care assembly plant sick-listed for 8 weeks with sub-acute low back pain. 98 subjects remained post-intervention. • Exclusion criteria included specific diagnoses.	Exercise.	Yes.	Treatment as usual.	Return to work, sick leave, recurrence of pain.	• t-tests and Log likelihood. • Assessed whether the groups differed on a number of potential confounds.	Return to work (+), sick leave (+), and recurrence of low back pain (+).	• Comparisons of 1-year pre-intervention, year of the intervention, and 1-year post. • The physicians who made the return to work decision were not blinded to their patients' experimental condition.
Alaranta et al., 1994.	• 293 patients (pre-intervention) with back disease without inflammation, pain duration at least 6 months, 30-47 years old, no claims, one back surgery maximum, no other rehabilitation. 287 patients at post.	Exercise.	Yes.	Traditional treatment.	Flexion, strength, pain, sick leave, symptom presence.	• Chi-square, t-tests, paired t-tests or Wilcoxon.	Subjective back pain (+), sick leave days (0). For males in intervention group, flexion (+) and rotation (+).	• 3 and 12 months follow-up evaluations. • Groups stratified by age and gender.
Kellet et al., 1991.	• One hundred eleven (85 at post-intervention) employees of a company. • Inclusion criteria: self-reported current or previous back pain; written communication; willingness to exercise at least once a week outside working hours for 1.5 years. • Exclusion criteria: any period of sick leave greater 50 days during 1.5 year prior to study; other medical reasons affecting the employees ability to participate.	Exercise.	Yes.	Yes.	Number of sick leave days, cardiovascular fitness, self-reported back pain.	• Paired t-test, t-test for independent groups. • Tested for between group differences at pre-intervention.	Change score in sick days leave (+) and in episodes of back pain (+). Within exercise group, # sick days (+), # of episodes of back pain (0), and cardiovascular fitness (0). Within control group, # sick days (0), # of episodes of back pain (0), and cardiovascular fitness (-).	• Follow-up at 1.5 years. • Prospective study.
Harma et al., 1988.	• 119 women volunteered for the physical training intervention study. Only 75 at post-intervention. • Criteria: at least 1.5 years of experience in shift work, age 20-49 years, and working as a nurse or nursing aide in a specific hospital.	Physical training.	No.	Yes.	Musculoskeletal symptoms, physical fitness.	• Wilcoxon test and Mann-Whitney U-test.	Physical fitness (+) and musculoskeletal (+) between groups. Within physical training group, physical fitness (+) and musculoskeletal (+).	• Follow-up at 4 months. • Groups were formed by matching subjects.
Moffett et al., 1986.	• 92 patients (pre-intervention) aged 18-67 (both genders) with more than 6 months low back pain in a clinic. 78 patients post-intervention. • Excluded for: history of spinal surgery, attending physiotherapy, evidence of an underlying disease.	Back school or exercise.	Yes.	No.	Pain, functional disability, activity limitations.	• Change scores with t-test and multiple regression. • Assessed whether the groups differed on a number of potential confounders.	At 6 weeks: activity (back school >), pain (0), disability (0). At 16 weeks: activity (0), pain (0), and disability (back school >).	• Follow-up at 6 and 16 weeks. • The physiotherapists and rheumatologists who assessed patients were blinded to the study conditions.

Table 3 continued.

Authors	Subjects	Intervention[1]	Random assignment[2]	Use of control group[3]	Dependent measures	Statistics	Results[4]	Comments
Donchin et al, 1990.	• 142 hospital employees with at least 3 annual episodes of low back pain.	Back school or exercise.	Yes.	Yes.	Flexion, strength, pain, back extension, back muscle endurance.	• Paired t-tests, Ancova, multiple regression. • Assessed whether the groups differed on a number of potential confounders.	Trunk flexion (exercise > back school > control). Abdominal strength (exercise > back school > control) at 3 months, and (0) at 9 months. Back extension and muscle endurance (0). Back pain (exercise > back school or control).	• Post-intervention assessments done after 3 and 9 months.
Bergquist-Ullman and Larsson, 1977.	• 217 patients with low-back pain (pre-intervention). 197 patients post-intervention.	Back school or physical therapy.	Yes.	Short waves of lowest possible intensity heat.	Pain, absence from work, duration of symptoms, number and duration of recurrences and absence due to recurrences.	• Chi-square tests, Anova, and Ancova.	Days between first treatment and recovery: back school and physical therapy faster than placebo. At 6 weeks, pain (0). At 1 year, incidence of recurrences (0), length of recurrence (0), and absence due to recurrences (0).	• Assessed the effects of covariates. • 6-weeks and 1-year follow-up reported (follow-ups occurred 10 days, 3 weeks, 6 weeks, 3 months, 6 months and 1 year after). • Subjects were stratified and randomly assigned to groups.
Greenwood et al, 1990.	• Worker's compensation fund population. • Coal industry sample. Sample of 284 claims.	Early rehabilitation.	Yes.	Cases handled in the usual way.	Days of disability, amount of medical and disability benefits.	• Two tailed studentized test, chi-square tests. • Test for between group differences at pre-intervention.	Length of disability (days) (0), disability benefits paid (0), medical benefits paid (0).	• Follow-up at 18 months.
Cooper et al, 1996.	• All registered or licensed practical nurses employed at a hospital that sustained a compensable soft-tissue back injury. • Sample was screened for concomitant non-occupational musculoskeletal lesion or confounding treatment. Pregnant subjects and those with absence leave of more than 5 weeks were excluded. • 40 (38) in the nurses intervention group, 118 (90) nurses in the control group [pre (post)].	Education and early rehabilitation.	No.	Yes.	Perceived pain and disability.	• 1-way Anovas, 3-way Anovas for repeated measures, 2-way Anovas regression models. • Compared groups for demographic characteristics at pre-intervention. • Used adjusted p-level of .01.	Perceived pain [levels low, mid, high] (0), perceived disability [levels low, mid] (0), perceived disability [level high] (+). Within intervention and control groups, perceived pain [high] (+), perceived disability [mid, high] (+).	• Intervention group drawn from high-risk wards. Control group from other wards. • Nurses were classified by blocking characteristics. • Follow-up at 6 months.
Mellin et al, 1989.	• 288 men, 168 women.	Rehabilitation or back treatment or exercise and ergonomic instruction.	Yes.	Written and oral instructions in exercise and ergonomics.	Index of physical measurements (IPM).	• One-way Anova and t-tests. Multiple linear regression. • Tested for between group differences at pre-intervention.	Change in IPM: better for inpatients vs. outpatients, better for inpatients vs. control, (0) outpatients vs. control.	• Same physiotherapist did the measurements at pre and post intervention. • 3-month follow-up reported. (study had 3, 8, and 18 months follow up, a second intervention at 1.5 years, and another follow up at 3 and 12 months after).

Table 3 continued.

226

Authors	Subjects	Intervention[1]	Random assignment[2]	Use of control group[3]	Dependent measures	Statistics	Results[4]	Comments
Harkappa et al., 1989.	• 476 at pre-intervention (459 post). • Selection criteria: physically strenuous or moderately strenuous work for at least 10 years; suffered from chronic or recurrent back pain for at least two years; working and physical capacity was affected; sick leave during last two years; low back pain was the major health problem, no other severe long-term illness present.	Rehabilitation or back treatment or exercise and ergonomic instruction.	Yes.	Written and oral instructions in exercise and ergonomics.	Pain index, disability index, compliance with treatment.	• 3 and 2 Way Anovas for repeated measures. 2-way Anovas and Chi-square analysis. • Tested for between group differences at pre-intervention.	Pain scores and disability scores were less for inpatients and outpatients compared to controls. Pain was less for inpatients compared to outpatients.	• 3-month follow-up reported. (study had 3, 8, and 18 months follow up, a second intervention at 1.5 years, and another follow up at 3 and 12 months after).
Harkappa et al., 1990.	• 476 at pre-intervention (402 post). • Selection criteria: physically strenuous or moderately strenuous work for at least 10 years; suffered from chronic or recurrent back pain for at least two years; working and physical capacity was affected; sick leave during last two years; low back pain was the major health problem, no other severe long-term illness present.	Rehabilitation or back treatment or exercise and ergonomic instruction.	Yes.	Written and oral instructions in exercise and ergonomics.	Pain index, disability index, compliance with treatment, days of sickness allowance.	• 1-way Ancovas. One-way Anovas and Chi-square tests. • Tested for between group differences at pre-intervention.	Pain index (0), disability index (0), compliance better for inpatients vs. outpatients and controls. Days of sickness allowance greater for controls vs. inpatients and outpatients.	• 2.5 year follow-up reported. (study had 3, 8, and 18 months follow up, a second intervention at 1.5 years, and another follow up at 3 and 12 months after).
Bru et al., 1994.	• 111 subjects. • Selection criteria: females; different professions; availability; reported pain in the neck, shoulder and/or low back over the last seven days; reported pain in the neck, shoulder and/or low back that caused leave of absence for some period over last 12 months; back pain had to be reported for at least 2 periods over the last six months. • Criteria to drop subjects: Medical conditions (e.g., rheumatoid arthritis, Bechterew's disease, epilepsy, previous surgery of spine, osteoporosis, breast cancer, fibromyalgia, pregnancy).	Cognitive or relaxation or cognitive and relaxation.	Yes.	Yes.	Neck pain, shoulder pain, low-back pain.	• Manova treating data as doubly multivariate, with repeated measures, Mancovas. • Used pre-test scores as covariates.	Directions of the changes between the groups were not provided.	• Follow-up immediately after and 4 months after intervention.
Linton et al., 1989.	• 66 female LPNs or nursing aids. Screening: had to have been sick-listed for back pain at some time during the previous 2-year period and had to be currently working.	Physical therapy, training, pain management	Yes.	Yes.	Pain, activities of daily living, absenteeism.	• Separate 2 X 2 (treatment group x assessment period) analyses of covariance for repeated measures. • Tested for group differences at pre-intervention. • Pre-test value of each measure served as covariate.	Pain intensity (+), pain behavior (+), activities of daily living (+). Pain-related absenteeism (+).	• Follow-up every 6 weeks for six months (no assessments during these) and at 6-months (assessment made).

Table 3 continued.

Authors	Subjects	Interven-tion[1]	Random assign-ment[2]	Use of control group[3]	Dependent measures	Statistics	Results[4]	Comments
Linton et al., 1993.	• **240 patients [pre] complaining of MSP (musculoskeletal pain).** • **Study 1: 106 patients [post] with history of MSP during the past 2 years but not sick listed during the most recent three months.** • **Study 2: 92 patients [post] who had not been sick listed for MSP during the past 2 years.**	Early interven-tion.	Yes.	Treatment as usual.	Pain, days off of work.	• t-test, chi-square tests. • Tested for between group differences at pre-intervention.	**Study 1:** <u>Within intervention and control group:</u> Pain today (+), pain/week (+), pain-free days (+), and activity index (+). Pain control (+) within controls. <u>Between groups:</u> Pain today (0), pain/week (0), pain-free days (0), activity index (0), pain control (0). Chronic pain (0) and sickness absenteeism (0). **Study 2:** <u>Within intervention and control group:</u> Pain today (+), pain/week (+), pain-free days (+), and activity index (+) Pain control (+) within controls. <u>Between groups:</u> Pain today (0), pain/week (0), pain-free days (0), activity index (0), pain control (0). Chronic pain (+) and sickness absenteeism (+).	• Follow-up 3 weeks, 6 and 12-months.

[1]If the interventions listed are separated by an "or", that means there were more than one intervention group. If several interventions are separated by commas, it means that a single intervention group received all of those treatments.

[2]Some of the studies used random assignment after stratification.

[3]A group that received no treatment, whether randomly assigned or not. This column may contain a description of the control condition.

[4](+) means that the intervention had better scores on the DV, compared to the control/placebo/treatment as usual . (-) means that the intervention had worse scores on the DV, compared to the control. (0) means that the intervention and control did not differ.

Table 4: Methodological characteristics of the healthy-subject intervention studies.

Authors	Subjects	Intervention[1]	Random assignment[2]	Use of control group[3]	Dependent measures	Statistics	Results[4]	Comments
Orgel et al., 1992.	• 23 (of 34) grocery store cash register employees at pre- and 19 at post-intervention.	Multiple changes at work-station.	No.	No.	Musculo-skeletal discomfort.	• Wilcoxon signed rank test.	Medication use (+), recovery days (+), discomfort on low back/buttock/leg (+), on neck/upper back/shoulder (+), and arm/forearm/wrist (0).	• Post-intervention measures taken 4 months post. • Controlled for hours of work at register.
May and Schwoerer, 1994.	• 800 production employees in 2 shifts of a meatpacking plant whose primary tool is a knife.	Multiple ergonomic improvements.	No.	No.	CTDs/employee, # physician referred CTD cases, production days lost, restricted working days.	• Wilcoxon signed ranks.	# of CTDs (+), # of doctor referred cases (+), production days lost (0), restricted duty days (+).	• Compared measures from 1 year prior to the interventions to 1 year post-intervention.
Lanoie and Tavenas, 1996.	• About 90 packers in a warehouse.	Multiple ergonomic improvements.	No.	No.	Accidents, back related injuries.	• Poisson regression. • Statistically controlled for various possible confounders.	# of accidents (0), # back related injuries (+).	• Assessed measures over the 3 years it took to complete all of the interventions.
Keyserling et al., 1993.	• Subset of 151 jobs with problems – taken from 335 jobs. • To be selected, jobs must have had at least one potentially hazardous ergonomic exposure.	Multiple ergonomic improvements.	No.	No.	Posture.	• Paired t-tests.	Trunk posture (+), shoulder posture (+), neck posture (-).	
Garg and Owen, 1992.	• 38 of 57 nursing assistants in one nursing home. • 95% female, age 19-61, .5-20 years experience. • 75% had suffered low back pain.	Training.	No.	No.	Injury incidence, severity rates, physical stress, and L5/S1 compression.	• 2 sample t-tests and Anova.	Hand force (+), L5/S1 force (+), Incidence back injury (+), severity back injury (+).	• Post-intervention assessments done after 4 and 8 months for some employees, and only after 4 months for the rest.
Wickstrom et al., 1993.	• 88 planers (age range 24 to 55 years) and 125 sheet metal workers (age range 19 to 56 years).	Training in biomechanics, physical training, ergonomic evaluation.	No.	All employees at a different metal industry.	Occurrence of low back pain, registered sick leave.	• Chi-square, t-tests.	Only for sheet metal workers: Fitness of low back tissues (+), occurrence low back pain (0), sick leave due to back pain (+).	• Follow-up 1 year after intervention. • Used participatory groups.
Feldstein et al., 1993.	• 45 nurse aides and orderlies on 2 surgical units (age range 19-62 years) at pre-intervention and 37 at follow-up.	Back education.	No.	Yes.	Pain.	• Chi-square, t-tests, or Ancova. • Statistically controlled for various possible confounders.	Back pain (0) for within and between groups.	• Post-intervention assessment after 1-month. • Control group was a unit not getting the intervention.

Table 4 continued.

Authors	Subjects	Intervention[1]	Random assignment[2]	Use of control group[3]	Dependent measures	Statistics	Results[4]	Comments
Daltroy et al., 1997.	• 4000 postal workers at 2 mail processing facilities.	Back education, pain management, lifting training, ergonomics.	Yes.	Yes.	Injury rates, likelihood of repeat injury.	• Extended log-linear models, Wilcoxon. • Statistically controlled for between group differences.	Low back injury rates (0), back injuries attributed to lifting and handling (0), other musculo-skeletal injuries attributed to lifting and handling (0).	• Study lasted 5.5 years. • Control group members could be re-assigned into the intervention group if they were injured. • Matched on job title and job characteristics.
Versloot et al., 1992.	• 500 bus drivers.	Back education.	Yes.	Yes.	Absenteeism.	• Manova. • Statistically controlled for between group differences.	Absenteeism (0).	• Compared 2 years pre-, 2 years during, and 2 years post-intervention. • Intervention and control groups came from 2 different geographic locations.
Parenmark et al., 1988.	• 33 newly hired assembly workers (19-45 years old) without arm, neck, or shoulder complaints. • 60 assembly workers with more than 1 year experience. None of them reported being ill.	Movement pattern training.	Not indicated.	Yes.	Sick days.	• Wilcoxon.	For new hires, total sick days (+) and upper extremity sick days (+). For experienced workers, total sick days (0) and upper extremity sick days (0).	• 48-week post-intervention assessment.
Gundewall et al., 1993.	• 69 nurses and nurse's aides between 18 and 58 years of age (1 male). 60 remaining at post-intervention. Subjects comprised people with and without back pain.	Exercise.	Yes.	Yes.	Strength, lost work days, pain.	• 2-sample t-tests, paired t-tests, Mann-Whitney test. • Tested for between group differences at pre-intervention.	Lost workdays (+), days with complaints (+), intensity of pain (+), back muscle strength (+).	• Subjects were stratified. • Investigators were not blinded. • Follow-up at 13 months.
Mitchell et al., 1994.	• 1316 warehouse workers in 5 different areas of an air force airport (mean age = 41.3, 974 males).	Use of back belt.	No.	Yes.	Back injury.	• Used chi-square and logistic regression. • Controlled for several possible confounders in the logistic regression.	Use of back belt (0).	• Retrospective study.
Reddell et al., 1992.	• 642 baggage handlers working for a major airline (572 males, age 19-67) in five different job types (though all manually handled baggage, mail, or supplies).	Use of back belt, training.	Yes.	Yes.	Lumbar injuries, lost work days, restricted work days, worker's compensation costs, hours worked.	• Anova.	Total case injury incidence rate (0), restricted workday case injury incidence rate (0), # lost workdays (0), # restricted workdays (0), worker's comp. rates (0).	• Experiment lasted 8 months. • No statistical comparison of possible differences between groups.

[1] If the interventions listed are separated by an "or", that means there were more than one intervention group. If several interventions are separated by commas, it means that a single intervention group received all of those treatments.

[2] Some of the studies used random assignment after stratification.

[3] A group that received no treatment, whether randomly assigned or not. This column may contain a description of the control condition.

[4] (+) means that the intervention had better scores on the DV, compared to the control/placebo/treatment as usual. (-) means that the intervention had worse scores on the DV, compared to the control. (0) means that the intervention and control did not differ. "Mixed" means that the intervention group differed from the control group on some of the outcome measures.